Social Experimentation

A National Bureau of
Economic Research
Conference Report

Social
Experimentation

Edited by   Jerry A. Hausman
and David A. Wise

The University of Chicago Press

Chicago and London

JERRY A. HAUSMAN is professor of economics at the Massachusetts Institute of Technology. DAVID A. WISE is John F. Stambaugh Professor of Political Economy at the John F. Kennedy School of Government, Harvard University.

The University of Chicago Press, Chicago 60637
The University of Chicago Press, Ltd., London

Library of Congress Cataloging in Publication Data
Main entry under title:

Social experimentation.

(A Conference report/National Bureau of Economic Research)
Papers presented at a conference held in 1981 sponsored by the National Bureau of Economic Research.
Includes indexes.
1. Evaluation research (Social action programs)—Congresses. 2. Negative income tax—United States—Evaluation—Congresses. 3. Electric utilities—United States—Rates—Time-of-use pricing—Evaluation—Congresses. 4. Housing subsidies—United States—Evaluation—Congresses. I. Hausman, Jerry A. II. Wise, David A. III. National Bureau of Economic Research. IV. Series: Conference Report (National Bureau of Economic Research)
H62.S6735 1985   361.6'072   84-8825
ISBN 0-226-31940-7

Contents

Introduction

Jerry A. Hausman and Davis A. Wise

During the past decade the United States government has spent over 500 million dollars on social experiments. The experiments attempt to determine the potential effect of a policy option by trying it out on a group of subjects, some of whom are randomly assigned to a treatment group and are the recipients of the proposed policy, while others are assigned to a control group. The difference in the outcomes for the two groups is the estimated effect of the policy option. This approach is an alternative to making judgments about the effect of the proposed policy from inferences based on observational (survey) data, but without the advantages of randomization. While a few social experiments have been conducted in the past, this development is a relatively new approach to the evaluation of the effect of proposed government policies. Much of the $500 million has gone into transfer payments to the experimental subjects, most of whom have benefited from the experiments. But the most important question is whether the experiments have been successful in their primary goal of providing precise estimates of the effects of a proposed government policy. This book is a collection of papers and comments from a conference held in 1981 under the sponsorship of the National Bureau of Economic Research and supported by the Alfred Sloan Foundation. At the conference papers were presented that addressed the question of the success of the experiments in achieving this evaluation goal.

In addition to the question of the success of the experiments for policy evaluation, whether the experiments were worth the cost was a recurring question among the conference participants. That is, could similar information have been provided by the use of econometric models and estimates on available survey data? It is important to remember that the policies that were evaluated in many of the experiments were far different from then-current policies that could be evaluated from survey data. For example the income-guarantee levels for male-headed households in the negative-income-tax experiments were far higher than any state provided in its welfare system. Similarly, time-of-use electricity prices for residential customers were unheard of in the United States before the experiments began. Nevertheless, estimated income elasticities from models of labor supply based on, say, the Survey of Economic Opportunity could be used to predict the outcome of the negative-income-tax experiments, and data from Europe might be used to predict the effect of the time-of-use electricity experiments. The authors of each of the first four papers that evaluate what we have learned from the four major groups of experiments focus on this question as well as the measured effect of the experiments.

It is important to keep in mind the conclusions based on hindsight, and they should be evaluated in this light. Even if the results of the experiments could have been well predicted by previous econometric estimates, no one could have been confident of this outcome before the experiments actually took place. Indeed this was a major motivation for the experiments. The authors of the four evaluation papers also consider what other purposes the results of the experiments are used for because experimental results may be superior to econometric estimates for these other uses. But since, to a large extent, the policy questions the experiments were designed to answer still have not been decided, the final accounting of the worth of the experiments in helping to decide the course of public policy is probably fairly far off into the future.

The methodology of randomized experiments was formalized and achieved wide acceptance due to the fundamental research of R. A. Fisher and his co-workers. Yet most of their research dealt with agricultural experiments. Complex statistical questions arise when this methodology is applied to social experiments. Individuals may refuse to participate in experiments or they may drop out while the experiment is underway. These effects must be accounted for in the evaluation of the experimental results. The next set of papers addresses questions of statistical and econometric methodology with respect to social experiments. Questions of sample selection and treatment assignment are analyzed. Also an overall model of how the results will be used is postulated. The possibility exists of a decision-theoretic approach to the evaluation of policies which could lead to a considerably sharper focus in the design of the experiments.

The last group of papers takes up the extremely complicated question of how the output of the experiments is actually used in policy formulation. Experiments provide new information that can lead to reevaluation of previously proposed policies or the formulation of new policy options. The analysis of the experiments and the policy-formulation process become intertwined, and yet the latter is constrained to some extent by the political process. What are the conditions under which the analysis of the experiments has the most influence on the policy process? Again the final impact of the experiments will not be known until more time passes, but these questions are important to the design and analysis of successful social experiments.

We now turn from this general introduction to a summary of each of the papers presented at the conference. Each paper was commented on by either one or two discussants, and we also summarize their comments. The authors had the opportunity to revise their papers after the conference and in some instances reacted to discussants suggestions. But most of the comments deal with broad questions motivated by or raised in the papers and raise valuable additional points about the success of social experiments and possible improvements in their implementation.

Dennis J. Aigner in his paper, "The Residential Electricity Time-of-Use Pricing Experiments: What Have We Learned?" evaluates the fifteen time-of-use (TOU) experiments that have taken place since 1975. The main question at issue is whether TOU prices would produce alterations in the demands of residential customers for peak-period electricity large enough so that the net effect on the customer's welfare plus the change in revenues and investments required of the electric utility would justify implementation of TOU rates. That is, the TOU rates are a close application of marginal-cost pricing by the utility. The experiments were designed to discover whether the change in rate pattern to a time-of-day basis would lead to an increase in social welfare. In his summary of the results, Aigner finds much less agreement among the price-elasticity estimates than is found in the labor-supply studies of the NIT experiments. However, he does find that the results lead to the conclusion that peak-period demands are inelastic when expenditure is held constant, which can have important implications for the effects of a TOU rate plan on utility revenues. Aigner then goes on to consider the welfare effects of the TOU rate plans. Based on the results of the experiments he concludes that only the largest customers are likely to benefit from the introduction of TOU rates. However, these large customers consume a significant proportion of total residential electricity demand. Lastly, Aigner takes up the difficult question of "transferability." Can the results of an experiment in one jurisdiction be used to predict the outcome of a TOU plan in another area? Aigner offers an interesting approach to this important problem.

Overall, Aigner concludes that only a very few experiments have led to reliable results. However, he does not find the differences in elasticity estimates too disturbing when considered across different service areas. His view is that better experimental design would have led to considerably better results. He also points out a potentially important limiting factor of the experiments. The experiments are best analyzed as short-run experiments since the appliance stock has been held fixed. He believes that the long-run response could be considerably different from the response suggested by estimates based on the experimental results.

Paul L. Joskow, in his comments, agrees with Aigner's conclusion on the limited usefulness of many of the TOU experiments. However, he doubts that the neoclassical welfare analyses used by Aigner to evaluate the TOU rates will be acceptable to state regulatory commissions. He also emphasizes that the short-run nature of the experiments will limit their usefulness. Therefore, he concludes that the TOU rate experiments will have little if any positive impact on regulatory decisions to implement TOU rates. Lester D. Taylor, in his comments on the Aigner paper, concludes that the evidence is not good enough to make a scientific evaluation of the desirability of TOU rate plans. Thus, all three authors feel that we have not "learned enough" from the TOU rate experiments although they all conclude that a limited amount of knowledge has been gained through the experiments.

Harvey S. Rosen reviews the housing-allowance experiment in his paper, "Housing Behavior and the Experimental Housing-Allowance Program: What Have We Learned?" This experiment granted housing subsidies to the poor to determine to what extent they would increase their housing consumption. The Experimental Housing Allowance Program (EHAP) was divided into two parts. The demand experiment was designed to determine the effect on housing consumption of the subsidies. The supply experiment was designed to determine the effect of the housing allowances on the rental housing market. Given the relatively inelastic short-run supply of rental housing units, it is important to estimate the effect of a subsidy program on market rents. Rosen analyzes the value of EHAP in terms of what additional knowledge we gained from the experiment which could not have been known from previous econometric studies on cross-sectional data. He bases his criterion on the argument that a structural econometric model is necessary to analyze housing consumption patterns, even with experimental data. He considers the problems that arise in econometric estimation of housing-demand functions, but he concludes that these same problems were present in the analysis of the EHAP demand data so that the experiment did not alleviate the usual problems that applied work in housing-demand encounters. His conclusions are quite similar for the problems that exist in the analysis of the EHAP supply experiment. Thus, overall Rosen argues that the problems faced by investigators who have used conventional survey data continue to exist in the experimental data except for variations in the price of housing induced by the experiments. He does not think that the social experiment was necessary and concludes "The money would have been better spent on augmenting conventional data sources."

John M. Quigley broadly agrees with Rosen's conclusions. He outlines some more complete analytical models for problems that arise in the housing experiment. He raises the additional problem that the duration of the EHAP demand experiment was quite short, since it lasted for only four years. Therefore inferences about the long-run response may be problematic. He feels that the effect of long-term subsidies might be quite different from the observed response to the EHAP subsidies. Gregory K. Ingram, in his discussion of the Rosen paper, also comes to similar conclusions about the value of EHAP. He does think, however, that program-participation rates which are an important determinant of program costs would be difficult to predict without an experiment. But his overall assessment is that EHAP did not help solve the many problems of measurement that exist in the analysis of housing markets. He concludes that the EHAP did have some value, but at too high a cost. He believes that only the demand experiment of EHAP was worthwhile.

In his paper, "Income-Maintenance Policy and Work Effort: Learning from Experiments and Labor-Market Studies," Frank P. Stafford reviews the evidence from the largest and perhaps most important group of experiments, the negative-income-tax (NIT) experiments. The five NIT experiments were designed primarily to analyze the effects of a potentially large change in the income support or welfare system in the United States. Since the cost of an NIT program would be closely related to the labor-supply response of individuals to the income guarantee and the tax rate, these parameters were varied across individuals or families in the experimental design. The response of individuals or families to the introduction of an NIT in terms of their work effort is closely related to their labor-supply behavior. Stafford's first question is "Why did we need the experiments at all?" He argues that from previous studies on survey data, labor economists had formed a consensus view on the range within which the labor elasticities would fall. Therefore estimates of the effect of the introduction of an NIT could be made from the coefficient estimates from these previous studies. The case for the NIT experiments from this vantage point he believes is perhaps not overwhelming.

Stafford discusses two reasons for the NIT experiments. One possible role is that the experiments would be easier to understand and to interpret by policy makers who would place more confidence in their results than in simulation estimates from survey data. The NIT experiments provide direct evidence on the alteration of work effort which could well be more convincing. The second reason for the NIT experiments, which Stafford finds less convincing, is that "model free" analysis of the experiments is possible while the related labor-supply studies must be based on econometric models of questionable validity. This latter reason is less convincing, in Stafford's viewpoint, because any actual NIT plan likely to be adopted is unlikely to be exactly one of the experimental treatments, and a model will be necessary to predict its labor-supply effects. Whether or not one finds the case for theoretical models to be strong, Stafford concludes that a strong case exists for the experiments to answer the main question of the effect of an NIT on work effort.

Besides the effect of an NIT on work effort, other outcomes of interest which Stafford identifies are on-the-job training, divorce or change in family structure, and labor-market outcomes of unemployment, work effort, and early retirement. In terms of the main variable of interest, work effort, Stafford finds the results of the NIT experiments broadly consistent with nonexperimental studies. Stafford argues that to answer the question of whether the experiments were "worth it" would require a decision theoretic model that could evaluate the possible policy alternatives and take account of the greater precision, or less uncertainty, that would result from the experimental evidence. Evidence from the NIT experiments on the other areas of labor-market behavior is valuable, but not conclusive, in Stafford's opinion. The effect of the experiments on greater divorce rates points up the important effects of transfer systems on family decision making. Overall, Stafford concludes that a great deal was learned from the experiments. Furthermore, he sees the possibility of continued research using the data that was collected, which would help answer other important questions.

Sherwin Rosen, in his comments, emphasizes the decrease in maintained model hypotheses which an experiment allows. He emphasizes that the finding of a similar work-effort response found in the NIT experiments as is found in survey data could not have been known in advance. While he thinks that room for improvement in design and analysis of the experiments certainly exists, overall he concludes that the NIT experiments led to a valuable increase in our knowledge in the area of work response to change in income guarantees and tax rates. In his comments, Zvi Griliches emphasizes the importance of randomization in experiments and the "exogeneity" introduced by experimental treatments. Griliches also emphasizes the importance of the experiments in providing increased variation in the data which in general will lead to better econometric estimates. Overall, he takes a somewhat stronger view than does Stafford on the value of the experiments.

Jeffrey E. Harris analyzes the health experiments in his paper, "Macroexperiments versus Microexperiments for Health Policy." His major point is that health experiments may be better designed and analyzed at the community or group level which makes them differ fundamentally from the microexperiments at the individual level of most other types of economic and social experiments. Harris first considers the problems inherent in the microexperiments that have been conducted so far. He concentrates on the Multiple Risk Factor Intervention Trial (MRFIT) and the Rand Health Insurance Study (HIS). He claims that data from

MRFIT are difficult to analyze because of the problem of participation bias. He also has doubts about the sample selection procedure in the HIS experiment. He then considers the potential problems of attrition bias, of interdependence among individual responses, and of Hawthorne effects. Overall, he thinks that these problems lead to quite complicated model designs to analyze the effects of the experiments. Harris feels that many of these problems could be minimized by the use of macroexperiments such as the Stanford Heart Disease Prevention Program (SHDPP) which uses as the unit of observation a complete community. While he does not find the SHDPP without fault, he believes that its main problem could be alleviated by a different experimental design. He argues that repeated cross-sectional sampling in macroexperiments is the preferred design. He favors the macroexperiments mainly because use of the mass media becomes a valued policy option since it does not affect the behavior of controls that are geographically distinct communities. He feels that further development of the theory of the design and analysis of macroexperiments would be useful since they offer the opportunity of more convincing experiments than do the microexperiments with their insurmountable difficulties.

Paul B. Ginsburg has reservations about Harris's claims for macroexperiments. He feels that the use of macroexperiments is limited by cost considerations. He thinks that many experimental situations have elements of both micro- and macroexperiments so that the choice between the two types is not often clear-cut. In his comments, Lawrence L. Orr takes sharp issue with Harris's conclusions. Orr thinks that a careful analysis is needed to decide which type of experiment is more useful in a particular situation. He disagrees most fundamentally with Harris over the question of whether the role of an experiment is to decide on the efficacy of a particular policy option or whether it is to analyze a range of possible policies. He believes that the latter situation is more typical so that microexperiments are needed to estimate individual response functions. The "black box" macroexperiment then becomes inappropriate. Furthermore, he believes that many of the problems inherent in microexperiments also exist in macroexperiments. Orr also believes that additional important problems of interpretation exist in the results of macroexperiments. Most important of these limitations is the sample-size constraint in macroexperiments together with the difficulty of control and administration. Orr concludes that the particular situation must be analyzed to determine whether a micro or a macro approach is more appropriate. He differs strongly with Harris's conclusion on the superiority of macro- over microexperiments.

The next set of papers considers the question of experimental design and analysis. Jerry A. Hausman and David A. Wise in "Technical Problems in Social Experimentation: Cost versus Ease of Analysis" attempt to set forth general guidelines that would enhance the usefulness of future social experiments and to suggest methods of correcting for inherent limitation in the experiments. They feel that more attention should be paid to the possibility of randomized design and its associated analysis. The experiments to date have utilized endogenous sample-selection procedures and treatment-assignment procedures which subvert the possibility of using classical analysis-of-variance procedures to determine the results of the experiments. Still, inherent limitations exist, even with randomized design, which are difficult or impossible to avoid. The problems of voluntary participation and of attrition from the experiment will continue to exist. But Hausman and Wise argue that these problems are considerably easier to treat if the confounding problems of endogenous stratification and assignment are not present. Lastly, they propose that the experiments be designed to estimate only a small number of treatment effects rather than a large range of policy options which often leads to imprecise estimates of the effect of any single policy option.

John Conlisk agrees with Hausman and Wise that endogenous stratification should be avoided if possible. However, he is in less agreement with the principle of random treatment assignment. He thinks that interactions between treatments and exogenous variables are of central importance to the behavioral response of the experiments. He also thinks that the number of experimental design points must be based on particular design considerations so that an overall judgment cannot be readily made. He concludes that self-selection and attrition problems are of great importance and that experimental design theory needs to be extended to deal with these problems. In his comments on the Hausman-Wise paper, Daniel L. McFadden concurs with the use of robust techniques such as ANOVA for the analysis of the experiments. He argues that random treatment assignment is the most important factor in an acceptable design in that it isolates the effects of other sample-frame difficulties. Endogenous sampling designs can then be used, although the statistical analysis is complicated somewhat. He agrees that problems of self-selection and attrition are important and suggests that the focus of future research should be on robust statistical methods to correct these problems.

Frederick Mosteller and Milton C. Weinstein consider the cost effectiveness of the experiments in their paper, "Toward Evaluating the Cost-Effectiveness of Medical and Social Experiments." Mosteller and Weinstein emphasize the importance of learning about the efficacy and cost-effectiveness of medical practices so that decisions about proper medical procedures can be made. They then proceed to consider the costs and benefits of the evaluation procedures. Therefore, they propose to evaluate the evaluations. They evaluate the procedure of a randomized clinical trial (RCT). To do so they consider the question of how the evaluations are actually used. They then specify a general conceptual model for evaluating the cost-effectiveness of the clinical trials. They do so by using a decision analytic model to assess the cost-effectiveness. They formulate a Bayesian model and after deriving the results consider the effect of relaxing some of the assumption of the model.

Mosteller and Weinstein then consider inherent problems in the assessment of cost-effectiveness of medical evaluations. They discuss both normative and positive models of response to the evaluations. The question of institutional design, to assure appropriate use of the information, is also covered. Other problems such as the assessment of information in the experiments and their utilization are discussed.

Then Mosteller and Weinstein turn to examples to examine the usefulness of their suggested approach. The examples deal with the gastric-freezing procedure and the treatment of hypertension. They conclude that further study is needed but that a potential cost-benefit calculation should be made before a trial is undertaken. Furthermore, they argue that controlled experiments cannot remove all the problems of evaluation but that they are of value and should be utilized more often. They believe that an incentive system which would lead to increased tests of efficacy would be advantageous policy.

In his comments Joseph B. Kadane agrees with the Mosteller and Weinstein conclusions about the need for more evaluation. He points out some of the limitations of their model and questions how the potential cost-benefit calculation that Mosteller and Weinstein call for could be made without additional information.

In "The Use of Information in the Policy Process: Are Social-Policy Experiments Worthwhile?" David S. Mundel argues that social-policy experiments are very expensive and therefore should be undertaken only in very particular situations. He argues that the potential utility of social experiments depends on the following factors: whether the experiments can answer the questions that are important to policy makers; whether the answers can be understood, given that important policy questions can be answered; and finally, whether the answers alter the beliefs of policy makers, given that they provide understandable answers to important questions.

Ernst W. Stromsdorfer examines the effect on policy of social experiments in his paper, "Social Science Analysis and the Formulation of Public Policy: Illustrations of What the President "Knows" and How He Comes to "Know" It." Stromsdorfer begins with the contention that policy makers will use whatever data are at hand to support their position whether or not the data come from a social experiment. He therefore considers the larger questions of how information is used in the policy-formulation process and how it interacts with the political process in the making of policy decisions. Stromsdorfer sees three processes for knowledge production in the federal government: management information-system (MIS) data, natural or quasi experiments, and classical experiments. He concludes that while a variety of experimental data exists of the natural, quasi-experimental, and classical experimental variety, they are of uneven quality and are not used in a consistent manner.

But Stromsdorfer does believe that this information has been used in the consideration of policy issues in recent Congressional and administration decisions. He points to the issues of welfare reform which have been affected by the results of the NIT experiments, unemployment insurance which has been affected by numerous studies for natural or quasi experiments, and social security reform. At the same time evaluation research often follows the lead of policy development. But Stromsdorfer also identified research categories that have had little or no impact. Overall, he concludes that program analysis and evaluation can be an extremely valuable policy tool. But at the same time, the reality of political constraint must be recognized since it sets limits on the collection, analysis, and usefulness of data and analysis which may be produced by experimentation.

Henry Aaron in his comments on Stromdorfer's paper agrees with the focus of research being used in an adversary process. Furthermore, Aaron emphasizes that the adversaries are contending for power, not the scientific truth that might arise from the experiments. But Aaron concludes that social experiments have been a force for slowing the adoption of new policies. Social experiments show problems to be more complicated than is commonly appreciated, with results more difficult to achieve. Lawrence E. Lynn, Jr., in his comments takes no view on whether the experiments have been useful. He warns against the overuse of the "rational actor" model of the political process.

1   The Residential Electricity Time-of-Use Pricing Experiments: What Have We Learned?

Dennis J. Aigner

1.1   Introduction

Over a period of six years, the Department of Energy (DOE) has been engaged in a cooperative program of residential time-of-use (TOU) rate experiments, involving time-of-day or seasonally varying prices. There are fifteen completed or ongoing projects, the first of which began in 1975 in Vermont.

The main goal of this program of experimentation was to determine whether TOU pricing would produce sufficient alterations in the load curves of residential customers to justify implementation of such rates. This "justification" involves three specific effects—the revenue impact on the utility, the amount of capacity reduction implied, and changes in consumer welfare. The experiments were designed, to a lesser or greater degree, to address one or more of these issues.

A number of design considerations have an impact on the ultimate usefulness of the experimental data that have been forthcoming, not the least of which is the amount of variation available in peak, midpeak and off-peak prices. Many of the DOE experiments have but one set of TOU prices, and therefore the inferences available are limited to a single statistical comparison of control-group and experimental households.

Dennis J. Aigner is professor of economics, University of Southern California.

This paper was prepared for presentation at the NBER Conference on Social Experimentation, 5–7 March 1981, Hilton Head, South Carolina. This version has been revised slightly to account for points raised in the general discussion of it as the conference, but not to such extent that the pertinence of the formal discussants' remarks are diminished.

Research on the experimental data discussed herein has continued at a rapid pace. In the interim since this paper was drafted several important pieces of work relevant to the task have appeared that were unable to be included.

While in other respects such an experiment may be well designed, its results are not generalizable to a situation where the TOU prices are different than those used in the experiment. Other design or sampling issues of some importance include the type of stratification used, the choice of a model used for an optimal allocation of observations to cells, whether sample size is adequate to allow for estimation of relevant parameters with sufficient precision, the influence of incentive or compensation payments, the means for handling attrition, the nature of the experimental environment, and so forth.

Design issues relate directly to how the data are developed and used for purposes of analysis. In addition, often latitude exists in the choice of a statistical framework for analysis apart from requirements or limitations implied by the data, its collection, and quality.

The purpose of the present paper is to consider the empirical results available so far from the DOE experiments in light of design and analysis concerns and the goals the experiments were ostensibly designed to serve. This is done by focusing on price elasticities as the important summary parameters of interest, since they feed directly into calculations of welfare and revenue impacts and impinge on the matter of rate design itself.

In the following section, the available elasticity results are summarized and discussed. Section 1.3 presents the basis for a welfare analysis of a move to TOU rates. In section 1.4, the question of implementation is considered. Finally, in the concluding section, we take a retrospective view and return to the initial design issues raised.

1.2 Summary of Elasticity Estimates

As might be expected, the early DOE projects are of highly variable quality from the standpoint of being able to make valid statistical inferences from them. Even some of the more recently established projects are of limited value for the purpose of estimating elasticities by time of use.

Table 1.1 summarizes the status of each project and its potential usefulness for estimating price elasticities. In assessing a project's suitability for price-elasticity estimation, the crucial factor in its experimental design is the degree of independent price variation offered to customers. Without rate-structure variation it is difficult to ascertain anything more than qualitative effects on customer demands resulting from the institution of a TOU rate-structure. Consequently, our primary criterion in judging a project's usefulness is the amount of rate-structure variation employed. Other design characteristics are also important, of course, but we regard these as being of secondary interest.

Detailed descriptions and comprehensive evaluations of all aspects of the experiments have been made by Research Triangle Institute (RTI)

Table 1.1   **Status of DOE Rate Demonstration Projects**

State	Status	Results/Potential
Arizona	ongoing	available; of interest
Arkansas	completed	available; of limited interest
California (LADWP)	completed	available; of interest
California (SCE)	ongoing	partially available; of interest
Connecticut	completed	available; of limited interest
New Jersey	cancelled	not available; of no interest
New York	completed	not available; of no interest
North Carolina (BREMC)	completed	available; of limited interest
North Carolina (CP&L)	completed	partially available; of interest
Ohio	completed	available; of limited interest
Oklahoma	completed	partially available; of interest
Puerto Rico	ongoing	not available; of no interest
Rhode Island	cancelled	available; of no interest
Vermont	completed	available; of no interest
Wisconsin	completed	available; of interest

(U.S. Department of Energy 1978) on behalf of DOE, and by the University of Michigan's Survey Research Center (Hill et al. 1979) on behalf of the Electric Power Research Institute. Thus only a brief description and evaluation of each project will be given here. In the appendix we discuss each project in greater detail and justify our evaluations of them.

The demonstration projects can be classified into two groups on the basis of when they were begun, since only midway into the program did the DOE issue guidelines on statistical sampling, experimental design, etc., to be used by new projects. These guidelines clearly are minimal when judged by the standards of some of the best projects, yet several of the most recently established projects do not meet them in important respects.

The first group oı experiments to be funded took place in Arizona, Arkansas, California (Los Angeles Department of Water and Power— LADWP), Connecticut, New Jersey, New York, Ohio, Vermont, and Wisconsin. The Vermont experiment has such serious flaws that we doubt the results should be utilized even on a local level. The Arkansas, Connecticut, New York, and Ohio experiments all suffer from a lack of variation in price treatments, with at most only two different TOU rate structures employed. The New York and Ohio experiments have additional serious design flaws, while the Arkansas and Connecticut experiments are otherwise well designed. The Arizona, California (LADWP), and Wisconsin experiments are all well designed with a wide variation in price treatments.

The group of newer experiments includes those in California (Southern California Edison—SCE), North Carolina (Blue Ridge Electric Membership Corporation—BREMC and Carolina Power & Light—CP&L), Oklahoma, Puerto Rico, and Rhode Island. The designs of these experiments for the most part benefit from the DOE guidelines, particularly in the crucial area of price variation. Only the Rhode Island experiment fails in this regard, employing a complex but unvarying rate structure that precludes isolation of TOU price effects. The Puerto Rico experiment, despite its favorable rate-structure design, has so many idiosyncratic features that it should be viewed at best as of local interest only. The California (SCE), North Carolina (CP&L) and Oklahoma experiments are all well designed in other respects in addition to their use of several price treatments.

Thus six experiments in various stages of completion offer the wide price variation desirable for estimation of TOU price elasticities. Data from the Arizona and Wisconsin experiments have been generally available for some time, with the Wisconsin data seeming slightly better in quality; a number of demand studies have been conducted utilizing these sources. We report the results of these studies, as well as some studies of the Connecticut experiment which utilize the data with a single price treatment. Data will soon be fully available from the California (LADWP), California (SCE), Oklahoma, and North Carolina tests, but at the time of this writing only preliminary reports on these experiments are available. To the extent that comparative results from those other projects that do not possess price variation but are otherwise well designed are pertinent, they are also discussed.

While the notion of price elasticity (own price, cross price, compensated, etc.) is certainly well understood, elasticity estimation within the context of a statistical model of electricity demand and/or consumption by time of use presents some unique methodological problems, solutions to which are still evolving. Earlier reports from the Electric Utility Rate Design Study (Electric Utility Rate Design Study 1977a, 1977b) contain reviews of the empirical work available on the average price elasticity of demand and introductions to the topic of TOU-demand modeling and elasticity estimation. Each of the studies cited contains a more detailed exposition of the models and methods used. General references are Aigner and Poirier (1979) and Lifson (1980).

The existing empirical elasticity estimates come in a variety of types, distinguished by whether they are compensated or uncompensated, "partial" or "full." The definitions of these elasticities and the concepts they measure are given in Aigner and Poirier (1979) and also in Hendricks and Koenker (1979). In our presentation of empirical elasticity results from the demonstration projects, the main focus is on the uncompensated partial own-price elasticities, the most commonly reported elasticities. After presenting and analyzing these in some detail, we turn to a discussion of other elasticity types and their usefulness.

Estimates from previous empirical work of uncompensated partial own-price peak-period elasticities are presented in table 1.2. Because of the single TOU rate structure employed in the Connecticut experiment, most researchers have not attempted to estimate price effects, but instead have focused on explaining load patterns as functions of socioeconomic variables, weather, and household demographic characteristics. Examples are the studies by Engle et al. (1979), Hendricks, Koenker, and Poirer (1978), and Hausman, Kinnucan, and McFadden (1979).[1] The Engle and Hendricks papers report on attempts to characterize and model the individual load curve.[2] The Hausman paper is insightful because it computes a welfare-based price index for electricity which suggests that the price of electricity went up for households facing the TOU rate (their welfare therefore went down), and thereby explains the reduction in monthly consumption experienced by them.

Lawrence and Braithwait (1977), however, do obtain estimates of price elasticities from the Connecticut data using the linear expenditure system of demand equations. By imposing a restriction on the consumption requirements of household appliances, they are able to surmount the problem of lack of variation in the price data. They find that peak-period elasticities hover around -0.5 while the midpeak and off-peak elasticities are quite a bit smaller.

Data from the Arizona experiment have received attention from several analysts. Indeed, the range of econometric work on this data set is more extensive than any other. Beginning with the work of Taylor (1977) and Atkinson (1979a, 1979b), further refinements to the econometric methodology and additional results were contributed by Aigner and Hausman (1980), Lau and Lillard (1979), and Hill et al. (1980). In DOE's assessment of the Arizona experiment, Miedema et al. (1978) also estimate TOU price effects.

Taylor's numerical results are not reported in the table because they are so anomalous. He fits both a straightforward linear-regression model and a model employing relative usage (for example, monthly kWh consumption in the peak period relative to total monthly consumption) as its dependent variable. In each instance the price variables perform poorly. There are no statistically significant price coefficients in any of the three equations, and in the peak and midpeak equations most of the own-price terms have positive signs. Income, temperature, and the measure of

1. The White et al. (1978) Research Triangle Institute report on the Connecticut experiment is also in this vein, since they too make no attempt to estimate price effects. They do not try to model the load curve or any aggregate thereof, but merely examine shifts in TOU consumption in response to the implementation of the TOU rate structure. They find that the TOU rates do cause some shifting of consumption out of the peak period.
2. The Hendricks, Koenker, and Poirer (1978) paper uses a methodology for approximating the load curve by a spline function. See Electric Utility Rate Design Study (1977a) for an introduction to these ideas.

Table 1.2   Uncompensated Partial Own-Price Elasticities of Electricity Demand by Time of Day

	Connecticut		Arizona		Wisconsin	
	Narrow Peak (4 hrs.)	Broad Peak	Narrow Peak (3 hrs.)	Broad Peak (5–8 hrs.)	Narrow Peak (6 hrs.)	Broad Peak (9–12 hrs.)
Peak Period Summer			−0.41LL −0.18HOTW −0.17AH		(−0.41, −0.66)	(−0.48, −0.84)CC (−0.81, −0.83)ATK
					−0.81	
Winter	(−0.46, −0.66)		−0.64	(−0.69, −0.79)AT		
Midpeak Period Summer			−0.26LL −0.24HOTW −0.47AH			
Winter	(−0.24, −0.50)		−0.70	(−0.38, −0.58)AT		

Off-Peak Period			
Summer	−0.46LL −0.19HOTW −0.36AH	(−0.51, −0.77)	(−0.30, −0.64)CC
		−0.09	(−0.21, −0.24)ATK
	−0.23	(−0.35, −0.57)AT	
Winter	(−0.29, −0.36)		

Sources: Connecticut: Lawrence and Braithwait (1977, table 6, p. 74). Arizona: Entry AT is from Atkinson (1979b, table 10, p. 92); AH from Aigner and Hausman (1980, table 4, p. 18); LL from Lau and Lillard (1979, table 3, p. 27); HOTW from Hill et al. (1980, table 4, p. 21). Wisconsin: Entry CC is from Caves and Christensen (1980b, tables 6 and 7); ATK is from Atkinson (1979b, table 11, p. 93).

Notes: Connecticut: Ranges for Connecticut are constructed over results for the months of November 1975 and January 1976, and over subperiods of the day (two of which were designated "peak," three "midpeak," one "off-peak"). The elasticity estimates given here are those estimated using the MIN assumption concerning appliance kWh requirements (see Lawrence and Braithwait 1979, 69).

Arizona: Since Atkinson (AT) pools the data over months, the ranged are constructed for the broad peak period only. Aigner and Hausman (AH) attempt to correct for truncation bias in their results. They use the one summer month of August 1976. Moreover, since length of the peak period is an independent variable in their model, a single elasticity is reported, although separate elasticities for individual pricing periods could have been calculated. Lau and Lillard (LL) work only with households that faced the narrow peak period, over the period May–October 1976. They pool the data over months. Hill et al. (HOTW) also attempt to correct for the influence of the incentive scheme in their work.

Wisconsin: Ranges were constructed by Caves and Christensen (CC) over the results for the months of July and August 1977, over alternative definitions of the peak period (in the case of "broad peak"), and over alternative TOU rate differentials from 2:1 to 8:1. Since Atkinson (ATK) pools the data over two available months and over prices, the ranges constructed are for the broad peak period only.

applicance capacity are significant explanatory variables in Taylor's equations, which would lead one to conclude that nonprice variables completely overwhelm price influence in explaining customers' response patterns.

Miedema et al. (1978) obtain similar results using monthly data over the same period as Taylor.[3] They estimate four different models of electricity consumption by time-of-day, employing as regressors prices, income, demographic characteristics, weather, lagged consumption, and allowance of prices to interact with the other variables. In none of the models, estimated individually for each of six months, do they obtain a single significant price-elasticity estimate.[4]

By way of contrast, Atkinson, Aigner and Hausman, Lau and Lillard, and Hill et al. all estimate significant price effects, although their estimates are dissimilar. These researchers take a neoclassical utility-maximization approach to the estimation problem and make a separability assumption about electricity consumption.[5] Their resulting partial elasticity estimates are presented in table 1.2.

Atkinson's (1979a) results are based on a translog model estimated over the same six-month period as Taylor and Miedema, et al. His results show significant own-price elasticities for all periods. When the peak is broadly defined, Atkinson finds the peak-period elasticity to be around − 0.7, larger (in absolute value) than those corresponding to the midpeak and off peak. For the narrowly defined peak he finds that midpeak elasticity increases to a level slightly above the peak elasticity. The conclusion from Atkinson's work is that manipulating the on-peak price would result in the largest quantity response, at least when the peak is broadly defined—as opposed to an alternative whereby the on-peak/ off-peak differential is changed by altering the off-peak price.[6] Although Atkinson's empirical work can be faulted on several grounds, subsequent attempts by others to improve on the econometric model and methods he employed still present a sharp contrast to the conclusions of Taylor and Miedema et al.

The work of Aigner and Hausman (1980) represents an interesting methodological contribution and contains empirical results that run

3. These results are similarly omitted from table 1.2.
4. In an appendix to their study, Miedema et al. (1978) employ a translog model and obtain for the most part negative and significant elasticity estimates. They dismiss these, however, as being mere artifacts of the assumptions inherent in this model specification.
5. For more on this approach see Aigner and Poirier (1979) or Hendricks and Koenker (1979).
6. Although the TOU experiments focus on manipulation of prices, there are other interrelated, controllable "parameters" of interest, such as the differential itself, length and/or starting time of the peak period, etc. Their corresponding elasticity measures are likewise interrelated. See appendix A of Aigner and Poirier (1979) for details on these matters.

counter to Atkinson's in both the computed levels of uncompensated elasticities and in their patterns. Aigner and Hausman attempt to correct the Arizona data for potential biases due to one aspect of the compensation scheme which protected sample households from paying any more for electricity under experimental rates than they would have paid under the prevailing (control) rate. Their results suggest that for these Arizona households the midpeak own-price elasticity is largest. The econometric specification they use is a powerful one.[7] With it, Atkinson's Arizona results are reconciled to those emanating from the Wisconsin project, which will be discussed shortly.

Similarly, Lau and Lillard (1979) offer a substantial methodological improvement over Atkinson's work—while keeping to his model in most other respects—by specifying a rich "pooling" model to exploit the cross-sectional/time-series nature of experimental data. They find the peak and off-peak elasticities to be about the same magnitude, with a relatively small midpeak elasticity. But there are shortcomings in their work (possibly only minor in nature) which need to be resolved before firm conclusions can be drawn.

A study related to the Aigner and Hausman work is the recent paper by Hill et al. (1980). These authors attempt to account for the effects of the rather complicated incentive structure faced by the experimental households in 1976. While Aigner and Hausman concentrate on the so-called maximum constraint, whereby households knew they would pay no more for electricity under TOU prices than they would have under standard rates, Hill et al. look at the more detailed aspects of the incentive scheme. If a household consumed the same amounts of electricity in each TOU pricing period in any month in 1976 as it did in the corresponding month in 1975, its 1976 monthly bill would have been 85 percent of the 1975 bill. In fact, very few customers bumped up against the maximum constraint during the experiment, so consideration of the exact details of the incentive scheme may demonstrate some further insights into the effects of it on TOU price response.

What Hill et al. find, using a different model than Aigner and Hausman (the same model used by RTI), is a similar pattern of uncompensated own-price elasticities to that reported by Aigner and Hausman, in that the midpeak elasticity is largest, followed by off-peak and on-peak values. The statistically significant cross-price effects are also negative, but the magnitudes of all these elasticities are quite different between the two studies.

Hill et al. also analyzed the 1977 data, where many changes were introduced in the experimental design, including elimination of the incen-

---

7. Their handling of socioeconomic variables is quite different from Atkinson's, although both use the same translog demand model.

tive scheme (the maximum bill constraint was still in force). Some differences in the estimated regression equations were evident, comparing the 1977 results to 1976. In particular, more of a tendency toward shifting peak-period kWh's into the midpeak and off-peak periods was observed.

Turning to the Wisconsin experiment, Atkinson (1979b) and Caves and Christensen (1980a; 1980b) use only two of the first available months of data when households were on experimental rates.[8] Thus their quantitative results must be viewed as very tentative. Atkinson processes the Wisconsin data through the same model he used to analyze the Arizona data, and with similar results. He finds a substantially higher on-peak own-price elasticity than for the off-peak period, whether the latter is broadly or narrowly defined.

Caves and Christensen approach the data cautiously, employing several demand models consistent with economic theory. In their earlier (1980a) study they evaluate three alternative models, rejecting the translog in favor of the constant elasticity of substitution (CES) and generalized Leontief systems (although they present elasticity estimates only for the latter). Their broad-peak results are similar to those of Atkinson in that the on-peak elasticity is larger (in absolute value) than the off-peak elasticity. Their narrow-peak elasticity results, however, show the on-peak elasticity to be smaller than the off-peak figure, a pattern that, while different from the one found by Atkinson, is in accord with Aigner and Hausman's result.[9] In their later (1980b) study Caves and Christensen employ the CES demand model and extend it to allow for the effects of nonprice variables like consumption level, appliance stocks, and household characteristics. They find that in addition to prices, appliance stocks have significant effects on time-of-day demands. Unfortunately, they present no own-price elasticity estimates, preferring to focus on the substitution possibilities between peak and off-peak consumption.

It is difficult to summarize the empirical results given in table 1.2 since the elasticity estimates frequently conflict with each other. While no consistent overall pattern emerges from the table, the estimates support the following conclusions. First, there is agreement that all the peak-period demands are inelastic when expenditure is held constant. Second, in all cases where the peak period is broadly defined, the researchers find that peak-period elasticity exceeds the midpeak and off-peak elasticities. This pattern, however, does not generally hold for the narrow-peak

---

8. Caves and Christensen (1980b) also use data on customers in the statistical control group for the same two months of the preceding year to improve the efficiency of their estimates.
9. Although Aigner and Hausman's finding is an overall and not just a narrow-peak-period result.

results or even for the Aigner and Hausman results which do not vary by peak length.

We now turn to a discussion of other elasticity types. Table 1.3 presents compensated partial own-price elasticity estimates from the previously cited empirical studies. These estimates are in all cases smaller than the corresponding uncompensated partial elasticities, a consequence of the fact that electricity has a positive expenditure effect.[10] Since these elasticities hold utility constant when prices change, they are of particular usefulness in analyzing time-of-day pricing policies where the goal is to induce consumers to shift their consumption patterns without causing them any loss in welfare. The compensated elasticity provides a measure of how much consumption would change in response to a price change if consumers' electricity expenditures were simultaneously adjusted (e.g., via a lump-sum payment that could only be used to purchase electricity) to prevent their welfare from changing. Unfortunately, many of the studies do not report compensated elasticities. The estimates that are reported are quite low, especially those obtained by researchers using the Arizona and Wisconsin data.

Cross-price elasticities are also estimated by a number of studies, and they are crucial to understanding how price changes affect the whole pattern of consumption by time of day. Because of the large number of cross-price elasticity estimates that would need to be reported, we refrain from presenting them in detail and opt instead for a more general discussion of the results. As with the own-price elasticities, the cross-price elasticity estimates vary widely across studies. Lawrence and Braithwait (1977) obtain small but positive estimates using the Connecticut data, indicating a slight degree of substitutability between electricity consumption by time of day. Working with the Arizona data, Atkinson (1979b) and Aigner and Hausman (1980) find, however, that the cross-price elasticities are generally negative, implying gross complementarity of time-of-day consumption. Caves and Christensen (1980b) also obtain negative uncompensated cross-price elasticity estimates with the Wisconsin data, although their compensated cross-price elasticity estimates are positive.

Almost all the studies report "partial" rather than "full" elasticities, the former not accounting for the indirect effects that price changes have on consumption through their effect on electricity expenditure. The full elasticities correspond to the common notion of the term "elasticity," and a compelling case is made by Hendricks and Koenker (1979) for them being the appropriate measures for public policy use (see Hendricks and

---

10. See Aigner and Poirier (1979, 9, equation [2.11]), for the relation between the uncompensated and compensated partial elasticities.

Table 1.3   Compensated Partial Own-Price Elasticities of Electricity Demand by Time of Day

	Connecticut		Arizona		Wisconsin	
	Narrow Peak (4 hrs.)	Broad Peak	Narrow Peak (3 hrs.)	Broad Peak (5–8 hrs.)	Narrow Peak (6 hrs.)	Broad Peak (9–12 hrs.)
Peak Period						
Summer			−0.01LL		−0.01	(−0.03, −0.04)ATK
Winter	(−0.15, −0.32)					
Midpeak Period						
Summer			−0.11LL			
Winter	(−0.18, −0.44)					
Off-Peak Period						
Summer			−0.01LL		−0.11	(−0.00, −0.01)ATK
Winter	(−0.19, −0.28)					

Sources: Connecticut: Lawrence and Braithwait (1977, table 7, p. 75). Arizona and Wisconsin: See table 1.2.

Notes: Arizona: Neither Atkinson (1979b) nor Aigner and Hausman (1980) report compensated elasticities. Wisconsin: Caves and Christensen (1980a) do not report compensated elasticities. See table 1.2 for further explanations.

Koenker 1979, 27). The problem lies in converting partial to full elasticities.[11] This procedure requires knowledge of the elasticity of electricity expenditure with respect to the price of electricity, so reliable estimates of the latter must be found. Caves and Christensen (1980a) and Hendricks and Koenker (1979) both compute full elasticities from partial ones, but both must rely on an assumed value of the expenditure elasticity.

Besides the projects reviewed herein, Research Triangle Institute has provided a summary report (Miedema and White 1980) that covers the efforts in Ohio, Rhode Island, and one of the North Carolina experiments (Blue Ridge Electric Membership Corporation). In these experiments, as in the Connecticut test, only one TOU rate was applied. In Ohio, the sample was small and the ultimate sample design so tenuous that the results of the test should probably be discounted entirely.

In the North Carolina BREMC test, again the sample was small (roughly one hundred experimental households) and one rate schedule was considered. In this experiment, which ran for twelve months only, no perceptible alterations from control-group behavior were observed in the test group.

The Rhode Island experiment provided an additional wrinkle to the menu of experimental tariffs by using a time-differentiated demand charge as well as the usual time-varying kWh prices. This test ran for thirteen months. As in the BREMC case, RTI found essentially no statistically significant TOU effects in Rhode Island.

These comparative results, along with their analyses of Arizona, Connecticut, and Wisconsin, prompted RTI to conclude:

> All studies showed some reduction in usage during the peak period under TOU rates. However, reduction in usage during the peak period was not accompanied by statistically significant increases in base-period usage. Total usage seemed either to decline or remain the same in all projects. . . . Peak-day usage shifts and average-day usage shifts appeared to be about the same. (Miedema and White 1980, 4)

Preliminary work on the Oklahoma and North Carolina (CP&L) experiments was recently made available at a DOE-sponsored conference in Denver. While no elasticity estimates were presented, there were summaries of the qualitative findings to date. In Oklahoma, Brown et al. (1980) report no significant TOU or seasonal effects. Flat rates proved to yield some conservation response compared to declining block rates, but otherwise no conservation or differential effects overall or by TOU price ratio were observed.

11. This conversion is not necessary if the demand model is formulated in such a way that the elasticities directly estimated have a "full" rather than a "partial" interpretation. However, as Hendricks and Koenker (1979) point out, these "simple" demand models have deficiencies that may very well more than counteract this benefit.

In the CP&L test, the RTI group (Miedma 1980) conclude that while some evidence of peak period and overall reductions in consumption can be found, for the most part these effects are not statistically significant to those test groups facing a two-part (customer and energy charge) tariff. With demand charges included, many of the TOU response effects are significant.

To date, there is but limited published work relating to the LADWP (Los Angeles) experiment being conducted by Rand, even though the test itself began in the summer of 1976. Some elasticity results are reported in Acton and Mitchell (1980). The primary use of these estimates is to fuel an illustrative cost-benefit calculation that provides the machinery for evaluating the question of TOU rate implementation, not to present an exhaustive collection of values for various rating periods, customer groups, etc.

What Acton and Mitchell do is to use the elasticity estimates in order to compute the welfare and bill changes that would occur to residential customers under an illustrative TOU tariff, organized by consumption level. In this way it is made clear that only for large users (≥ 1100 kWh/month) will the welfare benefits be sufficient to offset the additional costs of metering. For households with swimming pools, the verdict on TOU pricing is favorable for households at lower consumption levels (80 percent of the sample households with average monthly consumption ≤ 1100 kWh own pools).

An interesting sidelight of the Acton and Mitchell analysis is a brief discussion of the possible ramifications of going to a voluntary TOU rate. Customers who will experience bill reductions in excess of the cost of metering are likely volunteers, but they need not also be the customers who should be included from the point of view of welfare analysis (economic efficiency). For example, for the set of customers for whom it is beneficial in a welfare sense to be put under a TOU rate (monthly consumption ≥ 1100 kWh), most would experience a bill increase at initial consumption levels after incorporating added metering costs. Thus a voluntary program might discourage those customers who are prime candidates for inclusion unless they can be persuaded by the fact that their bills could be lowered by shifting sufficient usage out of the peak period.

That the target customer for implementation of TOU rates in Los Angeles is a large user or a user with a pool may be idiosyncratic of the service territory under consideration to a great extent. So while we may not encourage generalization of the Acton and Mitchell results to New York City, they should be roughly applicable in the southwestern part of the country. Their points about voluntary versus mandatory implementation and their techniques of analysis are worthy of widespread attention.

In a related study, Lillard and Acton (1980) analyze the seasonal-pricing portion of the LADWP experiment. This experiment involves 624 households. Using data covering twenty-three months through September 1977, Lillard and Acton find, in comparing the test customers to the statistical control group, that summer usage is decreased and winter usage is increased in response to the differentially higher summer price, but that the estimated price elasticities associated with these responses are very small—on the order of − .06. In an analysis of anticipated bill and welfare changes, again the estimated effects are so small that very little is to be gained on a per customer basis. But even so, over a large population the net gain (in welfare terms) can be consequential.

While a preliminary report on the California (SCE) experiment has been written (Aigner and Lillard 1980), to date no results from this test have been made public.

Finally, at this point not much is known about the behavior of peak demand (coincident or otherwise) as a function of (kWh) price. Moreover, reported results in all the studies apply generally to the "average weekday," not to the relatively few individual days on which the system peaks and similar extremes occur. The Connecticut data have been manipulated satisfactorily in this respect by considering changes in the customer's entire load curve, but owing to the lack of price variation in the experiment the resulting reductions in peak demand are difficult to generalize beyond the particular experimental conditions observed. This is not to say that information on daily peak-demand effects is not generally available. It is in any experiment where fifteen-minute data were collected. But to date almost none of the analysis work has paid it any attention, relying one supposes on the assumption that if peak-period kWh's are reduced, so must be the level of instantaneous demand.

1.3   Welfare Analysis of TOU Pricing[12]

In assessing the potential for gains and losses to customers who move to a TOU pricing scheme, it is not sufficient merely to examine bill effects. Projected bill changes may have a great deal to do with whether or not customers choose to accept a voluntary program of TOU rates but they are only part of the total impact a customer experiences. The other part of the total impact emanates from quantity adjustments per se. Granted that consumption of both peak and off-peak electricity has positive marginal benefit (more consumption implies more satisfaction), reducing peak-period consumption in response to its higher price, for example, must result in less satisfaction. The way these matters are handled in conven-

12. In preparing this section we have borrowed liberally from Acton and Mitchell (1980).

tional economic theory is through the concept of consumer's surplus. The basic idea is easily illustrated.

Consider figure 1.1, which shows a linear demand curve for, say, off-peak electricity. Prior to the implementation of TOU rates, assume the customer paid a flat-rate $\bar{p}$ per kWh and consumed $\bar{x}_1$ kilowatt-hours per month. At the new price, p_1, the customer now consumes quantity x_1. He pays a price p_1 for every unit consumed. But according to the demand schedule, he would be willing to pay a slightly higher price for consumption slightly less than x_1, a slightly higher price still for consumption slightly less than that, and so on back to the initial consumption level $\bar{x}_1$. But he receives these marginal units of consumption at price p_1 instead of at price $\bar{p}$. Thus, a "surplus" value accrues to him from the price change which is represented by the area of the shaded trapezoid $\bar{p}p_1ba$ (the amount $G + U$). A discriminating monopolist could price his product such a way that each additional unit (moving from $\bar{x}_1$ to x_1) is just that much less expensive so as to extract this surplus value from the consumer.

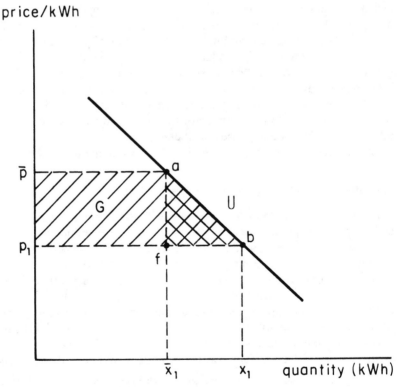

Fig. 1.1   Measurement of change in consumer's surplus from a price decrease from $\bar{p}$ to p_1

Otherwise the shaded area, which is in dollar units, represents a real gain in the customer's "welfare."

In a similar fashion, the increase in peak-period kWh's will result in a loss of this same sort of welfare. Figure 1.2 illustrates the situation, wherein the peak-period price per kWh is increased from a flat rate of $\bar{p}$ to p_2. At this price the customer will consume x_2 kWh's as compared to $\bar{x}_2$ when the price was $\bar{p}$. Using the same heuristic argument as before, the change in the consumer's surplus is a loss, in the amount of the area of the shaded trapezoid $p\bar{p}_2cd$ (the amount L).

Adopting a conventional notation, these areas are, respectively,

$$\Delta p_2 \left(\frac{x_2 + \bar{x}_2}{2} \right) \text{ and } -\Delta p_1 \left(\frac{x_1 + \bar{x}_1}{2} \right),$$

where the Greek delta means "change in" or "difference," i.e., $\Delta p_1 = p_1 - \bar{p}$ and $\Delta p_2 = p_2 - \bar{p}$. Then the change in the consumer's surplus from

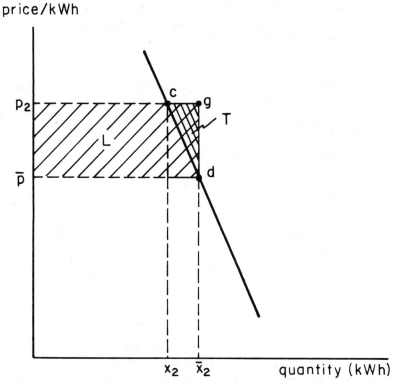

Fig. 1.2   Measurement of change in consumer's surplus from a price increase from $\bar{p}$ to p_2

the combined effects of adopting a higher peak-period price and a lower off-peak-period is given by:

(1)
$$\Delta CS = -\left[\Delta p_1\left(\frac{x_1 + \overline{x}_1}{2}\right) + \Delta p_2\left(\frac{x_2 + \overline{x}_2}{2}\right)\right].$$

From the producer's viewpoint, calculation of the gains and losses from moving to TOU pricing is simplified by assuming that $\overline{p}$, the flat rate charged in each period, is a quantity-weighted average of the marginal costs of production in each time period and that the customer charge recovers all fixed costs. If mc_1 and mc_2 are the marginal costs in the off-peak and peak periods, respectively, and ϕ_1 and ϕ_2 are the proportions of off-peak and peak consumption relative to total consumption for the class, then

(2)
$$\overline{p} = \phi_1 mc_1 + \phi_2 mc_2.$$

Assuming that the TOU prices, p_1 and p_2 are set equal to their respective marginal costs, mc_1 and mc_2, and again that the customer charge (E) is used to recover all fixed costs, then in figure 1.1 the producer will lose revenue by reducing the off-peak price (demand is assumed to be inelastic) in the amount $p_1 x_1 - \overline{p}\,\overline{x}_1$ for a change in production costs of $p_1(x_1 - \overline{x}_1)$. This gives a net change (loss) of

$$-\overline{p}\,\overline{x}_1 + p_1\overline{x}_1 = \Delta p_1\overline{x}_1,$$

a negative quantity. Similarly, in the peak period revenues are increased by changing from $\overline{p}$ to p_2 (again, demand is assumed to be inelastic), and costs are reduced, giving a net effect (gain) of $\Delta p_2\overline{x}_2$. In sum, the change in net revenue to the producer is

(3)
$$\Delta NR = \Delta p_1\overline{x}_1 + \Delta p_2\overline{x}_2.$$

If we adopt as our criterion for judging the overall benefits or costs to society of the adoption of the TOU pricing scheme (E, p_1, p_2) the sum $\Delta CS + \Delta NR$, then the change in welfare becomes

(4)
$$\Delta W = \Delta CS + \Delta NR$$
$$= -\left[\Delta p_1\left(\frac{x_1 + \overline{x}_1}{2}\right) + \Delta p_2\left(\frac{x_2 + \overline{x}_2}{2}\right)\right]$$
$$+ \Delta p_1\overline{x}_1 + \Delta p_2\overline{x}_2$$
$$= -\tfrac{1}{2}\left(\Delta p_1\Delta x_1 + \Delta p_2\Delta x_2\right).$$

This sum is equivalent to the sum of the areas U and T in the figures.

This welfare measure is only approximate. First, the demand curves used to develop these formulas are linear. Secondly, the contemplated price changes not only have direct influence on the quantities consumed that are depicted in the figures but also have indirect effects due to the interrelationship of each quantity on *both* prices. An exact measurement for ΔW depends on more adequate measurement of ΔCS and requires knowledge of this set of two interrelated demand equations.[13] This is what the TOU pricing experiments can provide.

For a representative customer, one who at the initial consumption levels $\bar{x}_1$ and $\bar{x}_2$ consumes electricity in the two periods exactly in the proportions ϕ_1 and ϕ_2, the equation (4) also can be interpreted as showing a direct welfare effect and a bill effect. At the initial consumption levels, x_1 and x_2, a movement to prices p_1 and p_2 will create a change in a customer's bill of exactly

(5) $$\Delta B_0 = \Delta p_1 \bar{x}_1 + \Delta p_2 \bar{x}_2$$

Whether this number is positive or negative depends precisely on how

$$\bar{x}_1 / (\bar{x}_1 + \bar{x}_2) \text{ and } \bar{x}_2 / (\bar{x}_1 + \bar{x}_2)$$

compare to ϕ_1 and ϕ_2. If they are respectively equal, which is the definition of the representative customer, then $\Delta B_0 = 0$. The shifts in consumption that are observed, Δx_1 and Δx_2, therefore represent unambiguous welfare improvements. Ultimately, the bill changes by an amount

(6) $$\Delta B = \Delta B_0 + p_1 \Delta x_1 + p_2 \Delta x_2$$

(in which $\Delta B_0 = 0$ for the representative customer).

Tracing through the changes in the bill and in consumer's surplus from the price changes to p_1 and p_2 for the representative customer, we are lead to the same formula for ΔW derived previously in equation (4). In figure 1.1 the representative customer's bill increases by $x_1 \bar{x}_1 bg$, whereas his surplus has increased by the trapezoidal area G + U. The net effect is a gain in welfare, the area U. Similarly, in the peak period his bill falls by the amount $x_2 \bar{x}_2 gc$, but surplus is reduced by the area L. The net effect is a gain, the area T.

For a nonrepresentative customer, one with consumption proportions different from ϕ_1 and ϕ_2, the calculations are the same, but $B_0 \neq 0$. Thus, there will be a shift in revenue either to the customer or to the utility at initial consumption levels in addition to the changes summarized in equation (4). As mentioned previously, calculating the exact welfare changes depends on a knowledge of the full demand structure; the above calculation should be viewed as approximate only.

The entire objective of this exposition lies in the identification of those customers for whom ΔW exceeds the additional costs associated with implementing the TOU rate structure. This desired set of customers may be identified by size, by appliance ownership, or by some other meaning-

---

13. See Acton and Mitchell (1980, 7) for more discussion.

ful stratifying variable. In their application to the LADWP service area, Acton and Mitchell found that under an illustrative mandatory program, the change in welfare was sufficiently large to offset the traditional metering costs only for customers whose average monthly consumption exceeds 1100 kWh. Although this is a small fraction of the population of LADWP residential customers (4.3 percent), they account for approximately 17 percent of residential consumption.

Offering TOU pricing on a voluntary basis creates a further difficulty in that the welfare-efficient set of customers may not be the ones attracted to the program. For example, in the Acton and Mitchell illustration, if customers were to be charged the appropriate monthly rate for TOU metering, the monthly bills of all but the very largest members of the $\geq$ 1100 kWh/mo. group would experience bill increases at initial consumption levels. Unless customers could be persuaded that their ultimate shifting response will result in sufficiently more "welfare" to make participation worthwhile—no doubt a hard concept to sell—the voluntary program will not work.

However, there may be other population subgroups that are almost as attractive in the welfare-efficiency sense whose bills at initial consumption levels show decreases large enough to offset metering charges, thereby making participation in a voluntary program attractive. In the LADWP case, Acton and Mitchell point to those households with swimming pools as likely candidates, but in this case also, bill changes at initial consumption levels do not make a voluntary program attractive, even though bill decreases would be experienced by most of this group once their peak and off-peak period consumption had adjusted to the TOU rates. Many households with electric space heating, on the other hand, would enjoy initial bill decreases in excess of additional metering costs and would, therefore, find a voluntary program attractive. However, only for the largest of these users are the welfare gains sufficient to offset metering costs. Therefore, the utility faces the problem of attracting a potentially large number of customers into a voluntary program for whom the ultimate composite welfare benefits are such that they should not have been included.

1.4   The Risks of Implementation

The previous sections have laid a foundation for possible implementation of TOU rates. But there are various uncertainties to cope with in assessing the risks associated with that course of action, given that the elasticity estimates upon which it depends are subject to sampling error at the very least (assuming there was a relevant experiment to provide elasticity estimates for the target population) and, more generally, subject to other risks, under the assumption that transference of results outside the target population and/or service territory is involved.

An important aspect of the risks involved in an implementation decision is that even if there is a relevant experiment available that can provide elasticity estimates for the target population of interest, the sampling errors associated with those estimates imply uncertainties for the revenue and welfare calculations. These can and should be traced through, by deriving the statistical confidence intervals on, say, revenue from the confidence intervals available for the estimated elasticities.

Finally, the more widespread problem of transferring results from an experiment of relevance to a different target population and, probably, a different service territory involves yet addititional uncertainty, still of the statistical variety. The methodology for handling the transference problem is available but has not yet been adapted to the issue at hand.

So, while there can be general discussion on all these points, the particular use of available techniques for applying them in specific cases remains one of custom fit.

1.4.1   Uncertainty in Using Experimental Results

In those few service areas where a reasonably good TOU experiment has been run, there still are some sticky issues to contend with in using the demand elasticities or, more generally, the estimated set of demand equations in evaluating the welfare and revenue impacts of adopting a TOU pricing structure. These issues are developed and illustrated herein. In those service areas where an experiment without induced price variation was completed, a similar exercise could be accomplished, but only if the contemplated rate structure were exactly the same as the experimental rate structure. Otherwise the situation is such that an evaluation would require the transference of results from another service area, a topic we address in the second part of this section.

A crucial feature of any of the experiments is the effective population to which they apply. In their initial evaluation of the available TOU-pricing projects, Research Triangle Institute (RTI) does a good job of addressing this point (U.S. Department of Energy 1978), and they reemphasize it in a recent report summarizing their findings on estimated price effects for several of the projects.

> The sample was drawn from a population consisting of all 1976 WPSC non-farm non-seasonal residential customers who had a 12-month billing history and whose average monthly usage exceeded 100 kWh in 1975. This sampled population (approximately 217,000) was stratified into nine groups according to their 1975 annual consumption. Simple random sampling was used within each stratum to produce the desired number of participants. Approximatley 43 percent of all WPSC residential accounts were represented by the sample.

Participation in the study was mandatory. Customers were billed under revenue-neutralized rates. The rates ensured that the average household's bill would be nearly identical to its bill under the existing rates, if its consumption level and pattern were unchanged during the experimental period. (Miedema and White, 1980, 66–67)

According to this quotation, 43 percent of Wisconsin Public Corporation accounts are represented by the sample; that is, this 43 percent is the effective population for which the sample results can be generalized. Since participation was mandatory, there is no apparent problem of sample self-selection to contend with.

In Ohio, the experiment was voluntary, and, according to Miedema and White,

Selection of sample customers excluded those without a 12-month billing history of April 1974 to April 1975, bulk-metered residences, company employees, residents on "frozen" rates, and customers with less than 6,000 kWh annual usage. The group that was sampled contained approximately 196,000 of the 337,000 residential customers living in the DPL service area.

About 80 percent of the customers selected to participate in the study were not included for such reasons as meter installation problems, refusal to participate, and moving plans. Based on the combined number of rejections for the experimental and control groups, customers in the final sample represent about 39,000 residential customers (the effective population). This group constitutes approximately 20 percent of the sample population and 12 percent of all residential customers. (1980, 55–56)

In this instance, many restrictions were imposed on the population ultimately sampled; so many, in fact, that the results (which are only comparative—one TOU rate was used) apply at best to 12 percent of all residential customers.

The point is simply that statistical inference involves generalizing sample results in the population from which the sample was selected. If that population is different from the target population, then the inference will be biased. In some situations the problem can be handled analytically,[14] but otherwise the best that can be hoped for is knowledge of the direction of the bias.

For the effective population, it is relatively simple to trace the effects of imprecision in the estimated demand elasticities on the revenue or welfare calculations discussed previously. For example, the revenue change derived from shifts in off-peak consumption in moving from price $\bar{p}$ to TOU prices p_1 and p_2 is a function of the quantity change $\Delta x_1 = \bar{x}_1 - x_1$.

14. See, for example, one of the attempts to correct the Arizona experimental results for bias introduced by the incentive scheme used (Aigner and Hausman 1980). While these authors do not specifically address the target-population–effective-population issue, the methodology developed is pertinent.

And that quantity change, as a function of the price changes p_1 and p_2, can be written

(7) $$\Delta x_1 = \frac{\partial x_1}{\partial p_1} \Delta p_1 + \frac{\partial x_1}{\partial p_2} \Delta p_2 .$$

The required partial derivatives, if not directly estimated from a set of fitted demand functions, are usually simple functions of other estimated model parameters, and a measure of the precision of their estimation can be readily obtained. For example, given direct estimates of $\partial x_1 / \partial p_1$ and $\partial x_1 / \partial p_2$ with their estimated variances and covariance, the variance of Δx_1 can easily be derived and used to put a confidence band around the predicted revenue or welfare change.[15] This would seem to be a very useful way to characterize the implications of uncertainty (imprecision) in estimated model parameters (slopes, elasticities) on the ultimate criterion for judging whether a particular TOU rate program should be adopted or not.

Unfortunately, there is not just one way to estimate the important parameters. In a previous section we saw how model specification had a pronounced influence on the estimated elasticities in the Arizona experiment. Each set of parameter estimates rests on different statistical assumptions, and therefore so do the inferences emanating from them. And, for the most part, these underlying assumptions cannot be tested. What is hoped for is robustness in the estimated parameters over models, but this almost never seems to happen. The range of parameter estimates over models, which implies a range of revenue and/or welfare changes, poses yet another source of uncertainty to cope with in evaluating a proposed TOU rate. In all such situations the most reasonable thing to do is to trace out the range of implications and assess their consequences in order to fully understand the risks involved, if not to completely resolve the matter.

1.4.2 The Transferability Problem[16]

When sampling is used to answer a question—test a hypothesis or estimate a particular population parameter—there is always the possibil-

---

15. If $V(b_1)$ and $V(b_2)$ are the variances of the estimates for $\partial x_1 / \partial p_1$ and $\partial x_1 / \partial p_2$, respectively, and $C(b_1, b_2)$ is their covariance, then

$$V(\Delta x_1) = \Delta p_1^2 V(b_1) + \Delta p_2^2 V(b_2) + 2 \Delta p_1 \Delta p_2 \, C(b_1, b_2) .$$

Extending to get a measure of precision for the revenue change from alterations in off-peak consumption, we have that

$$\Delta R_1 = p_1 x_1 - \bar{p} \bar{x}_1 = p_1 \Delta x_1 + \Delta p_1 x_1 ,$$

and that

$$V(\Delta R_1) = p_1^2 V(\Delta x_1) .$$

16. In preparing this subsection I have benefited greatly from discussions with E. Leamer.

ity of using previous studies or experience on the same topic in order to "guide" the sample design, to supplement it, or to replace it completely by prior information. If it is assumed that in any such application there is a primary population model that describes the relationships between dependent and independent variables and the statistical properties of error terms, and that this population relationship applies, with differences in parameters only, to all subpopulations, then all available information can be represented in terms of sets of estimated parameters of a "grand" model. The analytical question to be addressed is how the various sets of estimates are to be weighted in importance.

To be specific, consider the situation whereby a utility is considering increasing the sample size of its residential load research sample. The choices are limited to the addition of some calculable number of magnetic tape-recording meters and/or dependence on the load research data of a neighboring utility or group of utilities to use in lieu of an addition to its own sample. Assuming there is a statistical model that relates the load in any predescribed small interval (the meter resolution capability) to weather and various other exogenous factors (physical characteristics of homes, socioeconomic characteristics of families, appliance ownership patterns) for both utilities, it can be shown that there is an optimal estimator for the load at any moment which is a linear combination of the load data from both utilities.[17] This is not to say that additional sampling is not necessary; indeed, it may be. But at least a methodology exists that makes it possible to combine information in an appropriate fashion. Likewise, in any decision problem prior information can be considered in combination with sample data to decide whether further sampling is required, and, if so, how many additional additional observations should be taken.[18]

The transferability problem with respect to an analysis of the implications of a TOU rate can be viewed in exactly the same way. In general, the problem should be approached by allowing for the possibility that a fresh sample will be taken, that is, that the subject utility will design and operate its own pricing experiment. Then, given prior information based on the results of other experiments, the question is whether a new sample should be taken, and if so, what its size should be. Otherwise the decision problem is based solely on the available prior information. In a similar fashion, the combination of existing elasticity estimates for utilities that have run experiments with information from other utilities can be achieved.

A major problem in combining data sets or estimates concerns data

17. Lindley and Smith (1972). A very recent application of this methodology to a "transferability" problem is contained in the paper by DeMouchel and Harris (1981), which I became aware of at the conference.
18. Aigner (1979); a general reference is Raiffa and Schlaifer (1961).

quality and sample design. While it is possible to combine data from different utilities according to the Lindley and Smith (1972) methodology, a presumption must be made about their quality. Moreover, while the data themselves may be comparable, no doubt there will be differences in design—as summarized by which stratifying variables have been used, on which other explanatory variables data have been collected, etc. Thus in the combining process, recognition must be made of the fact that various specification errors will exist in fitting the so-called grand model. This problem has not been addressed so far in the literature that has grown out of the Lindley and Smith work. However, it must be confronted in order to properly characterize the data that are to be combined and to thereby determine whatever constraints may exist on the combining process from data that lack certain essential characteristics or "quality."

A general proposition is that "similar" utilities can properly make use of each other's load data or experimental results. The statistical modeling problem is how best to define "similar" and how to "partially transfer" information among dissimilar utilities. As an example, initially one might suppose that data could be transferred among warm-climate utilities and among cold-climate utilities but not between utilities drawn from different climates. However, climate might affect the average load in a given time period while leaving unchanged the responsiveness of load to increases in price. In that case information about the responsiveness of loads to price, possibly for predicting load increases, could be transferred between warm- and cold-climate utilities, but information about the average loads could not. Next suppose that after a study of several utilities it was found that the average load increased by 1 percent every time the average daily temperature departed from 68° by 2°. Then even the information about average load could be transferred between climates. This means that the transferability problem has to be addressed within the context of an econometric model of load demand.

As an example data-pooling problem, consider the one studied by Efron and Morris (1975), from which table 1.4 is taken. The batting average of eighteen major-league players after 45 turns at bat during 1970 are reported in column 1 of table 1.4. Anyone familiar with baseball statistics will recognize immediately that these averages are too dispersed to be end-of-season averages. In fact no one has batted over .400 for the season since Ted Williams did in 1941. A sensible prediction of Clemente's rest-of-season average would surely be less than his average of .400 after only 45 at bats. What Efron and Morris do is to pool Clemente's average with the averages of the other seventeen batters. An extreme possibility would be to assume that all players have the same batting ability and to predict the average for the remainder of the season to be the same for each, thus equal to the overall average of the 45 × 18 at

Table 1.4   1970 Batting Averages and Predictions for Eighteen Major League
                 Players

Player	Average after First Forty-five At Bats	Average for Remainder of Season	Pooled Prediction Based on Stein's Estimator	Limited Translation Pooled Prediction
Clemente (Pitts, NL)	.400	.346	.290	.351
F. Robinson (Balt, AL)	.378	.298	.286	.329
F. Howard (Wash, AL)	.356	.276	.281	.308
Johnstone, (Cal, AL)	.333	.222	.277	.287
Berry, (Chi, AL)	.311	.273	.273	.273
Spencer (Cal, AL)	.311	.273	.273	.273
Kessinger (Chi, NL)	.289	.263	.268	.268
L. Alvarado (Bos, AL)	.267	.210	.264	.264
Santo (Chi, NL)	.244	.269	.259	.259
Swoboda (NY, NL)	.244	.230	.259	.259
Unser (Wash, AL)	.222	.264	.254	.254
Williams (Chi, AL)	.222	.256	.254	.254
Scott (Bos, AL)	.222	.303	.254	.254
Petrocelli (Bos, AL)	.222	.264	.254	.254
E. Rodriguez (KC, AL)	.222	.226	.254	.254
Campaneris (Oak, AL)	.200	.285	.249	.242
Munson, (NY, AL)	.178	.316	.244	.218
Alvis (Mil, NL)	.156	.200	.239	.194

bats, namely .265. But the dispersion of the 18 averages after 45 at bats is
much greater than would be predicted if all players had identical abilities.
A better assumption would be that the players' abilities come from a
distribution with unknown mean and unknown variance. This assumption leads to the partial pooling of the 18 averages. The prediction of the
batting average for the remainder of the season is then a weighted
average of own average and overall average (.265). Clement's estimated
average is thereby reduced from .400 to .290. The last two columns of
table 1.4 contain different pooled predictions, the latter one being a
"limited translation estimator" that was designed to limit the pooling
effect on extreme averages, Clemente's for example. By a measure of
overall error, the pooled estimators perform better than the players' own
scores after 45 at bats as predictions of their future performance.

The statistical problem of predicting the rest-of-season averages of
these eighteen ball players is essentially the same as the problem of data
transferability for utilities. If no data are transferred from the other
seventeen players to Clemente, a prediction based on his average alone is
likely to be too extreme. If the other data are fully transferred with no
allowances made for individual differences, the resultant prediction of

.265 is likely to be too conservative. The statistical technique described by Efron and Morris allows the data to select the degree of transferability. If the 18 averages are sufficiently similar to support the hypothesis that all batters have the same ability, then the data are fully transferred in the sense that Alvis's .156 average has the same weight for predicting Clemente's rest-of-season performance as Clemente's own average. But if the 18 averages after 45 at bats are very dispersed, the degree of transferability can drop to zero, with Clemente's prediction being equal to his current average of .400.

This simple problem of pooling batting averages can be generalized in several ways that bring it closer to the complexities that must be handled in the problem of data transferability. The batting averages used for prediction purposes are all based on 45 at bats. In the case of the TOU experiments, sample sizes vary widely. And for most utilities that desire to evaluate a TOU pricing structure, sample size is zero. This is akin to a new player entering the league.

Of course, in the case of utility companies there will be many variables which could suggest reasons why a utility without data should not be treated as an average utility. Continuing the baseball example, we might expect to observe two kinds of batters—outfielders and infielders, with the latter selected with greater concern for their defensive abilities. A player with an initial average of .400 may with justification be considered an outfielder, and therefore his average should be shrunk not toward the overall mean of .265 but rather to the mean of the outfielders' averages. If it is not known which batters are offensive specialists and which defensive specialists, the data may nonetheless suggest the dichotomy.

Theoretically, the limitations on data transference will be defined by the weight placed on data from other utilities in the pooling process just described. In a sense, if all relevant variables are observed both in the parent utility and in the collection of utilities at large, there are no limitations to transferability. But because the data on concomitant variables may not be comparable, certain difficulties arise in the pooling process. As mentioned previously, the nature and extent of these difficulties remain to be worked out. From this research will come guidance as to what the limitations to transferability are. They will be defined in terms of geographical location, specific weather patterns, customer demographics, etc.

To conclude, there are no *conceptual* limitations on data transference but there are strong assumptions which may not be very attractive that are required to accomplish it through the Lindley and Smith (1972) framework. The existing methodology has not yet been applied to the case of transferring experimental results between utilities or, for that matter, to load research data in general. This major research focus remains to be undertaken. Finally, within the context of a general framework for transferability, even the information from experiments without price variation may be important and usable.

1.5   Conclusions

What are the primary shortcomings of the available estimates of the relevant short-run elasticities? First, there is the matter of discrepancies among the estimates within experiments. From a qualitative viewpoint, we can conclude that TOU- pricing "worked." Quantitatively, only the Arizona and Wisconsin tests provide enough integrity of design and at least a semblance of common findings on which to base a decision about implementation. Soon, but not just yet, detailed results will be available from Oklahoma, North Carolina (CP&L), LADWP, and Southern California Edison Co. These results may provide enough evidence for implementation, but we should also like to know if a better strategy than overall implementation might be phased or selective implementation, concentrating on large customers first. Presumably every experiment's results could be organized and reported according to size of customer (at least in some broad intervals) as in the LADWP case. Thus proper information to support selective implementation could be made available.

What then of the fact that the available reliable findings are confined to such a limited area (Arizona and Wisconsin—or Arizona, Wisconsin, Oklahoma, Southern California [LADWP and SCE], and North Carolina, when these latter results are available)? Ideally, one would hope that once all conditioning variables have been accounted for, there will be a unanimous verdict, even down to the actual numbers themselves. Yet there seems to be enough room for a lack of unanimity that, due to the basic latitude for mismodeling, present but undiscovered faults in the experiments, etc., one shouldn't be too surprised if in fact there is a hung jury on the specific magnitude of TOU effects across service territories.

Research on the transferability problem, made even more important by practical considerations imposed by the National Energy Act, may produce the comprehensive framework within which all such issues can be resolved. But the electric utilities will have to act (or at least defend their nonaction) on TOU- pricing very soon, probably before the transferability problem is resolved. In the interim, given a clear verdict on the qualitative results of the experiments, implementation may take place, for the rate setting and regulatory process itself is an experiment with inherent and accepted risks associated with errors of calculation and judgment. A decision made on TOU- pricing is no more or less irreversible than any other.[19]

19. Following this line of reasoning, presumably there are now quite a few examples of implementation, primarily of a voluntary nature, including Arizona Public Service Co., LADWP, and Wisconsin Power & Light.

Finally, what of the design issues raised at the outset? How have they contributed to or limited our knowledge of TOU- pricing effects from the battery of available experiments? Clearly the lack of significant price variation and the fact that in most experiments with price variation, peak, off-peak, and midpeak prices are not varied independently substantially limits the generalizability of the results even on a local level. Sample-size considerations are at issue here too, since more "treatments" (prices, definitions of pricing periods, etc.) require more observations in order to achieve a given level of precision for parameter estimates.

In these several respects, one of the experiments stands clearly above the rest: the Rand-LADWP experiment. It has a large sample size with wide (and, to some extent, independent) variation in prices. Definitions of pricing periods (peaks, off-peak, midpeak) were not rigid. Moreover, optimal design methods were used to further squeeze information out of the sample, but not to such an extent as to limit the variety of analysis models that could be applied once the data were in hand. Probably the only clear limitation on the LADWP experiment was its use of volunteers and an incentive scheme for participants.[20]

All the other experiments represent some compromise on the best features of the LADWP test, but some also improve on the LADWP experiment's major weaknesses. For example, both the Wisconsin and North Carolina (CP&L) projects have mandatory participation and no compensation payments.

In all cases, however, there are other, perhaps more severe limitations that customers face, imposed by the experimental environment and the fact that the experiments are short-run by nature. Many people contend that with a full-blown commitment to TOU- pricing, the responsiveness of customers will be different than that estimated by the experiments. This difference will occur because appliance choices will be made with an eye to TOU response; new appliances will become widely available, and there will be no choice but for customers to respond (assuming mandatory implementation). But it seems impossible to estimate these effects. The prevailing attitude is that if TOU- pricing can be shown to be cost-effective based on the available experimental evidence, the pricing strategy surely must be even more desirable in the long- run.

While both of these views are reasonable, it is important to note that none of the experiments allows us to estimate the effects (apart from TOU response) of changing the average price of electricity on the consumption of other goods. These expenditure elasticities, which convert partial price elasticities to full price elasticities, can mitigate substantially

20. It should be noted that the issues of independent price variation, voluntary participation, and incentive payments are not separate. Rates designed with revenue neutrality in mind (which therefore eliminates independent variation in peak and off-peak prices), of course eliminates the need for compensation payments and may be an important ingredient in achieving mandatory participation.

the anticipated long-run effects from mandatory implementation of TOU rates. It may well be that the apparent overall conservation effect of TOU- pricing observed in many of the experiments is merely an artifact of their short-run nature, wherein response was constrained by the present set of household appliances and closely reflects the potential response to higher electricity prices without regard to TOU influences.

Appendix: Project Evaluations

In this appendix we discuss the fifteen demonstration projects in more detail and explain our evaluation of each project. The projects may be judged on many facets of their experimental design and, as mentioned in the text, the Research Triangle Institute and Michigan Survey Research Center (SRC) studies do just that. The SRC paper, for example, evaluates projects on the basis of appropriateness of experimental conditions, noncoverage error, sampling error, treatment error, nonresponse error, and measurement error. The judgments we make in table 1.1 of the text are based on the descriptions and evaluations given in the SRC study, with the design of the experiment's price treatments being of primary importance in making our decisions.

In classifying projects on the basis of their ability to provide quality data for estimates of TOU price effects, we use the following procedure. First we divide the projects into two groups, depending on whether they employ a single price treatment or a wide variation in treatments. We then examine the nonprice aspects of each project's experimental design. Those projects with a single price treatment which also have other design problems are classified as being "of no interest." Those with a single price treatment which are otherwise generally well designed are termed "of limited interest." Any projects that have multiple price treatments but other design drawbacks are also considered to be "of limited interest." Finally, projects with multiple price treatments that are well designed overall are viewed as being "of interest."

Projects with a Single Price Treatment and
Other Design Flaws ("Of No Interest")

Projects in this category are those in New York, Ohio, Rhode Island, and Vermont. All employ single price treatments. The Vermont experiment is not even evaluated by the SRC study because of its unscientific design. The New York project has a severe problem with a biased sample, as the sample is made up in large part by nonrandomly selected volunteers who responded to a bill insert. The Ohio project is somewhat better in this regard, since the sampling was conducted randomly (after some customers were excluded for various reasons). However, because participation was voluntary, about 70 to 80 percent of the selected customers decided not to take part in the experiment. Other problems include possible customer confusion about the price they were being charged during a labor strike and insufficient documentation of many of the details of the experiment. The Rhode Island project appears not to have been designed to examine demand responses to TOU rates, as it employs a complex rate structure that is never varied. At the time of the SRC study, documentation was insufficient to judge the project on many other design characteristics.

Projects with a Single Price Treatment Which Are Otherwise Well Designed ("Of Limited Interest")

The Arkansas, Connecticut, and North Carolina (BREMC) projects come under this heading, as all are generally well designed except that they have only a single price treatment. The Arkansas project's favorable design characteristics include mandatory participation and no participation incentives. The Connecticut experiment employs a sampling procedure that results in high-quality consumption and survey data.

Projects with Multiple Price Treatments but Other Design Flaws ("Of No Interest")

The Puerto Rico project falls in this category. While it features varying time-of-day rates that allow for elasticity estimation, it has a number of unappealing aspects. There are many unnecessary exclusions from the sample, it is unclear whether allocation to treatment groups is random, and response is voluntary and quite low.

Well-Designed Projects with Multiple Price Treatments ("Of Interest")

The projects in this group are those in Arizona, California (LADWP and SCE), North Carolina (CP&L), Oklahoma, and Wisconsin. All employ multiple price treatments and generally have other favorable design characteristics. The North Carolina and Wisconsin projects are the best designed of these featuring widely varying rates since they have mandatory participation. These two experiments also use rate structures that contain demand charges, enabling researchers to estimate price effects on peak kW demand. The other experiments offer slightly lower quality data, and researchers have to contend with problems of volunteer bias and the effects of incentive payments on consumption.

Other Projects

TOU pricing experiments were also scheduled to take place in New Jersey and San Diego, California. Both were scrapped because of equipment problems.

Comment   Paul L. Joskow

Dennis Aigner has provided us with a useful paper that reviews the various residential time-of-use (TOU) pricing experiments and discusses a variety of important implementation issues. After nearly a decade of debate before state and federal regulatory agencies about the benefits and costs of TOU pricing and the expenditure of tens of millions of dollars on experiments, it is certainly an appropriate time to take stock of what we have learned.

The Aigner paper leads me to several general conclusions about the TOU experiments and their usefulness for public policy and electric-utility decision making. First, it is fairly clear that many of the experiments have serious flaws that limit their usefulness for estimating the price elasticities of interest. While there are numerous sampling, experimental design, and duration problems, the most important general problem is that many of the experiments failed to provide a sufficient number of different TOU price treatments to make econometric estimation of price elasticities possible. Of the fifteen experiments discussed, only six appear to be particularly useful for the estimation of TOU own-price and cross-price elasticities, and data from only two of these (Arizona and Wisconsin) have been made widely available for analysis to date.

Second, most studies that have analyzed the data from experiments which were structured so that price elasticities could be estimated have found that the own-price elasticities at various times (peak, shoulder, off-peak) are negative. This result comes as no great shock to most economists. The point estimates for the own-price elasticities vary widely, however. Peak-period elasticity estimates have a range of something like -0.2 to -0.8, and off-peak elasticity estimates range from about -0.1 to -0.8. Differences among the experiments in the definition of pricing periods makes useful comparisons of peak versus off-peak elasticities very difficult. Cross-price elasticity estimates also vary widely across studies, both in absolute value and sign. Analysts working with similar data come up with very different elasticity estimates because the analytic approaches differ with regard to the specification of the demand system to be estimated, the experimental time period for which data are utilized, and the extent to which they account for the compensation scheme used to "protect" participants from increases in their electricity bills.

Finally, at least in principle, the results of these experiments can be used by public utilities and their regulatory commissions to help decide on whether to institute voluntary or mandatory residential TOU pricing.

Paul L. Joskow is professor of economics, Massachusetts Institute of Technology.

There are three major issues that must be tackled here. First, since the implementation of residential TOU pricing requires relatively large expenditures on metering equipment, we want to determine the characteristics of those residential customers whose responses to TOU pricing will yield welfare gains that are greater than the additional transaction costs associated with TOU pricing. Aigner's discussion of the calculation of the welfare gains and losses from TOU pricing, that draws on the familiar Steiner/Boiteux peak-load pricing model and the application of this model to preliminary data from the Los Angeles experimental data by Acton and Mitchell, provides a simple methodology for making such calculations. Second, even when good experimental data are available to a regulatory commission, the elasticity estimates are uncertain, and statistical confidence intervals must be correctly calculated and applied in a meaningful way in any welfare analysis. Third, techniques must be developed to allow us to transfer what we have learned from the very small number of good experiments to other areas of the country with diverse economic and demographic characteristics. While Aigner sketches out possible solutions to these last two issues, it seems to me that a lot of work remains to be done before they can be adequately resolved.

The residential TOU experiments were conducted primarily at the behest of state and federal regulatory authorities and electric utilities interested in obtaining information to help resolve public policy debates over TOU pricing and to estimate the effects of TOU pricing on load patterns and revenues. These are the ultimate customers for the results of these experiments. I believe it is useful to evaluate them from the perspective of the regulators and the firms in the context of the problems they have been trying to grapple with at least for the past ten years.

The first issue that I want to discuss is why so many of the experiments were so poorly designed. I believe the answer lies in the true political and economic origins of these experiments. When the earliest experiments were structured, those involved had simply not thought very deeply about what the data generated might be used for. The earliest experiments were motivated more by narrow adversarial and litigation concerns than by a serious interest in sound economic analysis. The earliest efforts to estimate the effects of TOU pricing on residential electricity consumption patterns arose in the early 1970s in the context of enormous regulatory controversy about the desirability of marginal-cost pricing in general and TOU pricing based on marginalist principles in particular.

On the one hand, several environmental groups and a number of economists appearing before state regulatory commissions were pressing for the use of marginal-cost pricing principles in place of conventional average-cost pricing principles and argued that mandatory TOU rates for industrial customers and mandatory or voluntary TOU rates for residential consumers should be implemented. Proponents of TOU pricing pointed to the experiences in France, England, and Germany as examples of situations in which TOU pricing had been used successfully at both the industrial and residential levels. The efficiency rationale for marginal-cost pricing and the extension of marginalist principles to the development of peak-load pricing schemes for electricity service had long been a part of the economic literature. The major interest of environmental groups in TOU pricing was to give incentives to reduce the rate of growth in peak demand so as to reduce the need for additional power plants. These arguments were often congenial to state regulatory commissions because they too were looking for ways to reduce the need for new generating capacity, with costs two to three times average historical costs, as a way to moderate the need for rate increases. Most electric utilities opposed TOU pricing initially. Among other things, they argued that consumers would not respond to higher prices by reducing consumption on peak, that TOU metering was too costly and impractical, that it would increase uncertainty about revenues and profits, that it would only lead to shifting peaks, etc. Large industrial customers opposed marginal-cost pricing and, initially, TOU pricing primarily because they were concerned that major changes in rate structures would be used by state regulatory commissions to redistribute the relative contributions to total utility revenue requirements so that the industrial classes would pay more and the residential class pay less. The early TOU experiments were really fire-fighting exercises aimed at developing some crude U.S. evidence that the elasticity of demand for electricity was negative (yes indeed, back in the early 1970s some regulatory commissions and utilities refused to believe this). Furthermore, the experiments were motivated by a misperception that the residential class represented the greatest target of opportunity for TOU rates, despite the fact that countries like France had devoted most of their efforts to the industrial class. The early TOU experiments were also viewed by some as a convenient way of delaying regulatory decisions on TOU pricing.

These experiments had their origin in a heated regulatory controversy, and little thought was given to the kinds of cost-benefit analyses that Aigner spends a good deal of time discussing. There was no *inherent* reason for these early experiments to have been so poorly designed. There already existed a reasonably good model to build on in the English Domestic Tariff Experiment conducted between 1967 and 1972, and the analysts working with these early experimental residential data used precisely the same welfare model that Aigner presents in his paper. In short, the early experiments were poorly designed because they were poorly motivated and had very narrow objectives.

Some of the more recent experiments have been better structured and have yielded more useful information, both because the Department of Energy established some minimal guidelines and because some utilities have come to realize that it is in their interests to better understand how residential consumers respond to TOU rates, how such rates affect short-run revenues, and how such rates can be used strategically for system planning and load forecasting. Although there remains some utility hostility to TOU rates and skepticism about the value of the information generated by experiments like this, many utilities have come to realize that it is in their interest to squeeze as much information as they can out of such experiments since this information is potentially useful to them for planning and regulatory purposes. The best experiments have been done in situations where the ultimate consumers of the information (utilities and regulators) really cared about using it effectively and where the experiments were part of a broader-load research-and-system-planning effort. Furthermore, a major contribution of these experiments was to get utilities and regulators to begin to think seriously about rate-structure reforms and consumer responses to changing rate structures.

A second issue involves the neoclassical welfare analysis discussed at length in Aigner's paper. Are regulatory commissions and utilities likely to be guided by these kinds of calculations? I believe the answer is almost certainly no. Regulatory commissions appear to be guided in their policy decisions by three considerations: Can TOU pricing reduce the need for additional generating capacity and help to moderate requests for rate increases? Can the results of TOU pricing experiments be used to determine who gains and who loses as a result of changes in rate structure? Will TOU pricing reduce customer bills in the short run?

There is general acceptance among regulatory commissions of the notion that on the margin, all consumers should face prices that reflect the replacement costs of electricity. However, this intuitive understanding of the role of prices in consumer decisions and the relationship between consumption decisions and electricity supply has not been translated into broad acceptance of marginal-cost pricing principles by regulatory commissions. Whatever the academic interest in more refined welfare calculations, regulatory commissions do not understand what deadweight losses are, would not care much about them if they did, and, as a result, more refined calculations are unlikely to have any policy effects. I should note here that the decision to offer general TOU rates in England (the White Meter Tariff) was made before the Domestic Tariff Experiment was completed. Furthermore, the welfare calculations performed after the experiment was completed indicated that the welfare gains from TOU pricing were insufficient to cover the additional metering costs. The new rates went into effect before the experimental information was in and stayed in effect despite the negative welfare calculations. Regulatory commissions in the United States are primarily concerned with the average level of the electricity prices and issues associated with the distribution of the revenue burden among different types of customers. Their decisions for or against marginal-cost pricing and TOU pricing reflect these concerns. Any results based on conventional welfare calculations are only likely to have an impact if they can be placed in this context.

A third set of issues concerns the general usefulness of the TOU pricing experiments for long-range planning and load forecasting by utilities and their regulators. Most utility planners who understand the economic rationale for TOU pricing and are even sympathetic to the underlying objectives of efficiency based TOU pricing, do not find the experimental results to be particularly useful. A major reason for this view is the correct perception that by their very nature these experiments only allow us to estimate short-run elasticities of demand, given existing appliance stocks. Many utility planners envision the potential for substantial changes in the composition of appliance stocks as consumers repond both to generally higher energy prices and to TOU electricity prices. The changing appliance stock will draw on both existing appliance technology and appliance innovations. Of special interest are storage heating and cooling systems, storage hot-water heaters, dual fuel heat pumps, as well as changes in conventional appliances that will allow for better exploitation of TOU rates. System planners are most interested in examining the impact of TOU rates in the context of disaggregated appliance-specific load-forecasting models which can be conveniently coordinated with system dispatch and probabalistic planning models. As utility planning and load forecasting has become more sophisticated, the most progressive utilities have come to follow the European example of trying to coordinate pricing policy with appliance research and the provision of appliance information to consumers. Overall, utility planners have not found the aggregate econometric demand work that has been forthcoming from the experiments particularly useful because it reflects only short-run responses and has been conducted at too high a level of aggregation.

The lack of interest in the experimental results also reflects a perception that electricity pricing systems based primarily on time of use do not really represent the most effective way to give consumers signals reflecting the true marginal cost of production. In a number of cases utilities have gone well beyond conventional TOU pricing and are developing more sophisticated and efficient pricing systems. For example, for those systems in which peak demands are very sensitive to variations in temperature and humidity, there is a desire to tie the price signals more directly to weather-related periods of coincident peak demand than can be done with predetermined prices established for broad time periods of the day during several months of the year. A variety of radio, cable, and transmission-line communication devices are being developed. These will allow for more flexible interactive pricing systems, including interruptible tariffs that provide reduced rates but allow the utility to directly control appliances during peak periods. Coincident peak-sensitive pricing schemes are being offered to some industrial customers and experiments are under way with controlled storage heating, cycling of air conditioners, dual fuel heat pumps and other appliances. The residential TOU experiments simply do not provide the information on long-run consumer behavior that is of most importance in this effort.

TOU pricing experiments have had and will have little if any positive impact on regulatory decisions to implement TOU rates and have provided information on consumer behavior that is of only limited value in planning and load forecasting. The experiments have shown that consumers respond to higher prices by reducing consumption in the short run. For those who really doubted that such responses would occur, perhaps the results will finally convince them. Those studies that have found that peak and off-peak consumption were complements are of some potential interest, but I suspect that this result is an artifact of the focus on short-run responses given appliance stocks and are in any event presented at too high a level of aggregation to be of general use. Even where short-run elasticity estimates might be of value, the uncertainty ranges associated with the estimates obtained from the same data sets are so large that they are of limited use for pinning down anything of interest with great precision. To some extent the residential TOU experiments may have been counterproductive. They have led to too much of a focus on residential customers, where metering and other transactions costs are relatively high, and have diverted attention from industrial customers where TOU rates are likely to be more productive and where we have the most evidence based on foreign experience. Furthermore, the existence of ongoing TOU rate experiments may have served as a convenient excuse to avoid making decisions to reform electric utility rates so that they better promote economic efficiency.

This is not to say that there has been no progress on the rate-reform front. TOU rates are now available on a mandatory or voluntary basis in many states. Regulatory commissions and utilities have come to take rate-structure reforms, including TOU rates, much more seriously than they did ten years ago. The Public Utility Regulatory Policy Act requires states to consider the cost basis on which electricity rates are based and to determine whether TOU rates should be instituted. Recent Federal Energy Regulatory Commission rules for determing the rates that utilities must pay for power generated by cogeneration and other small power production facilities are based on the kinds of marginal-cost principles that have motivated economists to advocate the general application of marginal-cost pricing to electric-power rate making. But these reforms have proceeded largely independently of the residential TOU experiments. Commissions and utilities that have gone forward have taken the bull by the horns; they have recognized that consumption behavior is sensitive to prices and that rates based on marginal cost give better signals to consumers than rates based on average historical costs. They have recognized that TOU rates are almost certainly justified for large customers, given conservative assumptions about the relevant elasticities, that it takes a long time to economically re-meter the system anyway, and, therefore, that the most sensible thing is to gradually introduce permanent mandatory TOU rates starting with the largest consumers and to follow the behavior of these consumers with a carefully structured load research program. Mandatory programs have often been supplemented by voluntary programs in which customers wanting TOU rates must pay for their own meters and perform their own cost-benefit analyses. Some care in structuring the voluntary programs and gradual adjustments in the basic residential rates can help to avoid adverse selection problems that might otherwise develop.

Perhaps the most important change that has occurred during the past decade is that proposals for fundamental changes in all electric power rates are now taken seriously by regulators and utilities. TOU rates have come to be seen as one of several potential pricing and contracting innovations that must be viewed in the broader context of the development of a better understanding of appliance utilization, appliance choice, the development of new appliances that can use energy more economically, better sampling and load research work, and the development of more sophisticated load-forecasting and system-planning models. The TOU experiments and the econometric estimates of demand elasticities based on these estimates have provided some useful impetus to these developments, but I think it has been and will continue to be a small impetus. The most important effects have been indirect. The experiments have fostered more thoughtful discussion of rate-making alternatives that include TOU pricing, but have gone beyond pure time-related rates. The economic and statistical techniques that have been developed to analyze the data generated by these experiments will also certainly prove to be useful in the evolution of our understanding of consumer behavior as these techniques are applied to more extensive load-research information and new developments in pricing, metering, control, and appliance technology.

In short, the experiments have helped to focus the discussion and analysis of theoretical and empirical issues that arise when we consider broad issues of efficient pricing, consumer behavior, and load forecasting in the electric utility industry. The estimated elasticities themselves are of limited theoretical interest or public policy significance.

Comment   Lester D. Taylor

In April 1975, the Federal Energy Administration funded six demonstration electricity pricing experiments for the purpose of generating data that could be used in assessing the costs and benefits of pricing electricity according to the time of day it is used. TOU pricing was viewed by policy makers as a possibly important conservation-inducing response to the energy crisis that was triggered by OPEC and the Arab embargo. Economists, as is well- known, are drawn to TOU pricing because of its firm basis in theoretical welfare economics. Indeed, scratch an economist, and if he doesn't say "supply and demand," he will probably say "peak-load pricing," for if done properly TOU pricing is economically efficient and leads to a maximum social welfare.[1]

However, in any practical situation, this is a counsel of perfection, because whether or not an existing nonoptimal pricing system should be scrapped depends upon the benefits to be gained in relation to the costs. In other words, the implementation of TOU pricing can be justified on social-welfare grounds only if it can be demonstrated that the change in social welfare is positive. However, calculation of the benefits and costs that would be involved requires a great deal of very detailed information on the structure of demand and costs. Information on costs is in principle available in the utilities, but, unlike utilities in Western Europe, U.S. utilities in 1973 had never engaged in TOU pricing, so there were no historical data from which estimates of the demand for electricity by time of day could be obtained. This was the information that was to be forthcoming from the FEA time-of-use pricing experiments.

In his paper, Dennis Aigner has attempted to assess the knowledge that has been obtained in the experiments. Altogether fifteen experiments figure in Aigner's assessment—the six original demonstration projects, plus nine subsequent experiments. Aigner's was a difficult one, and he has done a very good job. Besides providing an excellent overview of results, he has produced a coherent description of a framework for calculating the benefits and costs of TOU pricing plus a statement of the problems that will be faced in transferring the results beyond the sampled population.

Drawing on earlier work at the University of Michigan and the Research Triangle Institute, Aigner gives a useful summary assessement of the strengths and weaknesses in the designs of the various experiments. By now, there is almost general agreement as to which are the well-designed experiments and which are the ones to avoid, at least in terms of

Lester D. Taylor is professor of economics, University of Arizona.

1. Social welfare in this context is defined as the sum of consumers' and producers' surplus.

yielding transferrable information about the structure of demand. As he notes, the Arizona, California (both LADWP and SCE), Oklahoma, North Carolina, and Wisconsin experiments have the most potential in this regard. Of these experiments, data from the Arizona experiment became available the earliest, and, together with the Wisconsin experiment, has been the most worked over to this point.

Having been a party to the Arizona experiment (Jack Wenders and I designed the tariffs and the incentive scheme), I agree with Aigner that the Los Angeles and Wisconsin experiments are more useful than the Arizona experiment, although the Arizona experiment does contain some prime information, especially concerning the effects of incentive payments. As Aigner notes, the first year of the Arizona experiment contained a complicated implicit incentive payment that was designed to ensure voluntary participation in the face of TOU rates that reached as high as 16¢/kWh during the peak period. Until the paper of Hill et al. 1980, the implicit incentive payment had not been properly modeled (including my own Aspen effort). That this is important to the price elasticities is evident by comparing the results in my Aspen paper, which Aigner kindly describes as "anomalous," with the results in Hill et al. 1980. However, to return to the comparison of the Arizona with the Los Angeles and Wisconsin experiments, the Los Angeles and Wisconsin experiments are much larger than the Arizona experiment and are better designed in their nonprice aspects.

The really important question in all of this, however, is the one raised in the title of Aigner's paper: What have we learned from the experiments? I had hoped that Aigner would conclude that enough information now exists to provide at least a preliminary assessment of the costs and benefits of implementing TOU pricing, but those hopes are clearly dashed. Although he doesn't say it in so many words, my conclusion from reading Aigner's paper is that any scientific assessment of TOU pricing is still a long way off. The experiments are in reasonable agreement on own-price TOU elasticities of demand, but there is virtually no agreement concerning cross elasticities. Until these are defined with reasonable precision, a scientific assessment of TOU pricing is not possible. However, my gut feeling is that events will not wait for this to occur.

References

Acton, Jan Paul, and Bridger M. Mitchell. 1980. Evaluating time-of-day electricity rates for residential customers. In *Regulated industries and public enterprise: European and United States perspectives*, ed. B. M. Mitchell and P. R. Kleindorfer. Lexington, Mass.: Lexington Books.

Aigner, Dennis J. 1979. Bayesian analysis of optimal sample size and a best decision rule for experiments in direct load control. *Journal of Econometrics*, 9: 209–21.

Aigner, Dennis J., and Jerry A. Hausman. 1980. Correcting for truncation bias in the analysis of experiments in time-of-day pricing of electricity. *Bell Journal of Economics* 11 Spring: 131–42.

Aigner, Dennis J., and Lee A. Lillard. 1980. Initial analysis of Southern California Edison's domestic time-of-use experiment. Department of Economics, University of Southern California.

Aigner, Dennis J., and Dale J. Poirier. 1979. Electricity demand and consumption by time-of-use. Report EA–1294, Electric Power Research Institute, Palo Alto, Calif.

Atkinson, Scott E. December 1979a. A comparative analysis of consumer response to time-of-use electricity pricing: Arizona and Wisconsin. In *Modeling and analysis of electricity demand by time-of-day*, ed. D. Aigner. Report EA–1304, Electric Power Research Institute, Palo Alto, Calif.

———. 1979b. Responsiveness to time-of-day electricity pricing: First empirical results. In *Forecasting and modelling time-of-day and seasonal electricity demands*, ed. Anthony Lawrence. Report EA–578–SR, Electric Power Research Institute, Palo Alto, Calif. (Also published in *Journal of Econometrics* 9 [January 1979]: 70–96.)

Brown, Michael, N. J. Dikeman, Jr., Upton Henderson, David Huettner, Charles Massey, Donald Murry, Suhas Patwardhan, and Frank Wert. 1980. A summary of the Edmond Electric Utility Demonstration Project and its findings. Paper presented at the April Electric Rate Demonstration Conference, Denver, Colo.

Caves, Douglas W., and Lauritis R. Christensen. 1980a. Econometric analysis of residential time-of-use electricity pricing experiments. *Journal of Econometrics* 14: 287–306.

———. 1980b. Residential substitution of off-peak for peak electricity. *Energy Journal* 2: 85–142.

De Mouchel, W. H., and J. E. Harris. 1981. Bayes and empirical Bayes methods for combining cancer experiments in man and other species. Technical report No. 24, Department of Mathematics, Massachusetts Institute of Technology.

Efron, Bradley, and Carl Morris. 1975. Data analysis using Stein's estimator and its generalization. *J. Amer. Stat. Assn.* 70: 311–19.

Electric Utility Rate Design Study. 1977a. Considerations of the price elasticity of demand for electricity. National Economic Research Associates.

———. 1977b. Elasticity of demand. J. W. Wilson & Associates.

Engle, Robert, Clive Granger, Allen Mitchem, and Ramu Ramanthan. 1979. Some problems in the estimation of daily load shapes and peaks.

In *Modeling and analysis of electricity demand by time-of-day. See* Atkinson 1979a.

Granger, Clive W. J., Robert Engle, Ramu Ramanathan, and Alan Andersen. 1979. Residential load curves and time-of-day pricing: An econometric analysis. *Journal of Econometrics*, 9 (January): 13–32.

Hausman, J. A., M. Kinnucan, and D. McFadden. 1979. A two level electricity demand model: Evaluation of the Connecticut time-of-day pricing test. In *Modeling and analysis of electricity demand by time-of-day. See* Atkinson 1979a.

Hendricks, Wallace, and Roger Koenker, 1979. Demand for electricity by time-of-day: An evaluation of experimental results. Paper presented at the Rutgers Conference.

Hendricks, Wallace, Roger Koenker, and Dale J. Poirier, 1978. Residential demand for electricity by time-of-day: An econometric approach. Report EA–704, Electric Power Research Institute, Palo Alto, Calif.

Hill, Daniel H., Robert M. Groves, E. Philip Howrey, A. Christopher Kline, Daniel F. Kohler, James M. Lepkowski, and Marc A. Smith. 1979. Evaluation of the FEA's load management and rate design demonstration projects. EA–1152, Electric Power Research Institute, Palo Alto, Calif.

Hill, Daniel H., Deborah A. Ott, Lester D. Taylor, and James M. Walker. 1980. The impact of incentive payments in time-of-day electricity pricing experiments: The Arizona experiment. Mimeo.

Lau, Lawrence J., and Lee A. Lillard. 1979. A random response model of the demand for electricity by time-of-day. In *Modeling and analysis of electricity demand by time-of-day. See* Atkinson 1979a.

Lawrence, Anthony, and Steven Braithwait. 1977. The residential demand for electricity by time-of-day: An econometric analysis. In *Forecasting and modelling time-of-day and seasonal electricity demands*, ed. A. Lawrence. EA–578–SR, Electric Power Research Institute, Palo Alto, Calif. (Also published in *Journal of Econometrics* 9 [January 1979]: 59–78.)

Lifson, Dale P. 1980. Comparison of time-of-use electricity demand models. Research Triangle Institute, N.C.

Lillard, Lee A., and Jan Paul Acton. 1980. Season electricity demand and pricing analysis with a variable response model. Rand Corporation working draft #WD–670–DWP.

Lindley, Dennis, and F. M. Smith. 1972. Bayes estimates for the linear model. *J. Royal Stat. Soc.* 34: 1–18.

Miedema, Allen K. 1980. North Carolina rate demonstration project: Preliminary results. Paper presented at the Electric Rate Demonstration Conference, Denver, Colo.

Miedema, Allen K., Jerome A. Olson, Dale P. Lifson, and Bryan Krakauer. 1978. Time of use electricity prices: Arizona. Report, Research Triangle Institute, N. C.

Miedema, Allen K. 1980. North Carolina rate demonstration project: Preliminary results. Paper presented at the Electric Rate Demonstration Conference, Denver, Colo.

Raiffa, H., and R. Schlaifer. 1961. *Applied statistical decision theory.* Cambridge: MIT Press.

Taylor, Lester. 1977. On modeling the residential demand for electricity by time of day. In *Forecasting and modelling time-of-day and seasonal electricity demands,* ed. A. Lawrence. EA–578–SE, Electric Power Research Institute. (Also published in *Journal of Econometrics* 9: 97–118.)

U.S. Department of Energy. 1978. Analytical master plan for the analysis of data from the Electric Utility Rate Demonstration projects. Research Triangle Institute, N. C.

White, S. B., C. A. Clayton, B. V. Alexander, and D. P. Duncan. 1978. Analysis of the effects of the time of use electricity rate in the Connecticut electricity utility demonstration project. Draft final report, Research Triangle Institute, N. C.

2 Housing Behavior and the Experimental Housing-Allowance Program: What Have We Learned?

Harvey S. Rosen

2.1 Introduction

In the United States and many other countries, attempts have been made to augment the real incomes of the poor by increasing their consumption of housing. Such schemes have taken a number of forms, for example, provision of public housing, construction subsidies, and so forth. It has been suggested that a better method than most might be to give poor people financial allowances that could be used to upgrade their housing standards. The success of such a program would depend upon the answers to several questions. Two of the most important are: Would low-income families respond to financial incentives intended to increase their housing consumption? To the extent that they do respond, would housing prices simply be driven up, resulting in windfall gains for landlords?[1]

To obtain answers to these important questions, the Department of Housing and Urban Development in 1970 authorized a social experiment, the Experimental Housing-Allowance Program (EHAP). The first part of EHAP, the "demand experiment," was designed to predict households' responses to housing allowances. In this experiment members of a random sample of low-income households were granted housing allowances and their behavior compared to a control group without allowances. The second part, the "supply experiment," was designed to

Harvey S. Rosen is professor of economics, Princeton University, and research associate, National Bureau of Economic Research.

The author would like to thank Joseph Friedman, Jerry Hausman, Edwin Mills, Mitchell Polinsky, and David Wise for useful conversations.

1. A more fundamental question, perhaps, is why housing allowances should be considered at all when direct income transfers would probably be preferable from the point of view of the poor. We will take it as given, however, that the public policy goal is to increase their welfare in some manner tied to housing consumption.

examine market effects of housing allowances. All low-income families in two communities were eligible to receive allowances, and the response of the overall level of prices in each community was carefully monitored. (The precise provisions of the programs are discussed in greater detail below.)

EHAP was not instituted in an intellectual vacuum. For years prior to the experiment, housing markets received considerable attention from economists. The purpose of this paper is to discuss what new insights EHAP has provided concerning probable responses to various types of housing allowances. Specifically, I intend to focus on what experimental data have taught us about these responses that could not have been learned from more traditional sources. This is admittedly a narrow focus, because EHAP produced a number of "serendipitous findings that had nothing to do with the research objectives used to justify them" (Aaron 1979, 48). For example, much of value appears to have been learned concerning efficient techniques for administering welfare programs. Nevertheless, the prediction of behavioral responses lies at the heart of EHAP, and it is on the basis of new knowledge about them that the experiment must be judged.

The existence of numerous studies that have used conventional data to answer questions similar to those studied in EHAP suggests a natural way to organize this paper. I will review the major problems that confronted previous investigators and for each problem discuss whether or not it has been mitigated by the availability of experimental data. I should emphasize that it is not my intention to suggest that the EHAP investigators were unaware of the fact that for some problems, experimental observations offer no particular advantage. Rather, their work has shown keen sensitivity to the limitations of their data.

The demand experiment is discussed in section 2.2 and supply in section 2.3. Section 2.4 contains the conclusions.

2.2   The Demand Experiment

The main purpose of the demand experiments was to obtain predictions of households' responses to various types of housing allowances. In this section I shall describe the experiment's structure and then discuss the problems that users of conventional data have faced in analyzing housing behavior, and the extent to which experimental data can alleviate these problems.

2.2.1   Description of the Demand Experiment

In the demand experiment,[2] a set of randomly selected low-income households received allowances, while members of a control group did

---

2. This subsection is based upon Allen, Fitts, and Glatt (1981), especially pages 28–30.

not. There were two basic types of allowances. Under the first, the payment received was the difference between the cost of "adequate" housing established for the program (C) and some fraction (b) of household income (Y):[3]

(1) $$M = C - bY,$$

where M is the size of the payment. (C was determined by a panel of housing experts, which considered both household size and the site in making its decision.) Equation (1) is referred to as the "housing-gap formula." Under the second scheme, known as the "percent-of-rent formula," the payment was some fraction (α) of the gross rent (R) paid by the family:

(2) $$M = \alpha R.$$

Essentially, the demand experiment consisted of confronting different families with various values of α, b, and C, and then comparing their housing decisions to those of the control group. In addition, some of the housing-gap households were told that their apartments had to satisfy certain minimum standards before they would be eligible for payment. For example, plumbing and kitchen facilities had to meet certain specifications; roofs, ceilings, and walls had to be in good repair, etc. (Friedman and Weinberg 1978, A-31).

In practice, values for b of 0.15, 0.25, and 0.35 were employed; the parameter α took on values that started at 0.2 and were incremented by 0.1 until they reached 0.6. C varied between 20 percent below and 20 percent above the levels set by the experts. The experiment was conducted for three years beginning in 1973 at two sites—Pittsburgh, Pennsylvania and Phoenix, Arizona. At each site about one thousand low-income families participated in the experiment,[4] somewhat under half of which were included in the control group. Only renters were eligible.

2.2.2 Problems in Predicting the Demand Response to Housing Allowances

Presumably, by appropriately comparing the responses of the control and treatment groups, one can infer the impact of the various types of allowances upon housing behavior. However, suppose for the moment that experimental data were not available and that an investigator was asked to predict the effect that allowances would have upon housing behavior. Most likely the investigator would begin by noting that the housing-gap formula is essentially an increase in income, and the percent-of-rent formula represents a change in the price of housing services from

3. The definition of "household income" was essentially posttax income less a $300 deduction for each worker in the family.

4. For example, in 1973 a Phoenix family with three or four members would be eligible only if its income were less than $8,150; for Pittsburgh, the limit was $6,250.

some price P to $(1 - \alpha)P$. Therefore, given income and price elasticities of housing demand, one can predict an individual's response to the housing allowance.[5] These considerations suggest the following strategy: Employ multiple-regression techniques (or some variant thereof) to estimate the demand for housing services, utilizing either cross-sectional or time-series data. This strategy yields a set of the relevant elasticities. Then, assuming that people would react to the price and income differences generated by a housing-allowance program in the same way as those generated "naturally," use the elasticities to estimate the program's impact on housing demand.

I shall now discuss some problems that face the investigator who wants to implement this strategy and whether or not the problems are eliminated when experimental data are available.

Specification of a Model

Users of conventional data typically begin by specifying a model that relates the quantity of housing services demanded for the ith observation (Q_i^D), to some function $f(\cdot)$ of price (P_i), income (Y_i), and a vector of demographic variables Z_i, which theoretical considerations suggest might be relevant:

(3) $$Q_i^D = f(P_i, Y_i, Z_i) .$$

In some cases $f(\cdot)$ is specified in an ad hoc but convenient form such as log linear (e.g., Polinsky and Ellwood 1979, Rosen 1979b), while other times it is derived from maximization of an explicit utility function (Abbott and Ashenfelter 1976).

Equation (3) is deterministic, so the next step is to assume that even observations with identical right-hand-side variables may have different Q^Ds because of random errors. Usually, an error term is appended additively. (For an exception see King 1980.) Now, given a set of observations on Q_i, P_i, Y_i, and Z_i and the stochastic specification, the model's parameters can be estimated using a variety of econometric techniques. The parameter estimates can then be used to compute behavioral elasticities;[6] indeed, in the case of log-linear demand curves, the parameter values themselves are the elasticities.

There are several major drawbacks with this standard procedure. First, economic theory puts very few constraints on the form of $f(\cdot)$, so the investigator must make an essentially ad hoc choice with respect to the specification of either the demand or utility function. Second, it must be

5. This assumes that individuals' choices are unconstrained by quality standards.
6. For example, the price elasticity of demand is $\partial f/\partial p \ P/Q$ where P and Q are (usually) evaluated at their mean values.

assumed that $f(\cdot)$ is identical across individuals.[7] (When time-series data are used, the analogous assumption is that $f(\cdot)$ does not change over time.) Finally, and perhaps most crucially, it must be assumed that the fitted relationship will continue to apply when a right-hand-side variable for a given observation changes. For example, if the investigator finds that $(\partial Q^D / \partial Y)\,(Y/(Q^D))$ is less than one, it does not imply that increasing a particular family's income 10 percent will increase its housing consumption by a smaller percentage. All one has really learned is that in the data, poorer families devote a larger fraction of their income to housing than richer families, ceteris paribus. Only by *assuming* that poor families would act like the richer ones if their incomes were increased, and vice versa, can one give any behavioral significance to elasticity estimates from regressions.[8]

In contrast, the situation facing the investigator with experimental data appears simple. There is no need to specify $f(\cdot)$, or to make possibly invalid behavioral assumptions. As Hausman and Wise (this volume) note, provided that the experiment is designed properly, all that is necessary is to compare the behavior of individuals in different treatment groups with each other, and with the control group. Indeed, EHAP investigators Friedman and Weinberg (1978) do exactly this. In a series of tables they exhibit information on housing expenditures for both the experimental and control groups at the time of enrollment and at two years after enrollment (see, for example, pages 8, 13, 14, A-54, A-55). Interestingly, however, only a small portion of Friedman and Weinberg's lengthy (and excellent) report on the demand experiment is devoted to discussion of such results.[9] Most of the document concerns the specification of models like equation (3) and their estimation with data from the experiment. But as Hanushek and Quigley observe, such "regression estimates . . . do not arise from experimental payments of income, but rather from the 'natural' experiment arising because 'otherwise identical' households of [e.g.] varying income are observed to have made different choices" (1979b, 20). In short, the experimental nature of the data is ignored, so that all the model-specification problems associated with conventional data must be confronted.

---

7. Note that this need not imply that the elasticities be identical across individuals; such will be the case only for the very simple Cobb-Douglas specification. One can also specify a random-coefficients model, which allows for a distribution of elasticities across people. See Hausman and Wise (1980).

8. This point is further developed in Mosteller and Mosteller (1979).

9. Friedman and Weinberg of Abt associates bring together a wealth of information on the demand experiment: the economic theory behind it, sample design issues, statistical analysis of the data, and more. Unfortunately, no similar major report has been issued by the Rand Corporation for the supply experiment.

Why is this the case? The main reason is the possibility that some of the key parameters that govern housing behavior depend upon variables that can change over time. For example, there is some evidence that the price elasticity of demand for housing is a function of income (Rosen 1979a). Thus, to the extent the economic environment changes, the value of simple comparisons between control and experimental groups will be diminished.[10] In contrast, a properly estimated structural model would allow an investigator to deal with such a situation.

Additional reasons are provided by Stafford's (this volume) discussion of the general circumstances under which experimental results are likely to be more useful than those from structural models. First, there must be reasonable certainty that the programs examined in the experiment are the ones that will eventually be considered by policy makers. This is because by its nature, an experiment can generate information only about the specific treatments being examined (or interpolations between them). Second, there must be some agreement on the relevant time horizon. Otherwise the experiment may not be long enough for one to observe all its effects upon the population.

The application of Stafford's criteria suggests that in the case of housing allowances, a structural approach is required. A multitude of housing programs have been considered in the past (see Aaron 1972); there is no reason to believe that society has settled into a consensus on the particular programs and parameters studied in EHAP. Furthermore, housing decisions are evidently made by families within a long-run framework, but the precise amount of time required is not known. As noted below, the problem of estimating lag lengths is not easy in structural models, but at least some interesting results have been obtained.

For all these reasons, it is almost inevitable that Friedman and Weinberg, as well as other investigators using the experimental data,[11] eventually turn to models of the kind used in the analysis of conventional data. Of course, it may be the case that there are other features of experimental data that make such models especially useful, an issue to be discussed below. But in an area like housing, they do not relieve investigators of the burden of constructing theoretical and statistical models.

Definition of Housing Services

Given that analyses of both experimental and conventional data require the construction of models, the important question becomes whether or not the experimental data better facilitate their implementa-

10. One can rescue the experimental approach from this criticism by building income-price interactions into the experimental design. However, as Hausman and Wise (this volume) point out, the more treatment groups, the less convincing are the results, ceteris paribus.

11. See, e.g., Hanushek and Quigley (1979a), Mills and Sullivan (1981), or Hausman and Wise (1980).

tion. Consider, for example, the problem of making operational the left-hand-side variable of the equation, "housing services." Housing is intrinsically a multidimensional commodity—a dwelling is characterized by its number of rooms, their size, the quality of construction and plumbing, etc. It is therefore very difficult to summarize in a single number the quantity of housing services generated by a given dwelling. Usually it is assumed that the amount of housing services is proportional to the rent paid, or, in the case of an owner-occupied dwelling, to the value of the house. (See, e.g., Polinsky and Ellwood 1979.) The difficulty here is that the rental value of a dwelling at a given time may reflect characteristics of the market that have nothing to do with the quantity of housing services actually generated. As King (1980) points out, for example, the special income-tax treatment of rental income will generally influence market values.

An alternative tack would be to abandon the possibility of summarizing housing services in a single variable, and instead to estimate a series of demand functions for various housing attributes. An immediate problem is the absence of observable market prices for attributes. Recently, Witte, Sumka, and Erekson (1979) have implemented the suggestion of Rosen (1974) that attribute-demand equations be estimated in a two-step process: (1) estimate the implicit attribute prices from a hedonic price equation for housing,[12] and (2) use these prices as explanatory variables in regressions with attribute quantities as the dependent variables. However, Brown and Rosen (1982) have shown that major statistical pitfalls are present in this procedure and that the validity of Witte, Sumka, and Erekson's results is therefore in question. Although some progress is being made in dealing with these problems (see Quigley 1982), the approach that continues to predominate is the use of rent as the single measure of the quantity of housing services.

Do the EHAP data allow the construction of more meaningful measures of housing services? The simple answer is no. Friedman and Weinberg, for example, struggle with the problem of measuring housing services in very much the same way as users of nonexperimental data (1978, 92–94). Similarly, Hanushek and Quigley's (1979a) analysis of EHAP data uses housing expenditures as the dependent variable in the demand equations. Experimental data do not remove this important stumbling block.

Price of Housing Services

Imagine an investigator with (nonexperimental) cross-sectional observations on a group of renters, all of whom come from a particular

---

12. A regression of the price of a commodity R on its characteristics (a vector X) is the basis of an hedonic price index for the commodity. The implicit price of the ith characteristics if $\partial R / \partial X_i$. See Rosen (1974).

community. If the housing market is competitive, it seems reasonable to assume that all individuals face the same price of housing services. However, in the absence of any price variation, it is impossible to estimate the price elasticity of demand. Investigators with conventional data therefore often analyze observations across cities. Of course, the problem of measuring intercity housing-price variation still remains. Because the price of housing services is housing expenditures divided by the quantity of housing services, the above noted difficulties in measuring the latter are bound to create problems in measuring price. Several possible solutions are found in the literature. A popular approach is to estimate hedonic price equations for different cities and use them as the bases for a housing price index. However, Alexander (1975) has pointed out several problems with this approach. One of the most important is that the selection of a set of attributes to be included in the hedonic price index must be decided on ad hoc grounds, but the substantive implications of the estimates often depend upon the choice made.

The user of EHAP data has an advantage in dealing with the problem of measuring price differences across observations. Recall that in a community the effective price of housing facing the individual, P_i, is

$$(4) \qquad P_i = (1 - \alpha_i)P_0 ,$$

where P_0 is the pretreatment price of housing and α_i is the EHAP subsidy rate (equal to zero for members of the control group). Because of the variance generated in P_i by the α_i, the fact that P_0 is identical across individuals in the community no longer precludes estimation of a price response. P_0 can be normalized at an arbitrary value and then equation (4) used as the price term. This approach is used by Friedman and Weinberg (1978) and Hanushek and Quigley (1980).

A potential problem is the possibility that the before-treatment price of rental housing may not be constant within a city. Polinsky and Ellwood (1979, 199) show that even if the market is competitive, variation in land prices within the community will lead to differences in the price of housing services.[13] However, Hanushek and Quigley (1980) argue convincingly that such differences in P_0 are unlikely to be of much importance in the EHAP samples. It seems safe to conclude, then, that the experimental data confer distinct benefits in estimating the price elasticity of demand for rental housing.[14] Ironically, the price elasticity per se is

13. If housing services include accessibility to the work place and the usual competitive assumptions hold, then the before-treatment price of housing services would be constant. But in this case, the dependent variable should be housing expenditures plus commuting costs. Note also that if owner-occupied housing were being considered (as it is in the supply experiment), an additional complication would arise because the effective price of housing services depends upon the individual's marginal federal-income-tax rate. see Rosen (1979a) or King (1980).

14. However, the value of these benefits is lessened to the extent that the program-induced price reductions are perceived as transitory.

unlikely to be of much use in designing a housing-allowance program. A percent-of-rent formula offers such attractive opportunities for mutually beneficial fraud on the part of landlords and renters that is hard to imagine it ever being implemented.

Shift Variables

Consider now the shift (i.e., nonprice) variables of equation (3). Standard theoretical considerations suggest that for income, Y, a permanent rather than annual measure should be used. Previous investigators have dealt with the problem of computing permanent income in various ways. Carliner (1973) and Rosen (1979a), analyzing longitudinal data, take an average of several years' income. Polinsky and Ellwood (1979), using Federal Housing Administration (FHA) data, assume that the FHA's estimate of "effective income" is a proxy for permanent income. Struyk (1976) uses the fitted value of a regression of income on a set of personal characteristics as his permanent-income measure.[15]

Turning now to the vector Z of other shift variables, note that investigators with conventional data have to make arbitrary decisions with respect to which ones to choose, their measurement, and how they interact with the other variables. Typical candidates for inclusion are race, sex of head of household, age, number of children, etc.

In an experimental framework, proper randomization removes the need for specifying the shift variables (Hausman and Wise, this volume). However, to the extent that structural models are required to obtain useful results, users of EHAP data are at no particular advantage when it comes to choosing shift variables and defining them appropriately. For example, Friedman and Weinberg's permanent-income measure (p. 54) is constructed using the same kind of averaging discussed above.[16] Similarly, their selection of demographic variables is made on an ad hoc basis (p. 81).

Disequilibrium

Most of the studies using cross-sectional data to examine housing demand implicitly or explicitly assume that all agents are in equilibrium.[17] Were this not the case, then a regression of housing services on price, income, and demographic variables could not be interpreted as a demand equation. On the other hand, analyses of longitudinal and time-series data often allow for the possibility that at a given point in time, house-

---

15. Of course, neither the necessity of using a permanent-income measure nor the types of solutions just mentioned are unique to the study of housing; they appear throughout the literature on the estimation of demand functions.

16. An additional problem arises because it is not clear how to convert the monthly EHAP payments, which are known to be temporary, into changes in permanent income.

17. An important exception is the work of King (1980), who considers rationing between different tenure modes in the United Kingdom.

holds may not be at their long-run-equilibrium positions because adjustment costs make it prohibitively expensive to respond immediately to changes in economic environment. It is usually assumed that such a disequilibrium is eliminated over time as households move gradually to their equilibrium positions (e.g., Rosen and Rosen 1980).[18] It is well-known that such models lack a strong choice-theoretic foundation, but a tractable alternative is lacking.

The equilibrium assumption is just as crucial to the analysis of EHAP data as to conventional data. Even simple comparisons of the behavior of the control and treatment groups are less meaningful unless both groups are observed in equilibrium positions. It is for this reason that Friedman and Weinberg (1978, 71) devote a considerable amount of time to separate analysis of those households that changed dwellings during the course of the experiment—movers are assumed more likely to be in equilibrium than stayers. (This, however, creates an important self-selection problem that is discussed in the next section.)

In addition, Friedman and Weinberg utilize the typical partial-adjustment model to study dynamic behavior,[19] and they find rather rapid adjustments in housing behavior (p. 125). Hanushek and Quigley (1979a) present an innovative method to estimate adjustment lags in the EHAP data, but their technique could just as well have been implemented using a conventional set of longitudinal data. Contrary to Friedman and Weinberg, they find rather sluggish adjustments: only about one-fifth to one-third of the gap between desired and actual housing consumption is closed in each year.

One aspect of the EHAP makes proper modeling of disequilibria especially important. For some treatment groups, individuals were ineligible for housing allowances unless their housing met certain quality standards. In other words, individuals were constrained to consume minimum amounts of certain housing attributes. To the extent that any of these constraints were binding, then demand functions for other attributes of the housing bundle would depend not only on prices of the attributes, but on the quantities of the constrained attributes. Estimation of attribute-demand functions in the presence of quantity constraints is clearly a complicated matter. Unfortunately, given the paucity of work on estimating attribute demands in the relatively simple unconstrained case, one cannot expect that the more complicated disequilibrium problem will be solved soon. Such work may provide an interesting use for EHAP data in the future.

18. This differs from the use of "disequilibrium" in much macroeconomics literature, where the term refers to a situation in which markets fail to clear because of some constraint(s). See, e.g., Barro and Grossman (1971).

19. Unfortunately, as Friedman and Weinberg (1978, 127) note, dynamic patterns might be affected by the limited duration of the experiment.

Selectivity Bias

In recent years econometricians have devoted a substantial amount of effort to the study of statistical problems that arise when the sample used in a regression analysis is nonrandom (see Heckman 1979). It has been shown that if selection into a sample is nonrandom, then, unless certain corrective measures are taken, parameter estimates may be inconsistent. For example, it is common to estimate separate demand equations for renters and homeowners. However, since individuals self-select into their tenure modes, the sample-selection process is not random, and inconsistent coefficients may result (Rosen 1979a). Similarly, if separate regressions are estimated for movers and stayers, sample-selection bias is a threat.

As Friedman and Weinberg (1979, 130) point out, although a random sample of low-income households was offered enrollment in the percent-of-rent plans, the demand functions were estimated from a nonrandom subsample; thus, "households that accepted the enrollment offer, were verified to be within the income eligibility limit, remained in the experiment, and moved sometime between enrollment and two years after enrollment." Each of these criteria introduces the possibility of sample-selection bias. Of course, users of EHAP data can take advantage of various statistical techniques to determine whether or not selectivity bias is present, and if so, to correct for it (Hausman and Wise, this volume). In experimental data, then, selectivity bias is not eliminated—it merely appears in new forms.

Participation in and Perception of the Program

To predict the aggregate response to a housing-allowance program, one needs to know the number of eligible families and the proportion of those who would choose to participate. Presumably at least rough information on the first item could be obtained from census or similar figures on income distribution. It is hard to imagine how nonexperimental data could be used to illuminate the participation issue. Although some conventional data sets have information on participation rates in existing welfare programs (e.g., food stamps), probably one cannot reliably infer from that data what the patterns of participation in a quite different program would be.

A related question concerns individuals' perceptions of the program. In order to use results from conventional data to predict the effect of housing allowances, one must first of all assume that people would understand the program. Furthermore, it must be assumed that percent-of-rent and (unconstrained) housing-gap payments are perceived as equivalent to price and income changes, respectively. Although one can test for rational perception of the provisions of existing welfare programs (e.g., Williams 1975), there is no reason necessarily to expect such results to carry over to the housing-allowance case.

With respect to both the participation and perception questions, the experimental data provide interesting insights, but no definite conclusions. Clearly, EHAP investigators can observe whether or not individuals participate in the experiment and correlate participation with various economic and demographic variables. The main problem is that the results may be affected by the individuals' knowledge that they are involved in an experiment, the "Hawthorne effect." To the extent that people act differently when they know that their behavior is being observed as part of an experiment, it will confound attempts to predict participation under a universal regime.[20] An additional difficulty is that participation rates may be affected by the knowledge that the program is only temporary.[21]

Friedman and Weinberg (1978) attempted direct investigation of the perception issue. Families in the percent-of-rent experiments were asked in what direction their housing allowances would move if their rent were increased by $10. Only about a half understood that their allowance would increase. However, when separate demand functions for both those who understood and those who did not were estimated, the hypothesis that their parameters were the same could not be rejected. Friedman and Weinberg (1979, 139) conclude that, even for persons who answered the question incorrectly, "their response to the allowance payment can be analyzed *as if* they understood."

A more convincing test would have been possible if there was variation in the pretreatment price of housing services. Suppose that the effective price P_i appears in logarithmic form on the right-hand side of the demand equation. Note that

$$\ln P_i = \ln(1 - \alpha_i) + \ln P_{0i},$$

where P_{0i} is the pretreatment price and α_i is as defined above. Thus, if $\ln(1 - \alpha_i)$ and $\ln P_{0i}$ are entered separately into the regression, a natural way to confirm correct perception is to test whether or not their coefficients are equal. Equality would suggest that individuals perceive treatment-induced changes in price the same way as those "naturally" induced. The advantage of such a test is that it does not rely on a direct question addressed to the participants. Unfortunately, as noted above, in the EHAP samples there is probably not enough variation in the pretreatment prices to make an attempt to calculate them worthwhile.

---

20. Of course, Hawthorne effects can be used to bring into question the results generated by all social experiments.

21. Participation was probably also influenced by the existence of minimum-housing standards. Some critics of EHAP have claimed greater variation in these standards would have provided useful information on the extent to which they influenced participation. See Downs and Bradbury (1981).

Another way to examine the perception issue would be to compare parameter estimates of structural models generated by data from different programs in the experiment (and the control group). If selection into the various groups were random and if individuals perceive program parameters correctly, then the underlying behavioral parameters should be about the same. Of course, to the extent that the particular specification of the structural model influences the results, they are rendered inconclusive.

2.3   The Supply Experiment

In most analyses of housing demand using both conventional cross-sectional and EHAP data, it is assumed that the pretreatment price of housing is constant. In effect, each household faces a perfectly elastic supply of housing services. From an econometric point of view, this assumption is justified because each household is sufficiently small to be regarded as a price taker.[22] However, sole reliance on such demand estimates to predict the overall behavioral response to housing allowances is potentially hazardous. If a considerable number of program participants increase their demand for housing services, then to the extent the supply of housing services to the community slopes upward, the pretreatment price will rise.

Considerations such as these led to the so-called supply experiment. In two communities, all individuals who met certain income qualifications were made eligible for housing allowances. The idea was to see whether or not the allowances would induce increases in prices or any other important disruptions in the housing market.[23]

In this section I shall summarize the provisions of the supply experiment and then, as before, discuss whether or not EHAP data provide substantial improvement over those from conventional sources. As might be expected, many of the issues that were important on the demand side are also present here. Such issues therefore receive only cursory discussion.

2.3.1   Description of the Supply Experiment

The supply experiment began in 1973–74, with a planned duration of ten years.[24] In the two sites chosen, Green Bay, Wisconsin and South Bend, Indiana, enrollment in the program was open to every eligible household. All payments were made according to the housing-gap formula, equation (1), with b, the implicit tax rate on income, set at 25

---

22. For many homeowners, the federal income tax generates an endogenous price for housing services.

23. Barnett and Lowry (1979, 10) discuss some predictions of the market effects of housing allowances that were made prior to EHAP.

24. This subsection is based upon Allen, Fitts, and Glatt (1981).

percent. In order to qualify for the payments, housing had to meet certain minimum standards. Unlike the demand experiment, homeowners as well as renters were allowed to participate. Perhaps the key methodological difference between the demand and supply experiments is that for the latter, there was no control group.

After four years of observation at both sites, it became clear that "the experimental program . . . had virtually no effect on housing prices, either marketwide or in the market sectors most heavily populated by program participants" (Barnett and Lowry 1979, 1). There are two principal explanations for this phenomenon: (1) because the income elasticity of demand for housing services apparently is quite low for program participants (about 0.3 for renters, according to Mulford (1979, 31),[25] the housing allowance did not shift the market-demand curve very much; and (2) the demand changes that did take place were spread out over time due to adjustment lags. Since both of these phenomena were observed in the demand experiment, some critics (Downs and Bradbury 1981) have argued that the supply experiment should not have commenced until the demand results were in. Nevertheless, it is useful to assess the benefits that the availability of experimental data will confer upon future researchers of housing supply.[26]

2.3.2   Problems in Predicting the Supply Response to Housing Allowances

Specification of a Model

Investigators who want to estimate housing-supply functions generally begin by trying to use economic theory to specify an estimable model. A popular approach is to assume some housing-production function, estimate its parameters, and use them to infer the shape of the supply function.[27] For example, Ingram and Oron assume that housing services are a constant elasticity of substitution (CES) function of "quality capital" and "operation inputs" (1977, 284). Polinsky and Ellwood (1979) also posit a CES production function, but assume that its arguments are land and capital. Field (n.d.) uses a transcendental logarithm production function with three inputs—land, capital, and labor. Poterba eschews selection of a specific form for the production function, and instead starts by postulating a supply function that is log linear in the price of housing, input costs, and credit availability (1980, 10). (Of course, duality consid-

25. In addition, only about half the eligible renters and 30 percent of the eligible homeowners had enrolled after four years (Allen, Fitts, and Glatt 1981).
26. Several researchers have used data from the supply experiment to estimate demand for housing schedules, e.g., Mulford (1979). These will not be discussed here.
27. Given the production function and input prices, one can derive the marginal-cost schedule which, under competition, is the supply curve.

erations suggest that one can work backward from the supply curve to the underlying production function.)

The specification of the underlying technology can sometimes predetermine substantive results. For example, since Ellwood and Polinsky assume constant returns to scale (1979, 201), the implied long-run supply curve of housing services is perfectly elastic, regardless of parameter estimates.[28] Postulating such a technology, then, guarantees the result that housing allowances will have no effect on the pretreatment price of housing, at least as long as input prices remain unchanged. The interesting questions then become: How high do prices rise in the short run? How much time is required to reach long-run equilibrium? These issues are discussed below in the section on dynamics; they are mentioned here to emphasize once again the importance that model specification plays in analyses of conventional data.

The presence of the supply "experimental" data does not remove the necessity for some kind of modeling, particularly since there is no control group. Barnett, for example, provides some simple comparisons of the increase in rents in the test sites relative to those in other U.S. cities (1979, 13). Even such relatively straightforward comparisons, however, require an implicit model of the determinants of housing costs, so that "other" costs can be subtracted out to find the "pure" housing-allowance effect. Rydell (1979) constructs a rather involved model of monopolistic competition in housing markets in order to assess the market impact of allowances. He simulates the model with experimental data, but this could have been done just as well with numbers from conventional sources.

Defining Housing Services and Their Price

The problem in defining housing services and their price are of course as central to supply as demand. Those studying the supply of housing with conventional data have made exactly the same sort of assumptions in constructing their price and quantity variables. (See Poterba 1980, Ingram and Oron 1977, or Rothenberg 1977.)

In this regard, the numbers generated by the supply experiment are no better than conventional data. Indeed, the difficulties associated with the multidimensional nature of housing are particularly vexing here, because one of EHAP's mandates was to find out what combination of rehabilitation of existing units, construction of new units, and improvement of neighborhood quality would be induced by housing allowances (Allen, Fitts, and Glatt 1981). To answer this question, one would need to

---

28. The assumption of a horizontal supply curve is quite common, e.g., see de Leeuw and Struyk (1975, 15). Of course, to the extent that input prices change with the size of the housing industry, the long-run supply curve will have a nonzero slope.

quantify these attributes, compute their implicit prices, and then estimate supply curves for each. As noted above, researchers have still not solved completely the problems associated with estimating demand and supply schedules for characteristics, and nothing about experimental data per se makes this task any easier.

Shift Variables

In a competitive model, the supply of housing services depends not only upon their own price, but upon input prices as well, so these are important shift variables. Housing studies using conventional data face serious difficulties in obtaining operational measures of housing-input costs. For example, Poterba (1980) uses the Boeckh index of the price of inputs for a new one-family structure to measure construction costs. Although this index is commonly used, it is well known to be deficient because fixed weights are used in its computation. Ingram and Oron (1977) use the fuel component of the consumer price index to account for the price of all operating inputs, but as Rothenberg (1977) points out, it is not clear that this index captures all the needed information.

With respect to measuring the prices of housing inputs, the experimental data provide no particular advantage. For example, Rydell (1979, 36) must make calculations regarding the costs of components of gross rent similar to those who use conventional data. It should be noted, however, that these computations appear to be some of the most careful available.

Disequilibrium and Dynamic Issues

As suggested above, many models of housing supply begin with a production function that exhibits constant returns to scale in the inputs. Given this specification, and assuming constant input prices, the long-run supply of housing services is infinitely elastic. Thus, any demand shift induced by a housing allowance will leave unchanged the long-run price of housing services. However, the question of supply response is still interesting, because the production function does not indicate the length of time required to reach long-run equilibrium or the path of prices during the transition. To understand the supply response, it is crucial to model both the process of adjustment to the new equilibrium and the presence of any factors that might impede the market from achieving equilibrium.

Thus, for example, in one of their models Ingram and Oron (1977, 292) assume that the most a landlord can invest each period is limited to the amount of cash generated by the existing investment, even if this amount is insufficient to close the gap between the desired and actual housing stock. Poterba (1980) argues that conditions in the credit market may affect the supply of housing, and he proxies these by the flow of savings deposits received by savings and loan associations. Poterba also assumes a delayed supply response to changes in all right-hand-side variables that are entered in polynomial distributed lags (p. 10).

The designers of the supply experiment clearly were aware of the importance of lags in the housing-supply process, as witnessed by the fact that the experiment was given a ten-year duration (although only five years' worth of data were collected). Because there was no control group, however, no simple comparisons can be made in order to learn how movements toward the final equilibrium take place. My guess is that even if there had been a control group (call it "South Bend Prime"), structural models would still be more useful than experimental comparisons for determining the lag structure. By the time a decade had lapsed, it is possible that a number of variables that influence adjustment patterns would have changed, so comparisons of South Bend and South Bend Price would not be very informative.

Market Environment

In the demand experiment it was unnecessary to study market environment, since the key question was how micro-units reacted to exogenous changes in their budget constraints. But to understand overall effects, the question of market structure is crucial—the impact of the housing allowances on pretreatment price clearly will depend mutatis mutandis upon the degree of competitiveness in the market, the amount of slack existing when the program is initiated, the extent of housing-market segmentation, etc.

The standard assumption is that competition prevails. As de Leeuw and Struyk (1975) and Poterba (1980) note, however, even given competition, complications arise because two markets have to be equilibrated by the price of housing services: the market for existing houses and the market for new construction. The situation is even more complicated when one takes into account the multiplicity of tenure modes. Each type of housing is traded in its own submarket, and each of these (interrelated) markets has a market clearing price. If the housing market is noncompetitive, the question of supply effects is even more difficult because of the absence of a generally accepted theory of price determination. Theoretically, one can imagine examining a group of cities that are identical except for housing-market structure and comparing the results when they are subjected to housing allowances. (Indeed, something of this notion was behind the selection of Green Bay and South Bend as the experimental sites.) In practice, such a course would be prohibitively expensive, even if it were possible to find an appropriate group of cities. Again, construction of structural models appears to be the more viable methodology. For example, using data from the supply experiment, Rydell (1979) attempts to explain the insensitivity of housing prices to apparent variations in market tightness by recourse to a theory of monopolistic competition. This approach is interesting, but the availability of experimental data provides no special advantage when it comes to testing its validity.

2.4 Conclusion

The Experimental Housing Allowance Program has generated a rich and valuable set of data on the housing behavior of lower-income Americans. These data appear to have been analyzed carefully and creatively by the EHAP investigators, although doubtless their conclusions will be challenged as the numbers are studied by other investigators.[29] The issue discussed in this paper is the extent to which the experimental nature of these data per se enhances their value. Specifically, are the problems faced by investigators, who have used conventional data to predict behavioral response to housing allowances, in any way mitigated by the availability of experimental data?

With the possible exception of experimentally induced variations in housing prices, it seems that the experimental data offer no particular advantages. Fundamentally, this is because housing behavior is so complex and the policy environment so uncertain that simple comparisons of experimental and control groups are unlikely to be of much interest. Rather, the data must be interpreted with the help of theoretical and statistical models. Thus, if the goal was to obtain new and improved estimates of the behavioral response to housing allowances, a social experiment was not necessary. The money would have been better spent on augmenting conventional data sources.[30]

References

Aaron, Henry. 1979. Policy implications of the housing allowance experiments: A progress report. Washington, D.C., Brookings Institution. Mimeo.

———. 1972. *Shelters and subsidies.* Washington, D.C.: Brookings Institution.

Abbott, Michael, and Orley Ashenfelter. 1976. Labor supply, commodity demand, and the allocation of time. *Review of Economic Studies* 43 (Oct.): 389–411.

29. For example, Mills and Sullivan (1981) have suggested that problems with econometric technique lead the EHAP investigators to underestimate income elasticities from the demand experiment.

30. A similar conclusion is reached by Hanushek and Quigley (1979b, 68).

Alexander, W. E. 1975. Comment. *Annals of Economic and Social Measurement* 4: 175–78.

Allen, Garland E., Jerry A. Fitts, and Evelyn S. Glatt. 1981. The Experimental Housing Allowance Program. In *Do housing allowances work?* ed. Katherine L. Bradbury and Anthony Downs, 1–31. Washington, D.C.: Brookings Institution.

Barnett, C. Lance. 1979. Expected and actual effects of housing allowances on housing prices. Working paper. Rand Corporation.

Barnett, C. Lance, and Ira S. Lowry. 1979. *How housing allowances affect housing prices.* Rand Report R–2452–JUD. Rand Corporation.

Barro, Robert J., and Hershel I. Grossman. 1971. A general disequilibrium model of income and employment. *American Economic Review* 61: 82–93.

Brown, James N., and Harvey S. Rosen. 1982. On the estimation of structural hedonic price models. *Econometrica* 50: 765–68.

Carliner, Geoffrey. 1973. Income elasticity of housing demand. *Review of Economics and Statistics* 55: 528–32.

de Leeuw, Frank, and Raymond J. Struyk. 1975. *The web of urban housing.* Washington, D.C.: Urban Institute.

Downs, Anthony, and Katherine L. Bradbury. 1981. Conference discussion. In *Do housing allowances work?*, ed. Katherine L. Bradbury and Anthony Downs, 375–404. Washington, D.C.: Brookings Institution.

Field, Barry C. N.d. Estimating substitution elasticities in housing with a translog cost function. University of Massachusetts at Amherst. Mimeo.

Friedman, Joseph, and Daniel Weinberg. 1978. Draft report on the demand for rental housing: Evidence from a percent of rent housing allowance. Working paper. Abt Associates.

Hanushek, Eric A., and John M. Quigley. 1980. What is the price of elasticity of housing demand? *Review of Economics and Statistics* 62 (No. 3): 449–54.

———. 1979a. The dynamics of the housing market: A stock adjustment model of housing consumption. *Journal of Urban Economics* 6: 90–111.

———. 1979b. Complex public subsidies and complex household behavior: Consumption aspects of housing allowances. University of Rochester. Mimeo.

Hausman, J. A., and David A. Wise. 1980. Discontinuous budget constraints and estimation: The demand for housing. *Review of Economic Studies* 47: 75–96.

Heckman, James. 1979. Sample bias as a specification error. *Econometrica* 47 (no. 1): 153–62.

Ingram, Gregory K., and Yitzhak Oron. 1977. The production of housing services from existing dwelling units. In *Residential local and urban housing markets*, ed. Gregory K. Ingram, 273–314. Cambridge, Mass.: Ballinger Publishing.

King, Mervyn A. 1980. An econometric model of tenure choice and demand for housing as a joint decision. *Journal of Public Economics* 14: 137–60.

Mills, Edwin S., and Arthur Sullivan. 1981. Market effects. In *Do housing allowances work?* ed. Katherine L. Bradbury and Anthony Downs, 247–76. Washington, D.C.: Brookings Institution.

Mosteller, Frederick, and Gale Mosteller. 1979. New statistical methods in public policy, part 1: Experimentation. *Journal of Contemporary Business* 8: 79–92.

Mulford, John E. 1979. The income elasticity of housing demand. Working paper R–2449–HUD. Rand Corporation.

Polinsky, A. Mitchell, and David T. Ellwood. 1979. An empirical reconciliation of micro and grouped estimates of the demand for housing. *Review of Economics and Statistics* 61: 199–205.

Poterba, James M. 1980. Inflation, income taxes, and owner occupied housing. Working paper no. 553. National Bureau of Economic Research.

Quigley, John M. 1982. Non-linear budget constraints and consumer demand: An application to public programs for residential housing. *Journal of Urban Economics* 12: 177–201.

Rosen, Harvey S. 1979a. Housing decisions and the U.S. income tax: An econometric analysis. *Journal of Public Economics* 11: 1–23.

———. 1979b. Owner-occupied housing and the federal income tax: Estimates and simulations. *Journal of Urban Economics* 6: 247–66.

Rosen, Harvey S., and Kenneth T. Rosen. 1980. Federal taxes and homeownership: Evidence from time series. *Journal of Political Economy* 88: 59–75.

Rosen, Sherwin. 1974. Hedonic prices and implicit markets. *Journal of Political Economy* 82: 34–35.

Rothenberg, Jerome. 1977. Comments on chapter 8. In *Residential location and urban housing markets*, ed. Gregory K. Ingram, 315–21. Cambridge, Mass.: Ballinger Publishing.

Rydell, C. Peter. 1979. Shortrun response of housing markets to demand shifts. Working paper R–2453–HUD. Rand Corporation.

Sixth annual report of the housing assistance supply experiment. 1980. Rand Corporation, Santa Monica, Calif.

Struyk, Raymond J. 1976. *Urban homeownership*. Lexington, Mass.: Lexington Books.

Williams, Robert George. 1975. *Public assistance and work effort*. Princeton University, Industrial Relations Section. Dept. of Economics.

Witte, Ann D., Howard J. Sumka, and Homer Erekson. 1979. An estimate of a structural hedonic price model of the housing market: An application of Rosen's theory of implicit markets. *Econometrica* 47: 1151–73.

Comment   John M. Quigley

Introduction

Harvey Rosen's paper provides a compact overview of the Housing Allowance Demand (HADE) and Supply (HASE) experiments; it focuses upon the extent to which the experimental nature of the longitudinal data collected enhances their value in scientific research. The Rosen analysis is well written and argued, and it is hard to disagree with his principal conclusions. I will begain by summarizing the conclusions of the Rosen paper, perhaps emphasizing his points in a slightly different way. I will then extend the discussion to include several important issues that the author chooses to ignore.

Rosen's review considers six of the seventeen treatment groups in the demand experiment and the single treatment group that comprises the supply experiment.

One of these groups—the unconstrained-housing-gap treatment—is simply a negative income tax. Imposition of this program nationally would adjust individual payments to reflect the cost of "standard" housing in each market, a good proxy for regional variations in the cost of living.

The other five HADE groups—the percent-of-rent treatments—are pure price reductions of various percentages.

The HASE treatment is a negative-income-tax schedule offered conditional upon the physical characteristics of housing chosen by recipients.

The principal conclusions of the author are three:

1. The experimental feature of the data obtained from the HADE unconstrained-housing-gap treatment group provides no additional evidence on the income elasticity of rental-housing demand.
2. The experimental features of the data generated by the HADE percent-of-rent groups "confer distinct benefits" in estimating the price elasticity of demand for rental housing.
3. The data obtained from the HASE treatments provide no particular advantages for the analysis of housing supply.

John M. Quigley is professor of economics and public policy, University of California, Berkeley.

The Experimental Data

HADE households in the unconstrained-housing-gap treatment group received transfers of varying amounts of additional income according to a single negative-income-tax formula for three years; households in the five percent-of-rent treatment groups received rent rebates of varying fractions (0.2, 0.3, 0.4, 0.5, and 0.6) for the same period. A large body of information was initially gathered about each household and its housing consumption; each household was re-interviewed and an identical body of data was gathered after six months, after one year, and after two years of program operation.

The Unconstrained-Housing-Gap Treatment

First, consider the problem of estimating the income elasticity of housing demand. Ever since Margaret Reid's (1962) revisionist analysis of the relationship between housing and income, the appropriate definition of income has been problematic. Clearly, the choice of a particular dwelling unit (an owned or a rental unit) is based upon a time horizon for consumption which is "long." The search, moving, and transactions costs associated with residential choices are large; presumably, these frictions play the same role as those associated with the purchase and sale of other durable goods. It is not helpful merely to state that these consumption choices are made on the basis of "permanent" income, at least not when confronting observations on individual households.

A number of researchers have used different, plausible, but essentially ad hoc methods to compute "permanent" income from data on individual households so that the income elasticity of demand can be estimated in a subsequent step.[1]

Consider those households receiving cash transfers; they receive thirty-six monthly payments after which their income reverts to its unsubsidized level. How is this stream to be converted into a change in permanent income so that it can be related to housing consumption?

If the problem were merely to establish the partial relationship between reported monthly income and contemporaneous housing consumption, the body of experimental information would suffice.[2] Note, however, that any cross section of households without any experimental payments would be equally adequate.

To take housing allowances seriously as a national program, however, knowledge of this partial relationship would never do. Some estimate of the long-run effect of these payments upon the housing consumption of

---

1. Many of these are reviewed in Quigley (1979).
2. Subject, as Rosen notes, to an assumed specification, an assumed functional form, and an assumption that within each market unit, price of housing services is constant.

poor households is required. Ironically, in the absence of a specific theory of permanent income, observations on a particular stream of known transitory payments might be a disadvantage in estimating the permanent response to permanent housing allowances.[3]

Joseph Friedman, one of the principal Abt researchers analyzing the demand experiments, estimates that the additional cost of providing lifetime guarantees of transfers to the (lucky) participants in HADE would have been about $10 million (or roughly 6 percent of EHAP program costs).[4] Had these transfers been truly permanent, it would have been possible, at least in principle, to isolate the housing-consumption response to a change in permanent income.

The Percent-of-Rent Treatments

Second, consider the problem of estimating the price elasticity of housing demand, where market observations on housing are in price-times-quantity units. Analysts have pooled observations on households across markets (SMSAs) and used SMSA housing price indexes (i.e., BLS average prices) in regressions to estimate the price elasticity of consumption. Unfortunately this procedure leads to biased estimates of the price-elasticity term (see Polinsky 1977 for details). Other analysts (Muth 1971; Polinsky and Elwood 1979) have employed an ingenious, if highly suspicious, method to derive unit prices for housing which vary within a single market. The method involves estimating the parameters of a housing production function (CES) and using exogenous information on the variation in unit prices and quantities of land to infer variations in unit costs, and hence output prices, for housing. Estimated housing prices are then used in a subsequent analysis to infer the price elasticity of demand.

Neither of these procedures is very satisfactory, but observations generated by the market do not isolate variation in housing prices, only in housing expenditures.

Thus observations generated by the HADE percent-of-rent experiment are extremely valuable. Each household faces housing prices of $P_0(1 - \alpha)$, where P_0 is the initial market price and α is the fraction of rent forgiven by the experimental treatment. If P_0, the initial price of housing, is constant but unobserved, then experimental variation in α permits estimation of the partial relationship between housing prices and housing consumption. This body of experimental data is the only evidence available that includes direct information on variations in the price of housing facing individual decision units. The most important problem in utilizing

---

3. At least researchers have analyzed empirically the problems of inference when income variations arise "naturally."

4. From a discussion of the EHAP research design at the Brookings Conference on Housing Allowances, November 1979.

this information is the transitory nature of the price reduction—rebate offers of α percent of monthly rent are made for only thirty-six months. Again, for (allegedly) small additional resources, this offer could have been extended indefinitely.

The Supply Experiment

Consider the data gathered from the supply experiment. A single tied-subsidy schedule is offered to each household that meets specific income criteria in two metropolitan areas. Detailed longitudinal observations are gathered on a sample of dwelling units, their occupants, and the behavior of their landlords.

What information do these data provide about the supply elasticity of housing services? The analytical problem is to identify the impact of an experimentally induced injection of demand upon the price of housing in the metropolitan area. To infer the effect of housing allowances upon housing supply requires that the experimental treatment be isolated from other factors—net inmigration, household formation, changes in input prices—that affect the supply of housing services according to some model or set of maintained behavioral hypotheses. Since these factors operate at the market level, it is difficult to see how any ingenious estimation strategy would disentangle them when observations are gathered from only two markets.

As Rosen reports, after four years of observing housing prices at both sites, there was little or no change in the relative price of housing at either site. From this fact, the HASE researchers infer "the experimental program . . . had virtually no effect on housing prices." Perhaps. But suppose that the relative price of housing had declined at either site—a possibility not logically excluded by anything in the experiment. What inference would be drawn by the HASE analysts?

In my view, the design of the HASE "experiment" and the organization of its principal reports makes it apparent that HASE can best be considered a "demonstration" from which a large body of behavioral data were gathered. The operation of a "real" housing-allowance program in two metropolitan areas provides a wealth of information useful in designing a national program, in estimating the likely administrative and monitoring costs, and so forth. (Some of the useful results of the demonstration are noted by Aaron 1981.)

In considering the political economy of a housing-allowance program, it is clear that if average housing prices had risen appreciably in Green Bay and South Bend, a universal housing-allowance program would be "dead." However, even if housing prices had risen at the HASE sites, it would not have been possible to conclude that the relevant housing-supply curve would be inelastic if a universal program were adopted—at least not on the basis of any model presented by the HASE researchers.

Inferences from Longitudinal Data

As a body of data on microeconomic behavior, the information generated by the EHAP program is unprecedented. The demand experiment provides multiple observations on individual households receiving transfers under seventeen different subsidy schedules, as well as a control group of households unaffected by the program. The supply experiment provides a rich body of information about particular dwelling units, their landlords and occupants over time. No other body of information contains longitudinal observations of demanders and suppliers of housing services within any single market.

The unique scientific advantage of these data lies as much in its panel design as in its experimental emphasis. The very existence of this rich body of information raises fundamental questions about the short-run dynamic behavior of economic agents.

As noted previously, decisions about changes in housing consumption are subject to substantial transaction costs—the time and out-of-pocket costs of searching and evaluating alternative units, the costs of moving household possessions, and the psychic costs of relocation. All these factors suggest that the quantity of housing services consumed by any household at any instant may deviate substantially from its "equilibrium" level—at least if equilibrium is defined as the quantity chosen given current prices, demographic characteristics, and income.

The concept of permanent income as applied to housing consumption is consistent with the instanteous "disequilibrium" between the current consumption and the current characteristics of households in the local market.

Theory says very little about the magnitude of adjustment lags in this (or any other) market or about the pattern of dynamic adjustment to changed circumstances. The dynamics of microbehavior in this market are, however, of real importance in interpreting the experiments and in evaluating their results.

Consider the percent-of-rent households. In response to a (permanent) reduction in housing prices, it is reasonable to presume that households desire to consume *some* additional quantity of housing services. Alternatively, the "disequilibrium" between current and desired housing services is increased when the price reduction is offered. Additional consumption implies moving, and only when the capitalized utility difference between current and desired housing consumption exceeds the utility costs of moving will an adjustment in consumption be made. Even then, there is likely to be some time lag before any adjustment is actually observed. The percent-of-rent experiment provides information on households at four points in time during twenty-four months of experimental treatment. Is it reasonable to presume that the entire effect of a price reduction is observed after two years? If it is, then the simple cross tabs or the more elaborate analyses of Friedman and Weinberg (1978) suggest a price elasticity on the order of -0.2. Is it reasonable to estimate the dynamic response pattern and the long-run price responsiveness simultaneously? If it is, then the simple stock-adjustment model of Hanushek and Quigley (1980) yields estimates that are, in the long run, two to three times larger numerically.

This is not to argue that one or the other of these results is preferred on methodological grounds. The different results do indicate, however, that the interpretation of the experimental "facts" is heavily dependent upon a model of the short-run dynamics of the market. With only a short time series and with at most only four observations on each individual household, it is difficult to estimate the asymptote of any assumed dynamic adjustment pattern with confidence. In fact, it does not take a very complex assumption about market dynamics to render the problem logically intractable.

The same difficulties in interpretation apply to each of the other treatment groups in the experiments.

The Constrained Households

Rosen's paper emphasizes the utility of the experimental evidence to estimate three parameters familiar to economists: a price and income elasticity of demand and a price elasticity of supply.

If households are highly sensitive to housing-price incomes in their consumption choices, a national percent-of-rent (housing-gap) program would increase the housing consumption of selected households. If households are relatively insensitive to prices and incomes, either program would reduce the high "rent burdens" that they face.

Clearly much of the popular and political appeal of housing allowances focuses on the provision of inducements to households to consume "adequate" housing. Indeed, as Rosen notes, it is unlikely that any percent-of-rent program would be implemented nationally—landlord-tenant collusion would then be profitable.[5]

Concerns about adequate housing (whether they arise from so-called externalities or simply paternalism) are reflected in the design of the HASE and HADE programs. All of the payments offered in the supply experiment were conditional upon verification that the recipient household was living in "adequate" housing, where adequate is defined programmatically. For five of the HADE treatment groups, housing-gap (i.e., negative-income-tax) payments were conditinal upon similar verification (but according to slightly different program definitions); six other HADE treatment groups offered payments conditional upon some mini-

5. It should be noted, however, that similar incentives exist in the food stamp program. In addition, there was no evidence of collusion among the eight hundred households and landlords participating in the percent-of-rent experiments.

mum rental expenditure. Overall 53 percent of the experimental households at both HADE sites waere assigned to treatments where subsidies were conditional upon verification of the physical condition of dwellings or minimum rental payments; 41 percent were assigned to unconstrained percent-of-rent treatments and only 6 percent to unconstrained-housing-gap treatments (see Allen, Fitts, and Glatt 1981).

The Ambiguous Evidence

In the absence of very rich models of consumer behavior (and, as noted below, in the presence of very small sample sizes), it is difficult to draw strong inferences from the housing-gap experiments where payments were tied to verification of physical standards.

For those households offered transfers subject to minimum rental payments, the sample sizes, after two years of the experiment, are reasonably large. Using comparisons with households in the control group, the HADE researchers estimate the effect of transfers-conditional-upon-rent- payments upon household rental expenditures. Further, in a series of complex analyses (Friedman and Weinberg 1979, chapter 6), they conclude that recipients of these transfers may have shopped less efficiently for housing services than control households.

The analysis of households receiving housing-gap transfers, according to different schedules, conditional upon the physical characteristics of their housing, is much more problematic.[6] In part, the HADE analysis is constrained by small sample sizes and low participation rates. For example, in Pittsburgh, 87 households in the minimum-standards treatment group met those standards after two years. However, 38 of those households met the standards initially, leaving 49 who were induced to meet the standards, at least in part, by the experimental payment offer. However, these offers were made under five different payment schedules. The difference in payments between the least-generous and the most-generous payment schedule is 183 percent.

More important than small numbers in interpreting the HADE analysis is the behavioral reason for small samples of program participants under the constrained treatment groups. Many of the comparisons reported are between participants and control households, or between moving households and movers in the control group. Presumably the analytical samples are selected on the basis of stronger tastes for housing consumption. This selectivity bias is clearly recognized by the researchers, and heroic efforts are made to "triangulate" on the "true" treatment effects by presenting parameter estimates for many different subsamples of households.

Nevertheless, it is difficult to interpret these estimates in the absence of a unified theory of household participation and household consumption.

6. This issue is discussed in detail in Hanushek and Quigley (1981).

Some Behavioral Models

For 53 percent of the households in the HADE treatment groups, payment offers were tied to specific adjustments in housing consumption—adjustments that had not been made in the absence of the experimental bribe. It is clear that in many circumstances the rational household may maximize its welfare by declining the payment and its associated strings. Unfortunately, neither Rosen's discussion nor any of the analyses of the constrained households pays much attention to the welfare economics of the choice problem solved by these low-income households. In response to the experimental offer, households choose program participation and levels of housing consumption; an economic model of behavior must address jointly the program-participation decision and the housing-consumption decision of those invited to enroll in the constrained treatment groups.

Each of the tied offers presents the potential recipient with a distorted and more complex opportunity set or budget constraint. If it is assumed that there exists a single index of housing services and that initial housing prices are constant in the market, then the minimum-rent treatment groups face a linear, but discontinuous budget constraint. If it is assumed that separate indexes exist for "housing-standards goods" and "other housing goods," and that initial prices are constant, then the minimum-standards treatment groups face a budget plane (in their choice of standards, other housing goods, and nonhousing goods) that is discontinuous. It is clear, moreover, that in the absence of these convenient assumptions, the budget constraint need not be linear in its traces; but it surely is discontinuous.

A microeconomic model of the participation and housing-consumption decision must use market information somehow to trace the shape of the indifference curve between housing and nonhousing goods or between standards components, other housing, and nonhousing goods.

Hausman and Wise (1980) have analyzed the choice problem when households face a budget constraint that may be nonlinear and discontinuous, but that can be represented by pricewise continuous functions; their methodology has been applied to the data from the HADE percent-of-rent households gathered after one year of experimental treatment. This methodology estimates the curvature of utility functions between "housing services" and other goods from the revealed participation and consumption decisions of the experimental households.

Assume a single linear price index of housing services, normalized to a value of one, so that rental expenditures R measure service consumption. Assume that household preferences can be represented by:

(1) $$U = (Y - R)^{1-\beta} R^\beta,$$

where Y is income and β is a function of household sociodemographic characteristics X and a random error n, i.e.,

(2) $\beta = X\delta + n$.

If income is not a determinant of β, then equation (1) is merely Cobb-Douglas in two goods.

More generally, maximizing utility implies

(3) $R = \beta Y + \epsilon = (X\delta)\, Y + nY + \epsilon$

where ϵ is a stochastic error.

Consider a household assigned to the minimum-rent treatment, i.e., a household i offered a cash transfer Δ conditional upon rental expenditures of R^*.

The household will accept the transfer and will participate in the program if its taste for housing is large enough, that is, if its β_i is greater than the highest value, $\bar{\beta}$, at which it would be indifferent.

(4) $(Y_i + \Delta - R^*)^{1-\beta_i}\, R^{*\beta_i} > (Y_i - R)^{1-\beta_i}\, R^{\beta_i},\ \beta_i > \bar{\beta}$.

Participating households will have housing expenditures of

(5) $\widetilde{R} = \beta_i\, Y_i + \epsilon_i > R^*$.

Analogously, a household will decline the transfer and will not participate if its taste β_i is less than the smallest value, $\underline{\beta}$, at which it would be indifferent.

(6) $(Y_i - R)^{1-\beta_i} R^{\beta_i} > (Y_i + \Delta - R^*)_{1-}{}^{\beta_i}\, R^{*\beta_i},\ \beta_i < \underline{\beta}$.

Nonparticipants incur housing expenditures of

(7) $\widetilde{R} = \beta_i\, Y_i + \epsilon_i < R^*$.

Thus for a sample of households in the minimum-rent treatment group, the likelihood function for the rental expenditures observed depends upon ϵ_i and β_i (for example, we will observe $\widetilde{R} > R^*$ if $\beta_i > \bar{\beta}$ and $\epsilon_i = \widetilde{R} - \beta_i\, [Y + \Delta]$).

Assumptions about the distribution of ϵ_i and about the distribution of β_i permit the function to be maximized and the parameters δ to be estimated.

Estimates of δ indicate the distribution of housing preferences across sociodemographic groups and the full response of individual households to the minimum-rent treatment.

The procedure is general enough to address choices made in response to any discontinuous monotonic budget constraint regardless of its shape. Indeed, it was first applied to the nonlinear case (Burtless and Hausman 1978).

The Hausman-Wise model may not be appropriate, however, for analyzing the responses to treatments tied to consumption of housing standards. At least two other approaches may be employed to estimate the curvature of indifference surfaces and hence to analyze jointly participation and consumption decisions. The first emphasizes the nonlinearity of prices for continuous-housing attributes. The second, and better known, emphasizes the discrete nature of housing choices.

First, assume that the m characteristics of housing standards (Z) and the n other housing characteristics (H) are priced jointly according to some hedonic rule,

$$(8) \qquad R = f(H,Z),$$

Where H and Z are continuous and differentiable. Households of income Y are assumed to have preferences over these components of housing as well as other goods, X, whose price is normalized to one.

Maximizing utility

$$(9) \qquad U = g(H,Z,Y - R),$$

subject to the nonlinear budget constraint

$$(10) \qquad Y = f(H,Z) + X,$$

means that housing prices are jointly chosen with housing commodities. Nevertheless, utility maximization implies a set of $i = 1,2, \ldots, m + n$ first-order conditions of the form

$$(11) \qquad f_i(H,Z) = U_i(H, Z, Y - R).$$

Joint estimation of the set of first-order conditions is possible as long as f is nonlinear and exogenous, at least for many forms of the utility function. Empirically, estimation may proceed by determining the parameters of the hedonic function, using Box-Cox or some other best-fitting procedure. The derivatives of the estimated function, evaluated at the (H,Z) chosen by each individual, become the dependent variables in the estimation of the parameters of utility functions.[7] These parameters would permit inferences to be drawn about the participation and consumption decisions of households offered tied subsidies.

The second technique would estimate the parameters of a stochastic utility function of the form

$$(12) \qquad U = g(H,Z,Y - R) + \epsilon.$$

These parameters could be estimated directly from observations on the dwelling unit chosen by each household in the treatment group and on a

---

7. For example, assuming the utility function is GCES (Murray 1975), Quigley (1982) provides an example.

sample of the rejected alternatives using the general model suggested by McFadden (1977).[8]

Conclusion

Inferences about the behavior of households offered subsidies tied to minimum rental payments or tied to the consumption of housing meeting minimum standards must address the decision to participate in the program as well as the housing-consumption decision, given participation. Since the opportunity sets of experimental subjects are distorted in peculiar ways by these treatments, an analytical technique that investigates the curvature of indifference surfaces seems necessary. Using somewhat different assumptions, the three strategies outlined above integrate the consumption and participation decision.

The first strategy has been employed by Hausman and Wise to analyze the minimum-rent households. The second strategy was discussed by Murray (1978) in the context of housing allowances. The third strategy is, in principle, a straightforward application of models successfully applied in other markets.

It should be noted, however, that even if the form of the utility function were known with certainty (on the basis of these or other investigations), the short duration of the experiment would still make inferences about the "long run" problematic. The effect of long-term tied subsidies upon the long-term consumption behavior of low-income households is difficult to infer from a very short time series.

References

Aaron, Henry. 1981. Policy implications of the housing allowance experiments: A progress report. In *Do housing allowances work? See* Bradbury and Downs 1981.

Allen, Garland A., Jerry A. Fitts, and Evelyn S. Glatt. 1981. The experimental housing allowance program. In *Do housing allowances work? See* Bradbury and Downs 1981.

Bradbury, Katherine A., and Anthony Downs, eds. 1981. *Do housing allowances work?* Washington, D.C.: Brookings Institution.

Burtless, Gary, and Jerry Hausman. 1978. The effect of taxes on labor supply: Evaluating the Gary NIT experiment. *Journal of Political Economy* 86 (no. 6): 1103–30.

Friedman, Joseph, and Daniel Weinberg. 1979. Draft report on housing consumption under a constrained income transfer: Evidence from a housing gap housing allowance. Abt Associates, Cambridge, Mass.

8. The most straightforward approach would be to assume that g is linear in its parameters and the ϵ's are i.i.d. weibull and to employ a sampling rule with the so-called uniform conditioning property to generate observations on rejected alternatives for each household. See McFadden (1974, 1977).

————. 1978. Draft report on the demand for rental housing: Evidence from a percent of rent housing allowance working paper. Abt Associates, Cambridge, Mass.

Hanushek, Eric A., and John M. Quigley. 1981. Complex public subsidies and complex household behavior: Consumption aspects of housing allowances. In *Do housing allowances work?* *See* Bradbury and Downs 1981.

————. 1980. What is the price elasticity of housing demand? *Review of Economics and Statistics* 62 (no. 3): 449–54.

Hausman, Jerry A., and David A. Wise. 1980. Discontinuous budget constraints and estimation: The demand for housing. *Review of Economic Studies* 47: 75–96.

McFadden, Daniel. 1977. Modelling the choice of residential location. Cowles Foundation Discussion Paper 477. Yale University.

————. 1974. Conditional logit analysis of qualitative choice behavior. In *Frontiers in Econometrics*, ed. Paul Zarembka, 105–42. New York: Academic Press.

Murray, Michael P. 1978. Methodologies for estimating housing subsidy benefits. *Public Finance Quarterly* 6 (no. 2): 161–92.

————. 1975. The distribution of tenant benefits in public housing. *Econometrica* 43 (no. 4): 771–88.

Muth, Richard F. 1971. The derived demand for urban residential land. *Urban Studies* 8 (no. 3): 243–54.

Polinsky, A. Mitchell. 1977. The demand for housing: A study in specification and grouping. *Econometrica* 45 (no. 2): 447–61.

Polinsky, A. Mitchell, and David T. Ellwood. 1979. An empirical reconciliation of micro and grouped estimates of the demand for housing. *Review of Economics and Statistics* 61: 199–205.

Quigley, John M. 1982. Non-linear budget constraints and consumer demand: An application to public programs for resident housing. *Journal of Urban Economics* 12: 177–201.

————. 1979. What have we learned about housing markets? In *Current issues in urban economics*, ed. Peter Mieszkowski and Mahlon Straszheim. Baltimore, Md.: Johns Hopkins University Press.

Reid, Margaret G. 1962. *Housing and income*. Chicago: University of Chicago Press.

Comment   Gregory K. Ingram

In his paper Harvey Rosen focuses on whether or not experimental data from the housing-allowance experiments have helped investigators resolve a number of analytic and empirical difficulties that plague the analysis of both the supply and demand sides of the housing market. He concludes that the experimental data have not been particularly helpful. His is a good summary of these issues, and I concur with his views. Rather than review his points directly, I shall take an approach, which I hope will be complementary to his, that focuses on a slightly different question: What have we learned from the housing-allowance experiments that can help us predict what the costs and effects of a full-scale national housing-allowance program would be, and could we have learned these things from nonexperimental data? The discussion of this question is organized around three subheadings: What would a national program cost? How would it affect housing consumption? How would it affect housing markets?

Program Cost

The total cost of a national housing-allowance program would be one of the crucial determinants of its adoption. Calculating these costs requires three pieces of information: the transfer payment and administrative cost per type of eligible household; the participation rate of each type of eligible household; and the total number of each type of eligible household (Khadduri and Struyk 1980). The payment for each type of eligible household would depend on the payment formula, household characteristics, and perhaps local market parameters. Data from housing-allowance experiments would not be particularly relevant. The experiments also provide estimates of administrative costs; these could arguably have come from nonexperimental sources.

The participation rate of households in the program, which is a crucial determinant of program costs, would be heavily dependent on data from the experiments. The experiments have revealed that the participation rates of eligible households in the experimental program were much lower (at 30 to 50 percent) than those of the AFDC programs (around 80 percent) that seemed to have been used as guidelines for the design of the housing-allowance experiments. Average participation rates for renters were 27 percent for the demand experiments, 42 percent for the supply experiments, and 53 percent for the administrative agency experiments, while they were 33 percent for owners in the supply experiment (Struyk and Bendick 1981, chap. 4). In fact, as Rosen states, these unexpectedly

Gregory K. Ingram is director, development research department, the World Bank, Washington, D.C.

low participation rates have been one of the factors that have compromised the success of the supply experiments. The experiments suggest that the variation in participation rates depends on several factors including the magnitude of benefits offered to eligible households (higher benefits raise participation); the level of standards used to inspect and approve dwelling units (stricter standards lower participation); the amount of "outreach" used (more promotion increases participation); tenure (owners participate less than renters); and market conditions (tighter markets may have lower participation). Although these factors seem to affect participation, it is not clear that the experiments have produced reliable models that can be used to predict participation rates as a function of the foregoing factors. Moreover, if a "treatment" other than one used in the experiments were to be evaluated, some kind of model or interpolation procedure would have to be used to predict participation rates.

Could we have learned about participation rates using nonexperimental data? Certainly many persons involved in designing the experiments were surprised at the low participation rates. Perhaps the experimental rates are biased downward. It is possible to argue that the true participation rates of a national program would be higher than those experimentally observed simply due to the temporary nature of the experiments. However, the results of the supply experiment, with its ten-year pay-out period, seem to mitigate this objection. A national program also might have higher participation rates because it would become more widely known than the experiments did, and more networks for "diffusion" of the program might become operative. Hence, although the participation rates from the experiments may be lower bounds for true rates, participation is an important determinant of total program costs that would be difficult to learn about without an experiment.

The total number of eligible households of each type, the last determinant of costs, might not be independent of the design of a housing-allowance program. It is possible that a housing-allowance program might alter rates of household formation or dissolution. For example, a housing-allowance program might encourage the formation of low-income, one-person households and thereby increase the number of eligible households. The housing-allowance experiments cast no light on this matter. Empirical studies, however, tend to find only weak relations between housing-market conditions and household formation (Williams 1978).

Housing Consumption

Two major formulas, the housing-gap and percent-of-rent specifications, were tested in the housing-allowance experiments, but it appears that the income-gap formula would be the most likely one to be incorporated into a national housing-allowance program. Although the demand experiments found no evidence for it, apparently there is a lingering suspicion that a percent-of-rent formula in a national program would be a prime candidate for fraudulent cooperation between landlords and tenants: it is feared that landlords would raise rents and split additional allowance payments with tenants (Struyk and Bendick 1981, 175). If the income-gap formula is the prime candidate policy, then the income elasticity of the demand for housing is the prime behavioral parameter of interest. This parameter has been widely estimated using cross-sectional data, and it does not appear that the housing-allowance experiments were necessary for its estimation.

The relatively low, income elasticities of demand obtained from the housing-allowance experiments are plausible and consistent with those obtained from other studies. They are certainly at the low range of cross-sectional estimates, but this is believable given the short time frame of the demand experiments and the low income levels of participants and control groups. Some analysts disagree with this characterization of the elasticities, and they believe that the "true" elasticities are higher. They argue that slow speeds of adjustment, model specification, and the omission of tenure change are biasing downward the experimental results (Hanushek and Quigley 1979). Change in tenure was possible in the supply experiments, but only about 1 percent of the participating households changed tenure (Struyk and Bendick 1981), 292). Many of these arguments are doubtless applicable to procedures used with traditional household survey data. In any case, it seems to me that the housing-allowance experiments were not necessary for the estimation of the required income-elasticity parameters.

As Rosen points out in his paper, data from the housing-allowance experiments do have a comparative advantage in the estimation of price elasticities because prices are not observed directly in housing markets. If a housing-gap formula were used in a national program, however, the price elasticity would be relevant only if housing prices changed due to the program. This price change would then have a secondary impact on housing consumption. Hence the price-elasticity estimates are interesting but not necessarily relevant to the consumption effects of a national housing program.

In addition to providing information about overall housing consumption parameters, several additional insights were gained about the consumption and choice behavior of households in housing markets and the usefulness of certain analytic approaches. Three of these are worth mentioning here.

First, several versions of the demand experiment and all of the supply and administrative-agency experiments required participating households to live in dwelling units that passed certain minimum physical standards. Where dwelling units failed these standards, the units could be upgraded or the household could move. Whichever response was used by a household, it appears that they adjusted their dwelling unit so that it passed the specific constraints imposed. There was usually no significant improvement beyond that mandated by the standards. Given this type of narrow and specific meeting of required standards, it appears that the standards used would be significant determinants of the outcomes associated with a national housing-allowance program. In particular, much thought needs to be given to the setting of standards in a national program. This specificity of response is a significant result that apparently could only have come from the experiments.

Second, a great deal of data were collected about household behavior in housing markets in the course of the demand experiments, and this data has been used to analyze empirically the search behavior exhibited by households in housing markets. It appears, for example, that search behavior does pay off in terms of finding dwellings with particular attributes desired by the households or in terms of finding dwellings that may be bargains (Dunson 1979). This analysis of search behavior has not exploited the experimental nature of the data, however, and in principle could have been done with traditional survey data that interviewed households during or just before their household moves. The existence of the allowance experiments obviously make the identification of this time interval straightforward.

Third, a number of results of the housing-allowance experiments were obtained by using hedonic indexes to control for variations in the price or quantity of housing. For example, it has been reported that households faced with minimum-rent standards tended to pay more per unit of housing quantity than households faced with minimum physical standards (Struyk and Bendick 1981, 140–43). Results of this type are based on hedonic indexes estimated for Phoenix and Pittsburgh. Although Rosen has already mentioned the shortcomings of these indexes in the analysis of housing-market outcomes, it is worth pointing out the particular properties of the Pittsburgh and Phoenix indexes. Using excellent data and sufficient resources for experimentation with alternative specifications, the hedonic equations for Pittsburgh and Phoenix had R^2 of 0.66 and 0.80, respectively (Merrill 1977). These are reasonably high levels of explanatory power. However, an analysis of the residuals from these equations indicates that the average absolute magnitude of the residuals was 22 percent of the average rent paid in Pittsburgh and 20 percent of the average rent paid in Phoenix (Dunson 1979, 208). Since many of the calculations done on price and quantity variation employ residuals from these hendonic equations, the large magnitude of the residuals is troubling. It suggests that there is a specification problem with the underlying indexes, or that hedonic indexes are operationally flawed when used in housing markets, even with the best data one could hope for. The magnitudes of the Pittsburgh and Phoenix residuals do not give one cause to be optimistic about the use of hedonic indexes to measure the small changes in price or quantity of the sort associated with the experiments. Again, experimental data was not necessary to demonstrate this.

Market Effects

The supply experiments tested for market-wide effects in two urban areas using a housing-gap-allowance formula. Since the housing-gap formula works through the income elasticity of demand, which is low, in combination with a low participation rate, the supply experiments increased housing demand very little. As a consequence, there has been no measurable market-wide effect of the supply experiment. This result is significant because one of the major objections to a national housing-allowance program has been its possible inflationary consequences. Do we really want to believe that a national housing-allowance program would have a similarly small market-wide effect? To answer this question, it is useful to do some simple sensitivity analyses on major-program parameters.

A number of different income limits have been used in the supply, demand, and administration-agency experiments carried out, but they all seem to yield an income-level cutoff that equals about one-half of median household income. About 20 percent of households typically have incomes below this level. In both the demand and supply experiments about one-half of income-eligible households enrolled in the program. Not all of those who enrolled decided to become participants. As noted earlier, in the demand experiment 27 percent of income-eligible households participated while in the supply experiments the participation rate was 42 percent for renters and 33 percent for owners. Thus participants ranged from about 6 percent to 8 percent of all households. Moreover, of those who participated, it is reported that about three-fourths stayed in their pre-enrollment dwellings (Struyk and Bendick 1981, 223). Hence, from 1.5 to 2 percent of all households moved because of, or in conjunction with, their participation in the experiment. This is not a large fraction of the roughly 20 percent of households that move each year. Using the percentage of all households whose moves are associated with allowances to proxy-demand increases suggests that slightly higher participation rates would not have much of an impact on market-wide housing-market outcomes. However, market-wide impacts might be observed if the percent of all households eligible for allowances was increased markedly, say from 20 percent to 40 percent.

One final number also merits reporting: three-fourths of those households whose original dwelling unit failed inspection in the demand experiment, but which eventually passed the standards, obtained a passing unit by moving (Struyk and Bendick 1981, 109). Given that three-fourths of participants stayed in their pre-enrollment dwelling unit, this implies that the majority of households participating in the demand experiments had pre-enrollment dwellings that passed the standards. The percent of households in the supply experiments that met the standards by moving after first failing the standards was much smaller, about 25 percent, but still over half of the participants in the supply experiments had pre-enrollment units that met the standards. Given this fact, it is not surprising that the demand increase stimulated by the housing-allowance experiments—and particularly the three-year demand experiment—was not large.

The basic behavior pattern implicit in these numbers seems to be as follows; households living in units that pass the minimum standards are likely to participate in the program and to stay in their original units. Households living in units that fail the standards originally are much less likely to participate in the program; those who do participate may move, especially if they are renters. Since the overall moving rates of participating households are similar to the moving rates of control households, and adjustments are made in housing bundles that narrowly and specifically meet the standards, it seems reasonable to conclude that a national housing-allowance program similar to the one tested in the experiments would not have significant market-wide effects. This conclusion depends heavily on the patterns of household behavior (e.g., participation, mobility, adjustment to standards) revealed by the experiments, and it would be difficult to characterize this behavior without the experimental data. However, most of the relevant behavior was observed in the demand experiments. We may yet learn something about specific landlord or supplier behavior from the supply experiments, but it will be difficult. For example, only 217 of the 3,720 monitored dwellings in Green Bay are occupied by program participants (Struyk and Bendick 1981, 301).

Conclusion

I agree with Rosen's view that the experimental data arising from the housing-allowance experiments have not helped us to solve many of the problems of measurement that underly the analysis of housing markets. However, I also believe that some of the experimental findings are crucial if we are to evaluate the case for a national housing-allowance program. The information on participation rates and the specific response of households to minimum standards are two results important to the assessment of a national program. Both would be difficult to obtain using traditional household interview data.

Does this mean that the housing-allowance experiments were worthwhile? The cost of the experiments, shown in table C2.1, are very high. So high, in fact, that one is forced to think there must be a better way to

Table C2.1   Estimated Cost of Housing-Allowance Experiment (in millions)

Experiment	Household Payments	Adminis-tration	Research and Monitoring	Total
Demand	$ 3.6	$ 2.0	$25.6	$ 31.2
Supply	42.5	18.5	41.7	102.7
Administrative Agency	9.8	3.4	9.2	22.4
Overall design and analysis	0.	0.	6.8	6.8
TOTAL	$55.9	$23.9	$83.3	$163.3

Source: Struyk and Bendick (1981, 297). Estimates by HUD, October (1979), of projected total costs.

learn what must be learned—or at least a cheaper experiment. With the benefit of hindsight (a crucial preamble), there was a cheaper experiment: the housing-allowance experiments without the supply experiment. But I do not believe there is a better way to learn what must be learned. Social experiments clearly have a place in the social scientist's tool kit.

Some would use the housing-allowance experiments to argue this conclusion more forcefully. First, they would state that a social experiment is much more credible to a decision maker (read congressman) than are empirically estimated equations or a simulation model. Second, they would invoke what I call the "Christopher Columbus principle of attribution" (one is judged by one's findings, not by success in discovering what was originally set out for), and claim that one year's savings from the improvements in administrative efficiency of HUD's existing programs stemming from results of the housing-allowance experiments will pay for the experiments (Struyk and Bendick 1981, 308). Finally, they would dispeal fears about fundamental flaws in social experiments by pointing out that the "Hawthorne effect," the hypothesis that people alter their behavior when under study, no longer has a strong empirical base. A new analysis (Lagerfeld 1979; Franke and Kaul 1978) of the original data collected at Western Electric's Hawthorne plant in Chicago does not support the study's original findings.

References

Dunson, Bruce H. 1979. A model of search behavior in rental housing markets: An empirical study. Ph.D. Diss., Department of Economics, Harvard University.

Franke, Richard H., and James D. Kaul. 1978. The Hawthorne experiments: First statistical interpretation. *American Sociological Review* 43: 623–43.

Hanushek, Eric A., and John M. Quigley. 1979. Complex public subsidies and complex household behavior: Consumption aspects of housing allowances. Working paper 825. Institution for Social and Policy Studies, Yale University.

Khadduri, Jill, and Raymond J. Struyk. 1980. Housing vouchers: From here to entitlement? Urban Institute Working Paper 1536–01.

Lagerfeld, Steven D. 1979. The end of the "Hawthorne effect"? Public Interest, no. 54 (Winter): 119–20.

Merrill, Sally R. 1977. Hedonic indices as a measure of housing quality. Abt Associates, Cambridge, Mass.

Struyk, Raymond J., and Marc Bendick, Jr. 1981. *Housing vouchers for the poor: Lessons from a national experiment.* Washington, D.C.: Urban Institute.

Williams, Roberton C. 1978. Household headship in the United States. Ph.D. diss., Department of Economics, Harvard University.

3   Income-Maintenance Policy
         and Work Effort:
         Learning from Experiments
         and Labor-Market Studies

         Frank P. Stafford

In the years since the welfare-reform proposals of Milton Friedman
(Friedman 1962) and James Tobin (Tobin 1965), social experiments have
been undertaken on the effect on individual behavior of changes in
income-maintenance policy. What has motivated these experiments?
Friedman and Tobin proposed a universal income-support system to
provide an income guarantee (G) or "negative tax" at a zero level of
income, and a tax rate (t) at which benefits are reduced as income rises. A
universal system of this sort, or negative income tax (NIT), was presented
as an alternative to a welfare system that provides income in kind and
discourages work through high implicit tax (benefit-reduction) rates.

    Changes in the welfare system to provide both a reasonable guarantee
and work incentives through reduced tax rates on earned income necessarily extend the income range of program coverage to persons previously
outside the welfare system. This is because lower tax rates lead to a higher
break-even income for a given guarantee of income support. As a consequence, a large number of near-poor come under the provisions of the
welfare system, and it is their behavior, particularly with respect to hours
of market work, that has attracted great interest and provided added
impetus to research in this area.

    The view expressed in this paper is that policy changes in the area of
income maintenance should be informed by economic research utilizing a
range of methodologies. Experiments are a new type of methodology in

    Frank P. Stafford is professor of economics, University of Michigan, and research
associate, National Bureau of Economic Research.
    The author would like to thank Ned Gramlich, George Johnson, and Carl Simon for
helpful comments. Research in this paper was supported, in part, by a grant from NSF
Special Projects Division. This paper was prepared for a Conference on Social Experiments, Hilton Head, South Carolina, 5–7 March 1981.

this area, but so too is the use of large-scale micro data bases designed for general-purpose research on household behavior. One important question is the relative use of experiments and field studies in the formulation of welfare reform along the lines of an NIT. Aside from questions of labor-supply effects of NIT, there has been a widening set of questions on policy-induced changes in training, unemployment, family composition, and marital stability. What have we learned from experiments and labor-market studies? Do the Friedman-Tobin proposals look as attractive today as they did before the research?

This paper is organized into three sections. Section 3.1 gives an overview of the role of experimental studies on the effects of a negative income tax. Section 3.2 summarizes what has been learned from the experiments. Section 3.3 suggests directions for future research and offers brief comments on the food stamp program as a form of NIT.

3.1   An Overview of Experimental Studies and Their Connection to Income-Maintenance Policy

3.1.1   Why Do Experiments?

By postulating a specific behavior model and utilizing nonexperimental (field) survey data, one can obtain an understanding of how an individual's labor-market hours change in response to changes in after-tax wage rates and lump-sum transfer payments. From such knowledge one could predict the labor-market hours of households under alternative income-support arrangements, which differ to the extent that they change after-tax wage rates and income guarantees.

From analysis of field studies, notably large-scale household surveys, labor economists have reached a consensus view that adult males have a labor supply that is relatively unresponsive to changes in income or wage rates, while adult women have a labor supply that is quite responsive to changes in income or wage rates. Given this prior research, a central issue is the role of experiments.

One possible role for experiments is to verify the impressions from field studies and to assure policy makers, who are unaccustomed to the ways of academic research. Policy makers can take the experiment as clearer evidence since experiments do not require one to make a commitment to any particular structural or behavioral model. Policy makers, it is argued, can remain agnostic or uninformed about scholarly research and can use the experiment to answer the direct question of whether a particular income-support system induces people to alter their hours of market work. A related, but simplistic view of social experiments is that they offer to social scientists as well as policy makers a major advantage over a modeling approach. One need not presuppose any particular behavioral model to learn whether a given form of income system would lead to increased or reduced market work. That is, one can proceed with a deliberately agnostic view of various conceptual models of labor supply and all their accompanying assumptions—including the characterization of individual behavior as optimizing subject to constraints.

3.1.2   Limitations of Experiment and Advantages of Theory

If experimental and control treatments are assigned randomly and the time horizon for assessing response is agreed upon, then, in principle, the experiment can answer the question of labor-supply effects of a particular income-support policy. As a practical matter people are never assigned randomly to experimental and control groups (see Hausman and Wise, chapter 5 this volume), and there is not a consensus on relevant time horizon. It could be argued that incentives for lifetime labor supply and training are what really matter, hence forty-five years is a necessary time horizon for the experiment. But if we skip over that argument, we can see a more fundamental deficiency in a solely experimental approach.

Suppose there are several policy alternatives. If the actual policy chosen ex post is different from the experiment, then one is unable to generalize to a "nearby" alternative without an explicit or implicit model. This is because "nearby" must be defined by some change in the levels of the experimental variables. Without a theoretical model there is no way to determine what changes might be significant. To emphasize this point, consider the research on the effects of substances on health—an area where the biological process may be understood poorly or (equivalently?) there may be several competing theories. Suppose no effort is made to understand the underlying structural process. If alcohol were discovered, experiments would demonstrate that ethanol has some effects but is not fatal in small amounts. Yet, extrapolation to methanol would be unwarranted and a separate experiment would clearly be essential. Just as there are many chemical possibilities, so too are there many income-support-policy combinations with different tax rates and income guarantees, and without an infinite amount of resources we could never check them all out by experiment. Further, just as some chemicals have adverse health effects after exposure twenty to twenty-five years earlier, so too may some labor-market environments have consequences that are only determined with a substantial time lag.

It seems obvious, therefore, that one major drawback of the structurally agnostic or "black box" approach that can be employed in an experiment is that it presupposes a single clear policy alternative. If, instead, a variety of policy alternatives is available, in principle one should have a separate experiment for each, and in practice there usually are several policy alternatives. In contrast, while one has to buy a general specification using traditional research methods, it is possible to evaluate a variety of proposals for welfare reform if, for example, one considers the income and substitution responses arising for different income-support systems. To see the advantage of relying on a theoretical model one need only consider the long-standing debate on whether the negative income tax or the wage subsidy is the preferred policy alternative. Recently wage subsidies have been given greater policy attention, and even though the experiments for the NIT are nearly complete the question arises as to their applicability to a wage subsidy. If the experiments are seen as support for the well-known model of labor-leisure choice and as a means to better parameter estimates of income and substitution responses in that model, then they can be seen as input for deciding on wage subsidies as a policy. Without such a theory the ethanol-methanol analogy seems valid.

3.1.3   Problems with both Theory and Experiments

Theory has a way of becoming partly obsolete through discoveries. (This notion is really a variation on the theme that behavioral research requires belief in some structural model.) To illustrate, recent empirical work gives support to the view that there is a wage-hours locus and that the labor market generates a wage-rate premium to persons working full-time rather than part-time (Rosen 1976). Almost all of the field research on labor supply is based on the assumption that individuals face a parametric hourly market wage rate that may be calculated from tax tables and survey information on labor earnings and hours at work. This assumption is an important restriction on the statistical model to identify underlying behavioral responses to wage and nonlabor income changes. If the correct specification is a wage-hour locus with rising wage rates for long hours, then the constant wage assumption will bias the estimated effects of high wage rates in reducing labor supply. We shall return to the issue of nonconvexity in section 3.3.

Use of panel data has shown that for many people, labor-market activity is best characterized by large year-to-year variations in hours as well as in intermittent spells of work and nonparticipation or unemployment (Duncan and Morgan 1977). A range of econometric models has been set out to capture some of the patterns of behavior,[1] and recently an increased level of theoretical work has provided an interpretation of why such behavior might be plausible. The theoretical models and empirical

---

1. See Heckman (1977). Data are presented on runs patterns from year to year over a three-year period on whether women worked at all in each year. Although 80 percent of the women either worked in each of the three years or did not work in any of the three years, 20 percent left or entered on this basis. Further, some may have been in and out within a year. Hours variations per year could be substantial even though participation may have occurred in adjacent years.

studies emphasize temporal changes in the value of time at home. Specifically, child care during the early part of the life cycle, particularly care of preschoolers, is offered as a major reason for periods of reduced market hours or nonparticipation.

Models of unemployment based on a search-theoretic framework regard spells of unemployment as optimizing behavior in a world where information is costly and where workers respond to wage cuts from a particular employer on the assumption that the cuts are firm specific and do not apply to the full range of market opportunities (Phelps 1970a; Mortenson 1970). Empirical evidence on a lack of active search by large segments of unemployed workers, particularly in manufacturing (Feldstein 1978), has led to interest in models where wages vary through time. In this setting, workers and firms form implicit contracts to allow for this variability, and layoffs occur with the understanding that subsequent reemployment will be with the firm. The effect of income-support systems on the form of the implicit contract has been emphasized (Feldstein 1976). While the specific models examine unemployment insurance, income guarantees can be regarded as a special case of unemployment insurance in which there is no experience rating of benefits and a specialized benefit reduction rate (Munts 1970). As a result the empirical work on unemployment-insurance effects can be used to gain insight into effects of an income-support system on unemployment.

Casual reflection on the nature of work leads to recognition that some jobs have a set number of hours of work and work pace. Work on assembly lines, the supermarket checkout, or administrative jobs can have a pace of work and hours set for an entire work group or organization. For example, production can be organized into several shifts of a given length so as to utilize more fully the capital stock (Deardorff and Stafford 1976). If so, workers then face a single wage-hours package at a given employer, and although they may adjust by choosing among employers, search and firm-specific training costs limits short-run mobility. Changes in labor supplied over the short and intermediate run may only be effected by decisions to work or not work, a simple all-or-nothing decision. To achieve a desired labor supply workers can work intermittently with the fraction of periods in the labor market as the decision variable. A somewhat related model is that developed by John Ham (1977), Orley Ashenfelter, and others in which unemployment is regarded as the consequence of temporary rationing on hours of work at a given wage rate. Still another model considers compensatory wage differentials to be necessary to attract employees when the job entails higher risk of unemployment (Abowd and Ashenfelter 1978). Here a relation between higher wage rates and fewer hours of work has quite a different interpretation from that given by the traditional labor-supply model.

If we define the traditional labor-supply model as one where a single person with a temporally stable objective function faces a temporally stable, exogenous wage rate with hours of work set totally on the supply side, then the share of the labor force for whom this definition applies is probably very small. The NIT-induced labor-supply responses, predicted under alternative approaches such as those suggested by the work of Ashenfelter and Abowd, Duncan and Morgan, Ham, Heckman, Phelps, Ashenfelter, Feldstein, and Deardorff and Stafford, differ from those predicted by the traditional model. Even where hours-of-work predictions are similar, these alternative approaches highlight periods in and out of employment.

If uncertainty arises as to which theoretical approach should be used, experiments look more attractive from the perspective of policy formulation. If the policy alternative is known in terms of both type (e.g., NIT versus wage subsidy) and magnitude (e.g., $G = \$5000$, $t = .5$), and the experiment covers a random assignment of those in the various labor-market circumstances, one can evaluate overall labor-supply effects regardless of the true theory. Either a total absence of theory or an abundance of theories seems to strengthen the case for experiment. This notion is summarized in table 3.1.

When the theory is "known" and the policy is certain (case 1), the choice of experiment versus field research should be determined largely by the costs of evaluation under the two methods. Yet analysis of the experimental data often employs a structural model just as does the field method. That is, experimental data may be used to fit structural models in the well-known theory—uncertain policy case, if it is believed that only the experimental treatments are likely to represent exogenous variations in the same variables reported in field surveys. The use of experimental data to estimate structural models characterizes much of the analysis in the experiments (Spiegelman and Yaeger 1980). If the real world generated observable variations in the exogenous wage and income variables,

Table 3.1   **Conditions for Using Experiments (E) or Field Studies (F) for Policy Evaluation**

		Policy Alternative	
		Certain	Uncertain
		I	II
	Known	E or F E	F E
		III	IV
Theory	Unknown or many	E	Neither will help much

then, on a cost basis, field studies would clearly dominate. Much of the debate on whether experiments are "worth it" depends on one's belief in the ability of the real world versus the experiment in generating truly exogenous variation in critical variables.

What are some of the sources of policy uncertainty? Voucher and categoric aid programs are common and combine with the cash transfer system. Some of the former programs such as the Food Stamp Program are income conditioned and thereby influence the effective marginal tax rate on labor income. For this reason it is often suggested that these programs be "cashed out" and blended with a universal cash transfer system. However, various categoric programs such as those for medical problems are not so simply dealt with. These needs-based programs will likely continue, and the issue of how they interrelate with the cash part of the system has never been resolved. This leads to uneasiness about the desirability of an NIT.

3.1.4   Long-Run Effects of Income Support

Income-maintenance research has traditionally focused on short-run labor-supply effects, but how sensible is this? Income-support systems can influence a range of individual and household decisions other than market work hours at a point in time. An intertemporal extension of the usual labor-supply model indicates that income effects toward reduced work hours will be greater if recipients expect the income support to continue through time and that if recipients believe the experiment to be temporary they will have leisure temporarily on sale; if so the short-run work-hours reduction could overstate the long-run hours reduction (Metcalf 1973, Lucas and Rapping 1970; Lillard 1978). As noted above, individuals may optimize by alternating their market work over eligibility periods from zero or few hours to full-time, receiving full benefits in the former periods and zero benefits in the latter periods. To discover effects such as these requires a longer period for each experimental sample point. These concerns motivated the long-term experiments (Seattle/Denver), and the issue arises as to their effectiveness in illuminating such impacts.

There are several important but rather subtle long-term effects that income-support systems may induce, including on-the-job training and timing of retirement. In models where the objective function is maximum-discounted present value of lifetime earnings and where on-the-job training consists of time inputs only, it can be shown that training need not be influenced by a proportional income tax. However, variations on these models suggest that there may be important effects of taxes, particularly if leisure is a time use that enters the utility function. Unfortunately, these models become rather difficult to work with and only point to such possible outcomes of income-support systems on work hours, training, and early retirement. Here there is a lack of understanding of how such structural models work to yield behavioral predictions, yet experiments as a substitute have the obvious limitation that the experimental period is long.

In addition to effects of welfare reform on training and work effort, there is a whole range of other possible longer-term effects. To illustrate, field research shows that the black-white individual-earnings ratio has improved secularly but that the black-white family-income ratio has not improved secularly. A reason for this disparity is that as incomes rise, families seek to alter their living arrangements to reduce the number of people outside the nuclear family in a given residence. As a result family income may decline through "undoubling" of families when individual incomes rise. Income-support systems often have price effects towards family-composition changes, and research has shown that AFDC payments increase the duration of spells of divorce in a fashion analogous to the impact of unemployment insurance on duration-of-unemployment spells. It is commonly assumed that such extended durations of divorce (or unemployment) are undesirable. Yet it can be argued that a desirable feature of a longer spell of divorce is a greater prospect for a more carefully chosen remarriage. These non-labor-supply aspects of income support have received much greater attention in recent years and raise important questions for experiments.

3.1.5 Experimental Strategy and Sample Size

Should the experiment have a central focus for effects (e.g., labor supply), with other outcomes considered to be subsidiary or add-ons? Should one perform separate experiments? These questions are important in deciding the scale of experiments because a sample size to achieve "sufficient" precision for one outcome may provide "insufficient" precision for another outcome. If one wishes to employ statistical decision theory in experimental design, the loss function for implementing the "wrong" policy drives the choice of sample size. The divorce example is interesting because some people interpret increased divorce rates arising from the policy as necessarily bad, whereas others may see rising divorce rates as possibly desirable—poorly formulated marriages may be dissolved. The former group may want to employ a large sample size to learn if the divorce rate is or is not that much higher than that of the controls, whereas those less concerned about divorce may define possible losses from the policy solely in terms of reduced output via labor-market incentives.

Choice of outcomes examined in the experiment depends on who the experiments are intended to influence. If the experiments are sufficiently technical, their initial impact is on research scholars. If a consensus on the findings develops, it will be passed on to policy makers in the form of testimony, reports, and the like. Alternatively, one can argue that the experimental structure should be kept simple deliberately with few outcomes examined so that the experimental results can be conveyed directly to policy makers. Regardless of the route through which the experimental inferences pass to policy makers, there is the issue of the ultimate influence of the experiment on policy choices. Unlike general-purpose research, many social experiments are intended to influence policy, and their budgets are implicitly determined by the resource payoff of better parameter precision insofar as decisions will actually depend on knowledge of certain parameters. If in fact no decisions stem from the research, then a decision-theory approach implies that the optimal scale of evaluation is zero.

Can social experiments be effective in assessing market-level outcomes? The NIT experiments were primarily oriented toward individual labor-supply responses, but what will be the market consequence of this behavior once individual supply decisions are aggregated and interact with the demand side of the labor market? One possibility is to use field research on labor demand in conjunction with experimentally given supply responses, but such a synthesis quickly begins to require much more structure on the problem than the purely experimental approach does. Another possibility is the use of entire markets as sample points. Here a large fraction of persons in a given labor market are treated, and the experimental sample point becomes an entire labor market. Obviously such a procedure is an expensive proposition, and the results will be difficult to interpret unless the treatment and control markets are selected on a probability sampling basis.

3.2   What We Know and How We Learned It

In this section we shall review the evidence on the impact of a negative income tax on a set of important behavioral outcomes. The outcomes of interest are hours supplied to the labor market, unemployment spells and intermittent labor-market activity, work effort or productivity, on-the-job training, early retirement, and divorce or other changes in family structure. In each behavioral area an effort will be made to utilize research findings based on both experiments and conventional survey data gathered from probability samples of households.

As argued in section 3.1, field research and model formulation are better seen as complements to rather than as substitutes for experiments. This can be seen in the progression of methods used to analyze hours of labor supply in the experiments. In the New Jersey–Pennsylvania experiment many of the early labor-supply findings are set out in a relatively atheoretical fashion, whereas in later work on the experiments, the data are used to estimate specific and more carefully drawn structural models.[2]

3.2.1   Hours of Labor-Market Activity

The Traditional Labor-Supply Model

Our starting point is the traditional labor-supply model—a model that has the longest research history and has received the greatest attention in the experiments. Coincident with the analysis of the first of the four large-scale income-maintenance experiments, Glen Cain and Harold Watts offered a review of the labor-market studies. Our purpose here is to offer a brief summary and update of that review given by Borjas and Heckman (1979) and to compare these studies with the experimental findings. What we will discover is that based on labor-market studies, there is a rather clear consensus on what changes to expect in labor-market hours when an NIT is introduced: men will not change their hours very much and married women will change their hours substantially.

From labor-market studies the major sources of disagreement about the responsiveness fall into two categories. The first category, emphasized by Borjas and Heckman (1979), is that of econometric implementation. They argue, quite convincingly, that within the confines of the traditional labor-supply model, correction for differences in econometric implementation with cross-sectional data leads to a narrowed range of wage and substitution effects for the labor supply of prime-age males.

If one is armed with parameter estimates and a belief that the traditional model is a valid specification, predictions of policy impacts can be developed as Ashenfelter and Heckman (1973) and Masters and Garfinkel (1977) have shown. The validity of the underlying theoretical model is the other major source of disagreement on NIT labor-supply effects, and such disagreements are more difficult to resolve. A brief mention of some of the problems arising from disagreement over "correct" structural models will be presented in this section.

Table 3.2 presents the Borjas and Heckman summary of selected estimates of the traditional model for adult males. The fourth column of the table indicates which of three estimation problems may have had a serious impact on the analysis. The three problems are those advanced by Borjas and Heckman, namely: (1) sample-selection problems and/or inappropriate measures of the dependent variable, (2) inclusion of asset income or transfer payments as nonlabor income, and (3) measurement error in the wage and income variables. The problem of sample-selection bias arises in many of the studies because researchers attempt to restrict analysis to poor families. By setting an income limit ($I = wh + y$) for sample inclusion, one generates a correlation between the error term (u)

---

2. The later results are from the rural, Gary, and Seattle-Denver experiments.

Table 3.2 Labor-Supply Elasticities for Adult Males: Conventional Analysis of Traditional Labor-Supply Males

Author	Uncompensated Wage Elasticity	Substitution Elasticity	Income Elasticity	Type of Estimation Problem (A,B,C)
1. Ashenfelter and Heckman 1973	−.15	.12	−.27	C
2. Boskin 1977	−.07	.10	−.17	B1, C
3. Fleisher, Parsons, and Porter 1973	−.19	.04	−.23	B1, C
4. Greenberg and Kosters 1973	−.09	.20	−.29	C
5. Hall 1973	−.18 to −.45	.06	−.24 to −.51	A, B1, C
6. Hausman 1981[a]	.01	.17	−.16	B1, C
7. Kalachek and Raines 1970	−.55	.86 to .76	−.31 to −.33	A, B1, C
8. Masters and Garfinkel 1977	.01 to −.11	−.04 to .06	−.06 to −.12	B1, C
9. Rosen and Welch 1971	−.27	.14	−.41	A, B1, B2, C
10. Stafford[b]	.11[c]	.21	−.10	C

[a]Hausman accounts for progressive taxes in his estimation.

[b]Frank Stafford, special tabulation for this paper.

[c]Preliminary.

and the "exogenous" variables, wage rate (w) and nonlabor income (y) in the equation:

$$(1) \qquad h = a_0 + a_1 w + b_2 y + u,$$

where h denotes hours of market work.

Nonlabor income often includes asset income, which would be increased by past market work, earnings, and savings and will generally lead to a downward bias in the absolute value of the effect of income on hours of market work ($B1$). Transfer payments depend on labor-market earnings, and earnings, in turn, depend on hours worked. Including transfer payments in y therefore generates a spurious negative relation between nonlabor income and labor hours ($B2$). The wage rate, w, is often calculated by dividing the flow of labor income in a time interval by hours during that interval. If so, positive measurement error in hours, given income, will lead to a negative measurement error in the wage rate (and conversely for negative measurement error in hours). Such measurement error is potentially very great (see section 3.3) and would lead to an apparent reduction in the wage elasticity of labor supply. Other forms of measurement error arise when hours of work in a single survey week are used in combination with annual earnings reports and when wage imputations are made for those with missing wage data.

Based on the Borjas and Heckman review of labor-market studies of adult males, there is a possible consensus on the labor-supply parameters for adult males, though the number of studies with few estimation problems is small. These studies are shown in table 3.2. Essentially all the studies have some kind of measurement-error problem which limits their validity. They argue for consensus estimates of the uncompensated wage elasticity, as in the $-.19$ to $-.07$ range, and of the income elasticity in the range of $-.29$ to $-.17$. Based on these estimates the effect of a negative income tax of $G = \$2400$ (1966 dollars) and $t = .5$ would lead to an 8 to 15 percent reduction in male labor supply for covered families. Can we believe this? As Hotz (1978) remarks, the work in this area is heavily based on the SEO data set. If other data sets are used, would similar results obtain? The Hausman study (1981) noted on table 3.2 uses 1975 data from the Panel Study on Income Dynamics and departs from the traditional model in that progressive taxes are accounted for. Despite these differences his results are not too far from the "consensus."

From a sample of U.S. adults in 1975–76, I have found a modest, positive, uncompensated wage elasticity for adult males. The data are unique in that hours in the labor market are obtained from four time diaries taken over a calendar year at quarterly intervals, and the wage rate is calculated from an independent report of work hours in the normal week and monthly labor earnings.[3] Thus, while there is presumably measurement error in wage rates, there is not a built-in negative covariance between errors in the wage rate and errors in hours.

Let us now turn to estimates of conventional analysis of the traditional labor-supply model for married women. The differences between many of the studies turn on whether the author is concerned with variations in hours of those who work (h) or variations in participation rates (p) or both $(h + p)$.

The consensus estimates from labor-market studies suggest that both labor-force participation and hours of work of married women are responsive to changes in (after-tax) wage rates. The participation elasticity (p) is commonly found in the range of .5 to 1.0, and the hours elasticity conditional on participation (h) is usually found in the .1 to .3 range, yielding a total elasticity $(h + p)$ commonly in excess of unity. The income elasticity is usually found to be substantial, with the exception of the Schultz (1980) study. This study excludes income-conditioned transfer payments and, in this regard, should have a better income variable. However, once these sorts of income exclusions are made, the residual category of nonlabor, nontransfer income from other sources is in most surveys a residual consisting of miscellaneous items such as short-run cash flow from financial assets (a measure of past market work and earnings?), alimony payments, income from rental of part of one's own residence, illicit income (?), gifts, and inheritances. In general, survey methods provide poor measures of nonlabor income.

Another way to get some idea of income effects is to consider the wife as a single utility maximizer and the husband's wage or income as the exogenous income variation. In this exercise there are indeed large income elasticities. From Schultz's work presented in table 3.3 these elasticities are on the order of -1.0. Based on these estimates, it is fair to say that the consensus is for a wage elasticity in the range of more than one for total labor supply and for large income elasticities as well.

The two outliers in the studies entered into table 3.3 are the studies by Leuthold (1978) and by Nakamura and Nakamura (1981). In the Leuthold study variables such as age, education, home ownership, and attitudes toward work are included in the labor-supply function. A reconciliation of her "low-elasticity" results with the "high-elasticity" consensus is that many of her exogenous variables are really various indicators of

3. The time diaries began with the question, "What were you doing at midnight of diary day?" After responding to the question, people were asked, "And then what did you do?" After going through an entire daily chronology for four days (two weekdays, a Saturday, and a Sunday in four separate quarters for our 1975–76 study) with each respondent, an estimate of average weekly hours of market work was constructed. For a discussion of the time-diary methodology, see Robinson (1980).

Table 3.3   Labor-Supply Elasticities for Married Women: Conventional Analysis of Traditional Labor-Supply Model

Author	Uncompensated Wage Elasticity	Income Elasticity
1. Ashenfelter and Heckman 1973	.3 (h)	
2. Cain and Watts 1973	1.0 (h+p)	
3. Cogan 1980	1.0 (h+p)	
4. Hausman 1981 (PSID data)	1.0 (h+p)	−.7
5. Leuthold 1978 (1971 data)	.03 (h)+p	0 to −.1 (h)
6. Nakamura and Nakamura 1981	−.2 (h)	
7. H. Rosen 1976	1.0 (h+p)	
8. T. P. Schultz 1980	1.0 (h+p)	0 to −.1 (h or p)
	.15(h)	

wages (age, education) and income (home ownership). Indeed the signs of these are as one would expect if they are considered to be measures of wage rate and income. The Hausman study differs from the others reported in table 3.3 in that it allows for a distribution of wage and income elasticities in the population. Thus while −.7 is the approximate mean-income elasticity, the median is −.2. Recent empirical work has attempted to identify the distribution of labor-supply preferences rather than to include variables that might be thought of as preference indications in the labor-supply equation. In the Nakamura and Nakamura study, the difference between their results and those reported elsewhere in the literature is based on the treatment of nonparticipants in the h equation, on control variables for children, and on the method used for imputing changes in the offered-wage equation. The methodology in this study appears well developed, yet the results are not in line with conventional wisdom. On the other hand, they do find a substantial effect of wages on participation probability, and this is consistent with the other studies.

A final important group for labor-supply analysis is single adults. This group presents a major problem in analysis because it includes a growing share of households and is enormously heterogeneous. It includes men or women who are single parents (some through divorce, some through death), single individuals, and "single" individuals living together. Although a universal NIT would cover all such groups, labor-supply research is only available in reasonable quantity for single parents and more specifically for "single female household heads." Work by Hausman with a small sample of female heads of households with children under eighteen indicates that the wage and income elasticities for this group fall somewhere between those for husbands and wives. The uncompensated wage elasticity is on the order of .5 and the income elasticity is on the order of that found for husbands. Another way to get some idea of the labor supply of female household heads is to look at the labor supply of married black women. Black families have historically had higher divorce rates than whites. Hence, a given married black woman is more likely to expect to be a single female household head.

If people formulate current labor-supply decisions in terms of their longer-run, expected marital status, and if current marital status is a less significant indicator of expected marital status for high-divorce-rate groups, evidence on the labor supply of black married women can be used for clues concerning the effect of "expected singleness" on labor supply. In this regard, Hausman's estimates are consistent with Schultz's results (see table 3.4). For virtually all age groups the total labor-supply elasticities for black married women are below those for white married women but above those for men (table 3.2). The results for nonmarrieds suggest that as more women (married or not) become "primary" earners or move along a continuum toward that end of the scale, they will have labor supply that is less responsive to the effects of income maintenance and tax systems.

With our illustrative estimates of the traditional labor-supply model from conventional analysis, we now turn to a review of experimental analysis. Estimates from the three experiments are reviewed in tables 3.5 and 3.6. The major difference between the experimental method and the conventional method is not that the experiment is "theory free," but that one hopes to obtain better exogenous variation in wage and income. As Rees argues, "in an experiment, differential tax rates create a truly exogenous source of differences in net wages" (Rees 1974). As the Hausman and Wise paper (chapter 5) demonstrates, there are serious practical problems that lead to voluntary participation and to selective attrition in the experiment. When this is so, a model of behavior, including both labor supply and participation in the experiment, is necessary. For purposes of this review, the assumption of random assignment will be made.

The results of the experiments, illustrated in tables 3.5 and 3.6, are consistent with the overall results from labor-market studies. In table 3.5 the major difference is between white and Spanish wives and all other groups. In table 3.6 the time response of labor supply is presented. Wives (two-thirds are white or Chicano) have a greater-percentage response to the treatment, and the temporal pattern is generally for a higher response the longer the duration of the treatment. This result is consistent with several of the hypotheses sketched out in section 3.1, including the leisure-on-sale model and the model of labor-supply choice subject to inertia from firm-specific work schedules and on-the-job training.

By using the experiments as a source of exogenous variation in wage rates and income, several authors have estimated labor-supply functions. These are illustrated in table 3.7. The results do not differ dramatically

Table 3.4 Elasticity Estimates of Labor Supply for Married Women

Variable	(1) Participation Probability (all persons) MLL		(2) Hours Worked (H > 0) OLS		(3) Expected Labor Supply (1) + (2)		Combined Labor Supply Model (all persons) (4) OLS		(5) Tobit		(6) Asymptotic t for (5) Tobit	
	White Wives	Black Wives	White Wives	Black Wives	White Wives	Black Wives	White Wives	Black Wives	White Wives	Black Wives	White Wives	Black Wives
Ages 14–24												
Own wage	1.542	.860	.024	.034	1.57	.894	1.58	1.13	1.83	1.12	(5.88)	(2.68)
Husband's wage	−.412	−.769	.047	−.195	−.365	−.964	−.288	−1.15	−.382	−1.06	(1.23)	(1.76)
Nonemp. income	.0003	−.0062	−.0087	.0150	−.0084	.0088	−.0040	−.0011	−.001	−.006	(.09)	(.40)
Ages 25–34												
Own wage	1.006	.861	.095	.209	1.10	1.07	.930	1.05	1.16	1.08	(4.12)	(5.53)
Husband's wage	−1.247	−.932	−.463	−.334	−1.71	−1.27	−1.49	−1.20	−1.65	−1.28	(6.40)	(3.98)
Nonemp. income	.0043	.0028	.0074	.0025	.0117	.0053	.0101	−.0003	.009	.002	(.80)	(.23)
Ages 35–44												
Own wage	.1793	.429	−.0448	.201	.135	.630	.160	.598	.254	.590	(1.08)	(3.83)
Husband's wage	−.9704	−.673	−.383	−.0579	−1.35	−.842	−1.23	−.681	−1.40	−.776	(7.08)	(3.11)
Nonemp. income	−.0207	.0208	−.0043	.0005	−.0250	−.017	−.0170	.020	−.024	.022	(2.14)	(2.49)
Ages 45–54												
Own wage	.7529	.409	.0719	.271	.825	.680	.761	.714	.946	.647	(4.74)	(3.58)
Husband's wage	−.9472	−.848	−.282	.0059	−1.23	−.842	−1.16	−.789	−1.32	−.952	(7.60)	(3.10)
Nonemp. income	−.0553	−.0117	−.0051	−.0056	−.060	−.017	−.0209	−.018	−.066	−.018	(3.98)	(1.33)
Ages 55–64												
Own wage	1.690	.681	.284	.115	1.97	.796	1.93	.945	2.09	.950	(7.09)	(2.37)
Husband's wage	−1.223	−.747	−.190	.297	−1.41	−.450	−1.34	−.707	−1.54	−.919	(4.95)	(1.52)
Nonemp. income	−.0346	−.0118	.0065	.0022	−.0281	−.0096	−.023	−.017	−.050	−.022	(1.60)	(.64)

Table 3.5   **Labor-Market-Hours Response in the New Jersey–Pennsylvania Income-Maintenance Experiments**

	Employment Rate (percentage)	Hours		Employment Rate (percentage)	Hours
Husbands			Wives		
White	−2.6	−5.6	White	−34.7	−30.6
Black	.08	.07	Black	−1.5	−2.2
Spanish	−2.4	−0.2	Spanish	−31.8	−48.3

Source: Rees (1974).

Table 3.6   **Labor-Market-Hours Response in the Seattle–Denver Income-Maintenance Experiment by Half Years (percentage)**

Experimental Quarter	Husbands	Wives
1–2	−.02	−.05
3–4	−.07	−.13
5–6	−.10	−.17
7–8	−.09	−.24
9–10	−.10	−.18

Source: Robins and West (1980, table 3) and Appendix.
Note: In SIME-DIME the average support level was about 1.1 times the poverty level with tax rates in the .5 to .8 range.

Table 3.7   **Labor-Supply Parameters Estimated from Experimental Data**

Author	Experiment	Uncompensated Wage Elasticity	Income Elasticity
Married Men			
Burtless and Hausman 1978	Gary	0	−.05
Johnson and Pecavel 1980	Seattle-Denver	−.06 short run	−.10 short run
		.02 long run	−.08 long run
Married Women			
Johnson and Pecavel 1980	Seattle-Denver	.08(h) short run	−.11(h) short run
		.12(h) long run	−.07(h) long run

from those in most of the labor-market studies summarized in table 3.2, though there are what can be regarded as small differences in the reported results between Burtless and Hausman (1978) and others.

From the experimental- or labor-market-study estimates one can proceed to cost out a national NIT program in the short run. A brief summary of such estimates is given in table 3.8. The reason for negative cost entries under plan 1 is that it is less generous than the current system of transfer payments. The budget costs are highest for plan 2 since a larger guarantee and a lower tax rate lead the program to draw in many more families who would be eligible. Increasing the tax rate, which lowers the break-even income, lowers the costs dramatically.

In light of the small disparity between the experimental and nonexperimental results, a question that arises is whether the experiments were worth it. How does one go about answering such a question? The question is really one on the optimal scale of evaluation. Much of the literature on sample design for the NIT proceeds on the assumption of a known evaluation budget and then seeks to answer the question of whether the sample should be apportioned into various treatment groups based on the fact that the treatment groups have different costs per observation.

Table 3.8   Costs of NIT Based in SIME-DIME Results (1975)

Plan	Percentage Change	Number of Families (million)	No Labor Supply	Cost with Labor-Supply Response
			Costs ($6 billion)	
1. $G = 50\%$, $t = .5$[a]				
Husbands	−7.0			
Wives	−23.3			
Total H-W	−10.3	2.4	−0.1	0.2
Female Heads	0	2.3	−1.9	−3.0
2. $G = 100\%$, $t = .5$[a]				
Husbands	−6.2			
Wives	−22.7			
Total H-W	−10.0	15.7	19.0	23.5
Female Heads	−12.0	3.6	4.0	4.5
3. $G = 100\%$, $t = .7$[a]				
Husbands	−10.1			
Wives	−32.0			
Total H-W	−20.6	5.8	6.5	9.6
Female Heads	−14.9	3.0	2.6	3.0

Source: Keeley et al. (1978).
[a]Plans are defined by tax rate (t); percentage of poverty line represented by the guarantee (G).

Another way to proceed is to regard the experiment as part of a problem in statistical decision theory. A full elaboration of this approach is well beyond the scope of this paper, but it does seem worthwhile to outline the general idea. The first two ingredients in such an approach are: (1) listing the critical parameters about which we are uncertain and (2) relating these parameters to a loss function for policy-decision variables. In the case of NIT let us assume that there are two critical labor-supply parameters and two policy variables, G and t. How large a sample should be drawn given some known cost per sample point?

To answer this sort of question we must first begin by defining a function that relates gains to selection G and t, conditional on values of the unknown parameters. This can be set out with a labor-supply function and an indirect utility function for the NIT recipients as is done in Burtless and Hausman. The labor-supply function is given as

(1) $h = k[w(1 - t)]^a (Y + G)^b,$

where h = hours of market work, w = wage, Y = nonlabor income, and a and b are the critical labor-supply parameters. Welfare of the recipients can be expressed as

(2) $V = V[w(1 - t), Y + G] = \dfrac{k[w(1 - t)]^{1+a}}{1 + a} + \dfrac{(Y + G)^{1-b}}{1 - b},$

where $v(\cdot)$ is the indirect utility function or maximum utility that can be obtained given $w(1 - t)$ and $Y + G$, for given values of a and b.

The "taxpaying" factors give a payment, P, of

(3) $P = (G - twh)n$

to the n recipients.[4]

Substitution of equation (1) for equation (3) provides an expression for the taxpayer costs. How does one translate this expression into a decision-theory framework to address the question of the optimal scale of evaluation? First, suppose we know a and b. What would be the optimal values of G and t? Here it seems necessary to impose an arbitrary social-welfare function. Following Orr (Orr 1976; Varian 1980, 1981), suppose the taxpayer gets Z utils from the utility of the welfare recipients.

(4) $Z = Z(V)$

where $Z' > 0$. One reason for this would be altruism. Another could be that the taxpayer assigns some probability that chance will place him or his heirs in the recipient category. If a and b are known, the task is to choose G and t to maximize taxpayers' net utility.

4. This is obviously an oversimplification because who is a taxpayer and who is a recipient depends on whether $G - twh$ is positive or negative for a given individual. Here we assume that all n recipients have known identical values of a and b.

(5) $$B = Z(V(w(1 - t), Y + G; a, b)) - P(G, t; a, b).$$

The reason for a social experiment or survey is to provide better information about a and b. These are not really known but are given by a joint prior probability density function (p.d.f.). Given the joint prior p.d.f., there can be defined an expected value maximizing choice of G and t in equation (5). Perhaps, however, we can do better through evaluation.

A sample that costs c per observation can be drawn to carry out the evaluation. As we contemplate samples of differing sizes, we may expect to leave the mean of the p.d.f. unchanged but to reduce the posterior variance. The incremental gain in the expected maximum value of B as we contemplate incremental sample sizes can be compared to the marginal sampling cost, c,[5] to determine an optimal sample size. In such an analysis the scale of the program (here, n) will be important and could lead to a large evaluation expenditure of the magnitude involved for the NIT experiments.

Actual implementation of the approach set out in equations (1)–(5) would require a computer simulation and some prior-joint-density function for a and b. Those skeptical of previous labor-market studies would want to use a diffuse prior, while Borjas and Heckman would want to use a rather tightly drawn prior. Simulation results would show a range of optimal sample sizes depending on the prior-density function. An important point of such an approach is that if the posterior mean values of a and b turn out to equal the prior means, this is not the basis for concluding that the experiments were not worth it. The expected postexperimental parameter precision will be greater and the expected value of the best policy can therefore be increased above its pre experimental value.

3.2.2 Unemployment Spells and Intermittent Labor-Market Attachment

Research on unemployment is based on two broad groups of theoretical models, which for the sake of discussion can be called rationing models or rational models. Rationing models postulate unemployment to be the consequence of events that limit a person's ability to achieve a desired labor supply. The Keynesian involuntary-unemployment model is a rationing model. Constraints arising from lay-offs or reduced work hours lead to involuntary unemployment. In rational models people respond to exogenous events in a purposeful way. For example, the job-search models of unemployment regard informational investments as the source of time out of employment (Phelps 1970b), or in the models of Lucas and Rapping (1970) and Feldstein, (1978), in a downturn workers

---

5. The cost per observation also depends on a and b but we can ignore it here.

take advantage of temporary discounts on leisure time and are not induced to work longer hours because the usual effects toward more market work when income falls are mitigated in an intertemporal setting.

Rather than develop a lengthy discussion of these theories, we will proceed by indicating some results from labor-market studies and the findings from research on SIME-DIME data.

The three labor-market studies we will discuss are those of Ehrenberg and Oaxaca (1976), Feldstein (1978), and Hamermesh (1980). These studies rely on what may be termed rational models. The Feldstein (1976) model postulates an implicit contract between the firm and its workers. The contract covers anticipated periods of high and low wages (based on high and low values of the firm's output price) in light of knowledge of the unemployment insurance (UI) system. The UI system, by favorable income-tax treatment of benefits and imperfect experience rating of the tax for employer contributions to the UI system, encourages an implicit contract that places greater reliance on variations in the number of workers employed than on variations in hours per worker. Unemployed workers do not search but are only temporarily laid off in the sense that they anticipate eventual recall to their pre–lay-off job. The Ehrenberg and Oaxaca model postulates search behavior of the unemployed as motivated by a known dispersion of reemployment wages and knowledge of UI benefits. The Hamermesh model postulates maximization of the utility of expected income in light of a known value of the layoff probability, rules for UI benefits per week, and rules for potential duration of benefits.

Defining hours not on the job as reductions in labor supply, all three studies indicate possible labor-supply effects of the UI system. Ehrenberg and Oaxaca report that for older males who change employers, duration of spells of unemployment is increased by 1.5 weeks as a result of an increase in the replacement ratio from .4 to .5. Feldstein reports that for the mean replacement rate (.55) about half of the temporary unemployment rate of 1.6 percentage points, or about 0.8 of a percentage point, is accounted for by UI benefits. The Hamermesh results also indicate that UI increases time not on the job for women by increasing the unemployment-spell duration. His work indicates that anticipated benefits also increase weeks worked per year. This suggests that the UI system creates incentives for intermittent labor supply on the part of women who would otherwise have a still weaker attachment to the labor force.

The labor-market studies are suggestive of the impacts one could expect from an NIT, but NIT benefits are not enhanced by previous labor-market earnings, and UI benefits are financed by experience-rated payroll taxes on employers, though some authors seem to believe it is so imperfectly experience-rated as to not be experience-rated at all. In the United States, UI benefits have been untaxed so annual earnings have not affected benefits beyond their effect on eligibility. Because of substantial policy differences, a simple carry-over to NIT from labor-market studies on UI would be most tenuous. For these reasons the experimental results take on greater importance in evaluating a connection between unemployment and NIT.

A research memorandum by Robins and Tuma (1977) reports on treatment-control differences in the proportion employed and not employed, with an attempt to disaggregate those not employed into groups of "involuntarily unemployed" and "voluntarily unemployed." The voluntarily-unemployed category may be termed "out of the labor force." The results for wives (table 3.9) provide some interesting contrasts with those of Hamermesh. Despite the large differences in theory and method between the two studies, it does seem that the NIT leads to reduced employment and increased unemployment at the expense of employment, whereas UI leads to an increase in both employment and unemployment at the expense of time out of the labor market.

3.2.3   Work Effort and Productivity

Both experimental methods and labor-market studies have treated respondent reports as the appropriate measure of labor supply, but it seems likely that work effort varies substantially across different jobs and that a person could respond to an income guarantee by reducing work effort rather than reducing elapsed hours on the job. As an empirical matter, work effort does vary substantially across types of jobs. For example, union members, particularly those in blue-collar operative jobs, report greater work effort (Duncan and Stafford 1980), partly because in capital-intensive production processes such as the assembly line, cost minimization by firms will lead to a faster work pace.

Suppose the rate of depreciation of the capital is, over some range, independent of the flow or rate of production per unit time. Then the rental rate for capital as a function of the production rate or work pace is a rectangular hyperbola with the hourly capital rental rate rising at a slower

Table 3.9   **Observed Proportions in Employment States in SIME-DIME Control Treatment**

	Husbands		Wives		Female Heads	
Employed	.81	.78	.37	.31	.55	.52
Involuntarily unemployed	.13	.16	.12	.14	.22	.22
Voluntarily unemployed	.06	.05	.50	.54	.23	.26

Source: Robins and Tuma (1977, 28).

work pace and falling at a faster work pace. Consider a situation where workers have a U-shaped reservation wage function for work pace. Too slow a pace is boring and too fast a pace is fatiguing. Then cost minimization will lead to an outcome where workers are compensated to work at a pace beyond the minimum of their reservation wage function. The greater the capital-labor ratio, the further beyond the minimum will be the equilibrium work pace.

It is easy to imagine a slower work pace as a normal good. As income rises, the entire reservation wage function will shift upward and to the left, yielding a slower equilibrium work pace at a lower rate of capital utilization per unit time as well. Some empirical work by Scherer (1976) is consistent with this view, and causal reports of reduced work pace in U.S. auto assembly plants as income grew secularly are consistent with this sort of model. The income effects of the NIT should lead to a slower work pace or, more generally, reduced work effort.

A preliminary analysis of work pace and nonwork time on the job has been based on data from the Time Use Survey by the Survey Research Center of the University of Michigan (forthcoming). In addition to detailed time diaries, information was gathered on time spent in formal or scheduled breaks, in socializing, or in "personal business or just relaxing." In an estimated equation to test some predictions of life-cycle training and labor-supply models, it was found that netting out training and nonwork time at work led to stronger age and education elasticities with effective work hours rather than elapsed hours on the job. As Harvey Rosen remarks, "To the extent that age and education are proxying for the wage, these results suggest that improper measurement of effective hours may be obscuring a positive wage response" (Rosen 1980, 173).

3.2.4 Training and Retirement

Do tax rates affect incentives to invest in human capital? In the well-known human-capital model of Ben-Porath (1967), this depends on whether the production of human capital requires both time and market inputs. When labor income is subject to a proportional income tax, the cost of investing is lowered along with the returns (Becker 1971). If the sole input to education is time, then both costs and returns are lowered by the same proportion. In the "neutral" case of the Ben-Porath model with no market inputs to human-capital production, the investment decision is unaltered by a proportional tax. In the simple model, leisure is not included in the objective function, so the question of income effects cannot be addressed.

If investment requires both time and market goods, a proportional income tax discourages investments since the price of only one input is reduced by a proportional income tax. As a result, investment declines. If on-the-job training is regarded as using fewer market inputs, then we could expect a smaller training effect for adults than for those still in formal schooling.

In more complete models that include labor supply, clear results are difficult to obtain (Ghez and Becker 1975; Ryder, Stafford, and Stephan 1976; Blinder and Weiss 1976). This finding is of major importance in attempting to think of long-run incentive effects of NIT. Very difficult problems of theory combine with a paucity of long-term panel data from household surveys with exogenous tax-rate variations. The absence of good labor-market studies or experimental results leaves life-cycle training effects of taxes as true terra incognita, though Weiss, Hall, and Dong (1980) report a reduced training effect of NIT from the SIME-DIME study.

If one fears the unknown, one will not be comforted by the anomalous results in this literature which indicate that small changes in lifetime income and initial human capital can lead to a choice of radically different lifestyles: from one of little initial training with labor supply declining and leisure rising monotonically after an early life-cycle period, to one of large initial training with labor supply rising throughout most of the life cycle.[6] The choice between these equal-utility life-styles could be training biased because one would receive all of the guarantee through the early life cycle when time is specialized to leisure and training.[7] On the other hand, an NIT adds to the overall taxes on labor-market earnings and thereby would probably discourage training through substitution effects.

Research on the latter part of the life cycle has analyzed early retirement decisions with human capital exogenous. These studies imply that assets and Social Security "wealth" (discounted expected benefits) lead to early "retirement" (labor-market withdrawal or sharply reduced hours). Studies by Boskin (1972), Burkhauser and Turner (1978), and Quinn (1977), and research in progress by Tom Fraker (1981) clearly indicate impacts of Social Security wealth.

Fraker studies older unemployed male workers, using panel data to determine the resolution of unemployment spells. His question is whether, given health and other conditions prior to the unemployment spell, Social Security wealth induces a higher probability of "retiring" instead of becoming reemployed. The answer is clearly yes. For an older unemployed worker with a .5 probability of reentering the labor market, a one-standard-deviation increase in Social Security wealth would reduce the participation or reentry probability by .28.

6. Ryder, Stafford, and Stephan (1976, 666). Recently several authors have emphasized aspects of income taxation that could encourage human-capital investments via insurance effects. See, for example, Eaton and Rosen (1980); Varian (1981).
7. This issue arises in the debate over college students being eligible for food stamps.

Based on these results for Social Security, is there anything that could be said about an NIT? One way to assess this is to consider the discounted NIT guarantee value as "NIT wealth." This idea does not seem too far off. Even though the level of NIT wealth depends on a time path of labor supply, starting from any given possible "retirement" date, so too does Social Security wealth, at least over the age range of sixty-two to seventy-two. In this way it seems clear that a prediction of early retirement with an NIT is a warranted expectation. Moreover, Quinn's results indicate a positive interaction of Social Security wealth and private pensions. In a similar fashion, if an NIT is available to increase retirement income or to tide one over until Social Security eligibility is obtained, this interaction could accentuate the increase in early retirements.

3.2.5 Divorce and Remarriage

One of the findings in the New Jersey–Pennsylvania and SIME–DIME analysis was that NIT treatments led to higher divorce rates (Bishop 1980). This finding can be regarded as a surprise in that, unlike the current public-assistance programs in many states, NIT payments are made to families regardless of whether or not the male adult is present. This result is less surprising in light of labor-market studies that show a strong effect of AFDC payments on the duration of spells of divorce.

One can develop a simple model of the sort implicit in Bishop's discussion of marital instability. He talks of "independence effects" and "income effects." To see these, suppose the husband (M) and wife (F) have separate utility functions, U_M and U_F. Within marriage there is defined a utility-possibility frontier that can be obtained by optimal variation in labor-market hours and nonmarket activity of both spouses in the absence of an income-support system. This is given in figure 3.1 as UPF.[8] Outside of marriage there is some maximum utility attainable from becoming single (or finding another spouse), and this is given as U_{RM} for the husband and U_{RF} for the wife.

Without the transfer system marriage continues, and the spouses may occasionally quarrel about where along the AB segment the family should be. The introduction of an income-support system should make the family better off (shifting the UPF outward to UPF'), but it can also increase well-being outside of marriage because some payment is available to single persons as well. Consequently, the U_{RM} and U_{RF} shift out from the origin to U_{RM}' and U_{RF}'. As drawn in figure 3.1, the posttransfer

---

8. This sort of approach is adopted by Brown and Mauser (1977). See also Gerson (1981); Hill and Juster (1980). Rather than assume a common utility function, one can postulate family public goods as well as private goods for each partner entering into the individual utility functions. Empirical evidence indicates that time in household chores by one spouse substitutes for the other's time in the household chores, but that spouses' leisure-time activities are complementary.

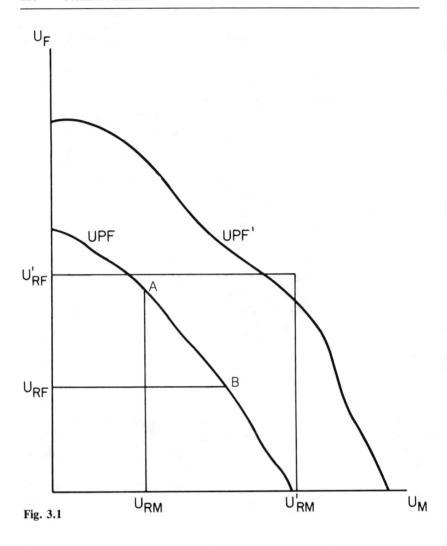

Fig. 3.1

equilibrium would lead to dissolution. Here the independence effects dominate the gains within marriage effects.

To push the analysis a bit further, while the introduction of a cash transfer system can increase divorce rates when newly introduced, it may have a smaller *long-run* effect on divorce rates because marriages formed subsequent to its introduction will be based on new reservation utilities. It is *changes* in reservation utilities out of marriage rather than their level that affects divorce rates most strongly. This implies that the short-run effects of an NIT on divorce rates could be larger than the long-run effects.

AFDC payments conditioned on maintaining single status are another matter. Analogous to UI, if AFDC is available contingent on maintaining a particular state (not married rather than not employed), then we would expect an effect on the duration of spells of divorce. Specifically, Hutchens estimates that if the AFDC guarantee of the high AFDC states (about $300 in 1971) were applied to the low AFDC states (about $60 in 1971), the two-year remarriage probability for a woman with three children would fall from .50 to .15 (Hutchens 1979). This response seems to be very substantial.

A question would seem to be not whether NIT has an effect on remarriage but whether it has a smaller effect than a system it could replace, such as AFDC. In the NIT experiments one would expect that the remarriage rates conditional on divorce are affected less by the experimental treatment than by an AFDC-type system. If so, an NIT may affect duration of divorce spells, but less so than a system that has payments explicitly conditioned on marital status.

As we consider the areas of behavior, what have we learned from the experiments? To me it seems that, with the exception of areas productivity, training, and work effort, we have learned a substantial amount. Results based on the analysis of data collected in the experiment tell us there will likely be substantial behavioral responses to an income-support system. It would be unwarranted to conclude that a transfer-payment system can be designed without careful regard for work-incentive effects as well as other aspects of family decision making, including marital stability.

Avoiding unintended outcomes for national programs is extremely important. Better precision on various behavioral parameters is important because it can help us avoid such unintended outcomes. While a formal model of the optimal scale of evaluation for something as complex as an NIT is very difficult, my impression is that we have learned a great deal from the experiments. At a minimum, the experiments have reduced the variance of labor-supply parameters, even if they have not shifted the means very much. Such improvements in parameter precision are valuable when applied to such an important social issue as income support. Further, the experiments represent a large social science data base that will help answer other important questions as more experience is gained in working with the data.

3.3 Directions for Future Research

Future research on labor supply, whether based on experimental variations in exogenous variables or on conventional household surveys, should focus on a number of shortcomings identified in section 3.2. These include pure measurement problems and problems with the theory. Neither of these areas received much attention within the experiments.

3.3.1 Some Methodological Problems

One of the universal labor-supply findings is that adult males have labor-supply responses that do not change much in light of wage and income changes. Although I do not think this finding is too far off, it could be quite wide of the mark on methodological grounds. Table 3.10 shows a comparison of hours per week from the time diary with hours per week based on respondent reports of usual hours on the job. In response to direct questioning, a remarkably high percentage of employed adult males claim to work forty hours per week and fall into the forty to forty-nine hours per week category. Generally, the off-diagonal entries to the southwest outnumber the off-diagonal entries to the northeast by about two to one.

One reason for believing that the time diary is a better basis for a point estimate of labor-market time is that the diary method is not directed to highlight a particular activity. Methodological work with beepers programmed to emit a signal at random intervals led us to conclude that diaries provided unbiased estimates of most activities and that respondent reports usually overstate time in the specific activity.

Suppose that respondent reports of market work, particularly for men, are concentrated at forty hours per week when in fact the hours of market work have a lower mean and a greater variance. Then experimental or household surveys based on direct questioning will lead to a small apparent labor-supply response.

From our study we also estimated non–work time while at work in the market. Socializing, formal and informal breaks, and on-the-job training all reduce current labor supply. The disparity between respondent reports of work hours and diary hours adjusted for on-the-job training and leisure is very large. For men in the age groups under 25, 25–35, and 34–44, they are 40.1, 24.5; 42.8, 32.0; 41.1, 31.2, respectively (Stafford and Duncan 1980).

Table 3.10	Comparison of Alternative Hours at Work Measures for Employed Adult Males				
	Time Diary Report of Minutes Worked per Week				
Reported Hours per Week (average week)	Under 1770	1770–2369	2370–2969	2970 or more	No Diary Time
Under 30	13	10	2	1	2
30–39	12	12	10	1	2
40–49	45	35	105	36	3
50 or more	6	10	23	27	0

3.3.2   Labor Supply through Time

Is there a connection between income-support systems and intermittant labor supply? Here we define intermittant labor supply as a temporal path of time at market work, with large variations including possible periods with no time at work and subsequent return. The traditional labor-supply model, particularly with progressive taxes, is virtually guaranteed to lead to a stable interior equilibrium provided wage rates and nonlabor income are unchanged. Intermittant labor-market activity is usually seen as the consequence of wage rates, that change through time because of business-cycle influences. The individual is postulated to take advantage of transient wage opportunities that arise through time from business-cycle or market specific wage changes. In such a setting various policies designed to stabilize income over the high- and low-demand periods can exacerbate cyclical swings in labor-market activity (Feldstein 1976).

A number of ways exist to explain intermittant labor supply in a world where wages do not vary through time because of changes in product demand. If the opportunity set is nonconvex and the utility function is subject to random fluctuations from period to period in the parameters that determine the relative value of leisure (e.g., simple shifts in the slopes of indifference curves), then rapid swings in desired work could appear from period to period even though the opportunity set is stable. An interpretation of such a model is that random events, such as a child's illness or other nonmarket events, change the utility-function parameters from period to period.

The approach here is to develop a simple illustrative model that captures the inherently variable nature of labor supply, at least for some sectors of the labor market, and then to ask what influence government policy could have on the path of labor-market effort, including periodic nonparticipation. Motivating factors for such a model include the secular rise in the unemployment rate and the evidence of intermittant labor-market behavior reported in section 3.2. The two critical elements that lead to periodic behavior in the model are scale economies in work effort as it relates to potential output (a type of nonconvexity) and a negative-feedback effect from sustained work effort to productivity potential. This type of specification squares with the observation that most labor markets are characterized by a wage premium for longer-duration employment spells and employment spells characterized by a larger fraction of time devoted to market activity.[9] Part-time jobs with short tenure usually pay

9. Note that measurement error in work hours will lend to a small apparent relation between average wage rates and hours, if wage rate is defined by dividing labor earnings by hours. Further, even if average hourly wage rises modestly for longer hours, the marginal wage can be rising sharply.

much lower wage rates to the same individual. The literature on firm-specific human capital highlights the incentives for firms to formulate work contracts that encourage employment over a longer duration, in order to realize returns on early investments. A second motivating fact is that most people actually work on an intermittant basis. They take weekends off. They take vacations. They have spells of non-participation in the labor market.[10] These occur in the absence of business cycles, though business cycles may certainly affect them. In the model set out below, such periods outside the labor market can regenerate market productivity.

A Model of Intermittent Work Effort and Unemployment

A decision to work leads to an output path that grows through time, but it also leads to a build-up of fatigue. The fatigue or reduced individual well-being acts to limit output and creates incentives to withdraw from work (or reduce work effort) to regenerate well-being. The disutility from work derives from work effort but also from fatigue. Just as in the traditional model, the gains from work include claims to output, but the model differs in that fatigue as well as work effort affect well-being. The disutility of work can be determined largely by cumulative effects of fatigue with a possibly small role for actual work effort.

The relationships between output, π, the well-being state, R, and work effort, u, are given by

(1) $$\dot{R} = \pi,$$

(2) $$\pi = -c^2 R + g_1 u,$$

where c^2 and g_1 are parameters with $c^2 > 0$ and $0 < g_1 < 1$, and $|u| \leq 1$.

The individual well-being state is a supply-side factor. It can be thought of as fatigue, and negative values imply that one is "fresh" and full of enthusiasm for work. Work output can be motivated on the demand side as well as on the supply side. On the demand side, firms have an interest in a sustained period of work effort, both because of job-specific training costs as well as other setup costs. On the supply side a worker can be more effective with a period of concentrated effort and attention at a given job. The intensity of work effort, u, can range from $+1$ to -1. The parameter, g_1, can be thought of as a policy or productivity variable that affects the rate at which work effort is transformed into output available to the firm and its employees. It can include payroll taxes, personal income taxes, or any policy that alters the relation between work effort and output. A more complex specification could allow for a direct relation between u and $\dot{R}$ or a separate decision variable influencing $\dot{R}$.

10. Another example is periodic urban migration from rural villages in less developed countries.

Consider a simple linear objective function where the flow of gains is defined as

(3) $$L = a\pi - R - \gamma u.$$

In terms of an intertemporal objective function, we have a control problem of minimizing the negative of L over an infinite horizon. The intemporal objective function is

(4) $$J_0 = \int_0^\infty - [a\pi - R - {}^\gamma u] \, dt,$$

which is minimized subject to equations (1) and (2), and initial conditions on π and R.

To analyze this system it is convenient to transform the state variables R and π so that

(5) $$x_1 = \frac{c}{g_1} R \text{ and}$$

(6) $$x_2 = \frac{1}{g_1} \pi.$$

We have the transformed-state equations as

(7) $$\begin{bmatrix} \dot{x}_1 \\ \dot{x}_2 \end{bmatrix} = \begin{bmatrix} 0 & c \\ -c & 0 \end{bmatrix} \begin{bmatrix} x_1 \\ x_2 \end{bmatrix} + \begin{bmatrix} 0 \\ u \end{bmatrix}.$$

The system (7) is known as the harmonic oscillator and is the basis for representing a wide variety of physical systems (Athans and Falb 1966). In this labor-supply model we will see that for our objective function, the model leads to an outcome of intermittent labor supply with piecewise continuous-control sequences of $+1, -1, +1, -1, \ldots$

What is the control law for our system? If we define

(8) $$g_2 = g_1 a,$$

then our transformed system is

(9) $$\min J_1 = \int_0^\infty - [g_2 x_2 - g_1 x_1 - \gamma u] dt$$

plus equation (7).

The Hamiltonian for the transformed system is

(10) $$H = -g_2 x_2 + g_1 x_1 + \gamma u + P_1 c x_2 - P_2 c x_1 + P_2 u$$
$$= -g_2 x_2 + g_1 x_1 - P_2 c x_1 + P_1 c x_2 + u(P_2 + \gamma).$$

Behavior of the System

Based on the general principle that

(11) $$H(x^*, u^*, P^*) \leq H(x^*, u, P^*),$$

for all admissable u and $t \in (0,\infty)$ (where * denotes values of the variables satisfying necessary conditions for an optimum), we can conclude that the optimal control is piecewise constant and is given as

(12) $u^* = -\,\text{sgn}\,(P_2 + \gamma)$

where sgn denotes signum function.[11]

In analyzing this system we are interested in points where u^* switches from -1 to $+1$ and from $+1$ to -1. Given the system costate equations

(13) $\dot{P}_1 = -\delta H/\delta x_1 = -g_1 + cP_2\,,$

(14) $\dot{P}_2 = -\delta H/\delta x_2 = g_2 - cP_1$, and if $\dot{P}_2 = 0\,,$
              then $P_1 = g_2/c\,.$

We are interested in points where

(15) $P_2(t_1) = -\gamma$ $\Big\rbrace$ u^* switches from $+1$ to $-1\,,$
and $\dot{P}_2(t_1) > 0$

and where

(16) $P_2(t_1) = -\gamma$ $\Big\rbrace$ u^* switches from -1 to $+1.$
and $\dot{P}_2(t_1) < 0$

We know $H = 0$ ($t_f = \infty$ and no specific time dependence in H) (Athans and Falb 1966). If $P_2 = -\gamma$, then from (10) we have

$$-g_2 x_2 + g_1 x_1 + u(-\gamma + \gamma) - (-\gamma)cx_1 + P_1\,cx_2 = 0$$

or

(17) $P_1 = \dfrac{g_2}{c} - \dfrac{(g_1 + \gamma c)}{c}\,\dfrac{x_1}{x_2}.$

From substituting equation (17) into equation (14) we have the following expression for $\dot{P}_2$:

---

11. $n = \text{sgn}\,(m)$ means

$$n = +1 \text{ if } m > 0,$$
$$n = -1 \text{ if } m < 0,$$
$$n \text{ undefined if } m = 0.$$

A possible difficulty is that the control law is not defined if $P_2 + \gamma = 0$ over some interval $t \in (t_1, t_2)$. If so, it can be shown that

$$P_1 = 0 => P_2 = g_1/c > 0.$$

This would contradict $p_2 = -\gamma$, which implies that singular controls (where n is undefined) are not a concern here.

$$\dot{P}_2 = g_2 - g_2 + (g_1 + \gamma c)\frac{x_1}{x_2}.$$

(18) $$\dot{P}_2 = (g_1 + \gamma c)\frac{x_1}{x_2}.$$

We can conclude then that

(19) $\dot{P}_2 > 0$ if $x_1, x_2 > 0$ or if $x_1, x_2 < 0$.

(20) $\dot{P}_2 < 0$ if $x_1 > 0$, $x_2 < 0$ or if $x_1 < 0$, $x_2 > 0$.

The control law is defined by into which of the four quadrants the state variable pair falls. In quadrants I and III, $u^* = -1$ and in quadrants II and IV, $u^* = +1$. The path of the state variables subject to a control sequence $+$ (II), -1 (I), $+1$ (IV), -1 (III) can be constructed by noting that if $u = 0$ through time, then (7) defines a circle with an origin of $(0, 0)$. If $u = +1$ through time, then the path is clockwise along a circle with an origin of $(1, 0)$, and if $u = -1$ through time, then the path is clockwise along a circle with an origin of $(-1, 0)$. These trajectories are given in figure 3.2. A path satisfying equations (15), (16), (19), and (20) is given as a linking of segments of the various circles.

Discussion

An economic interpretation of the path suggests that there are two major phases—a work phase and what may be called a regeneration phase. Starting at A and moving clockwise the person begins from a period outside of the labor market with fatigue at its minimum. Entry into work is characterized by full effort ($u^* = +1$), and combined with a low fatigue level, output rises rapidly until we reach B. From B on the person "coasts," having built up a large productive capacity. One counterintuitive result is that work effort slacks off ($u^* = -1$) when productivity is high. Does this make any sense? One way to consider it is to imagine an alternative plan, say, $u = 0$ or $u > 0$. In the case where $u = 0$ the path would be on a circle with the origin $(0,0)$. This would lead to a future crossing of the x_1 axis to the right of C and would hinder what can be termed the regeneration subarcs of CD and DA. In a sense $u^* = -1$ over BC forestalls an excessive build-up of fatigue. The regeneration phases consist of a segment of capital rebuilding and leisure (CD and DA). On the CD segment, $u^* = +1$ is required to build up productivity for a future work period given fatigue effects. On the DA segment, $u^* = -1$; this can be viewed as prework recreation which will lead to a more productive work period.[12]

Before turning to effects of changes in the parameters c and g_1, it can be

---

12. One colleague has remarked that the full path reminds him of the academic year with DA late summer, AB fall semester, BC winter semester, and CD early summer.

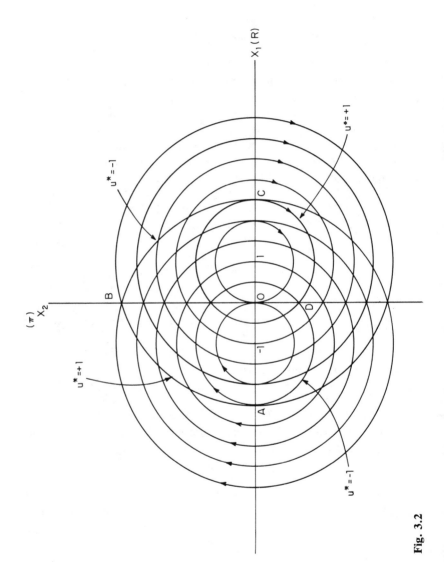

Fig. 3.2

remarked that part of the BC segment could be thought to correspond to income support contingent on recent labor-market history. A large number of proposals have been advanced to make income transfers available only for those "willing to work." If this translates into recent work history as a condition for income support (as with UI), then the BC segment could consist of drawing down on income eligibility. In part, an eligibility for future benefits can be thought of as defining our state equation which has an inherent scale economy in that $\dot{\pi} = f(u)$, rather than $\pi = f(u)$. This has been discussed in several recent models of labor-market behavior.[13]

What are the effects of reducing g_1 on labor-market behavior? A lower value can be thought of as an increased tax. Consider initial values of $g_1 = c = 1$. In this case the transformed system (7) is coincident with the original system (1) and (2). If g_1 is reduced, the absolute value of R and π are reduced by that proportion in figure 3.2. This implies that with a "tax" on work effort, the work phase is characterized by smaller positive output. The time required to move along an arc in figure 3.2 is given by the angle defined by the two line segments connecting the origin of the circle to the endpoints of the arc. What this implies is that time in the labor market is not influenced, though output from the path through the positive half-plane is reduced.

Effects of changes in other parameters on the solution are less readily interpretable as policy measures. A reduction in c^2 leads to a path that moves through the $x_1 x_2$ plane at a slower rate. If one thinks of adult workers as better conditioned to cope with fatigue effects of work, we would expect longer duration work spells in comparison with teenagers, who are less socialized to the world of work.

The point of our model is to indicate that a theory specifically oriented to represent intermittant labor supply can be developed. Research along these lines seems an important complement to the rapid growth of econometric studies on panel data and evidence from the NIT experiment on hours of work through time. These empirical results indicate that a great deal of labor-market activity is intermittant, a finding that takes on importance if the introduction of income-support systems leads to not only reduced average work hours but to a greater number of switches between market and nonmarket states. Moreover, our model suggests that while the time on the job and the frequency of switch may not change, the output can be reduced via taxes.

One puzzle in the model is that parameters in the objective function do not appear to alter the system behavior. My belief is that the simplicity (linearity) of the objective function reduces the system dependence on

13. Concerning UI effects see Mortenson (1977). Burkhauser and Turner (1978) have employed a model where Social Security leads to a connection between current work and future-income eligibility. This model leads to greater work effort in the prebenefit period.

these parameters. However, the potential for a model of this sort is not restricted to the linear objective function or the linearity in (1) and (2). In fact, as long as u enters equation (2) linearly, and $F(\pi)$ and $G(R)$ in $\dot{R} = F(\pi)$ and $\dot{\pi} = -G(R)$ are increasingly weak concave functions, a much more general objective function will still lead to solutions characterized by closed orbits.

3.3.3   Taxes, Television, and Work Effort

Based on current knowledge of labor supply, the issue of whether an NIT plan will ever be adopted can be raised. My guess is that a consensus still exists among economists that a modest scale NIT is a good public policy. Perhaps it does not appear as straightforward a matter as when Tobin and Friedman proposed it some fifteen or twenty years ago, but the idea does not look that bad either.

Although Congress has voted down NIT proposals with remarkable regularity, there has been an evolutionary series of changes in the federal food stamp program which have gradually moved it from a program to help with the distribution of "surplus" food to something close to an NIT. The change adopted in January 1979, which eliminated the purchase requirement,[14] reduced substantially the voucher aspects of the program. As a consequence we have something close to an NIT in the current federal food stamp program. Did research have anything to do with this change? I think so, since many of the policy analysts concerned with the program felt that a move toward an NIT program was desirable.[15]

Has the evolutionary adoption of an NIT-like food stamp program reduced work incentives? I believe that it has had some effects based on the empirical evidence reported above and the fact that longer-term responses to wage and income effects are expected to exceed short-run effects. Further, the measurement of hours and the calculation of wage rates by dividing earnings by the same hours measure is likely to lead to an underestimate of the labor-supply response to wage rates. This tendency for errors in variables to convert what would be a positive labor-supply function to a negative one has been termed "division bias," and recent evidence suggests it could be substantial (Borjas 1980).[16] If in fact labor-supply functions are positively inclined for men, then the wage

14. Here is an illustration of the system before 1979. If a family eligible for $100 a month of food stamps at zero income had a monthly income of $200, then they had to pay $60 cash as the purchase requirement (with a benefit reduction rate of .3) to receive the $100 of food stamps. Although the "bonus value" of the stamps was only $40 ($100 less $60), barring illegal resale of the stamps, they had to spend at least $100 on food if they participated in the program. Now such a family would simply receive $0 worth of food stamps.

15. Research shows that the pre-1979 program did have voucher-like impacts. The marginal propensity to consume food out of food-stamp benefits was much higher than for other income sources. See Benus, Kmenta, and Shapiro (1976).

16. This has occurred to a minor extent with home repairs being the only market or nonmarket work activity to experience an increase between 1965 and 1975.

effects of an increase in the tax rate t would lead to reduced work, as would the guarantee. The benefit-reduction rate in the Food Stamp Program of about .3 can be regarded as a tax on labor income.

Another phenomenon is the secular rise in "full-employment rates" of unemployment in the United States. My view is that some specific theoretical work, perhaps along the lines suggested in this section, would lead to some empirically testable implications. Out of this we may gain a better understanding of the links between types of income-support systems and intermittent labor supply, including unemployment. In any event, it would seem desirable to explore a wider range of possible labor-supply models.

One of the findings from our time-use survey appears to lie outside the realm of accepted wisdom. Data comparing time use of those in the labor market between 1965 and 1975 show a rather strong shift away from work time, both in the market and at home, toward passive activities such as personal care and TV viewing. This shift can be seen in table 3.11. Part of this finding may be a cohort effect, since the 1975 cohort of 19 to 24 years old has a far smaller amount of total labor-market time (328 minutes per day) in comparison to the 1965 cohort of 19 to 24 year olds (408 minutes per day). However, the 25 to 34 and 35 to 44 year olds of 1965 who are 1975's 35 to 44 and 45 to 54 year olds respectively, exhibited declines in total market work time of 415 to 387 minutes per day and 409 to 373 minutes per day. Further, the 45 to 54 year olds of 1965, who worked 397 minutes per day in the labor market, were working 323 minutes per day as the 55 to 64 year olds of 1975. Hence, the decline in labor-market time appears to hold across all age cohorts rather than simply being less hours worked by fresh cohorts of young people.

Other notable changes in time use between 1965 and 1975 include the very dramatic rise in time spent viewing TV by the college-educated, higher-income, professional and female respondents and a large percentage rise in active leisure and household repairs such as maintenance and gardening. However, the groups with the largest increases in active leisure and household repairs are quite different. For the former those with the largest increases are in the lowest-income groups, and for the latter the largest increases are for managers, professionals, craftsmen, and operatives.

The overall shift toward passive activities is not consistent with a rising wage rate, since many such activities are very time intensive, and rising taxes on market earnings should lead to a shift toward nonmarket work. One can employ a household-production approach to gain some insight on the matter. The widespread availability of color TV and the attempt of the networks to capture a better-educated and higher-income audience can be regarded as a home-technology shift that has favored this activity and led to more time in passive activity. What this suggests is that the

Table 3.11   Time Use of Men and Women by Minutes per Day at Work and at Home, 1965 and 1975

| | Labor-Market Time[a] | | | | | | | | Work at Home | | | | | | | | |
| | Total[b] | | Main Job | | Second Job | | Travel to Work | | Housework | | Household Repairs, Upkeep, Gardening | | Child Care | | Shopping, Financial | | Total Work Time | |
	1965	1975	1965	1975	1965	1975	1965	1975	1965	1975	1965	1975	1965	1975	1965	1975	1965	1975
Average	409	367	350	318	7	3	37	33	76	64	8	13	19	19	47	40	559	500
Married men	451	428	383	365	9	7	43	40	23	25	13	18	17	15	44	37	548	523
Unmarried men	454	353	394	309	8	2	33	34	37	38	2	10	5	5	36	29	534	435
Married women	337	276	294	242	2	0	28	21	181	143	4	10	29	31	51	55	602	515
Unmarried women	350	353	300	305	5	0	31	32	121	89	2	7	19	27	56	41	548	517

| | Personal Care | | Education | | Organizations | | Social Events | | Active Leisure | | Passive Leisure | | | | Total Nonwork Time | | Sample Size[c] | |
| | | | | | | | | | | | TV Viewing | | Other Activities | | | | | |
	1965	1975	1965	1975	1965	1975	1965	1975	1965	1975	1965	1975	1965	1975	1965	1975	1965	1975
Average	647	662	11	20	16	15	39	34	24	34	84	117	60	55	881	937	864	557
Married men	639	642	10	18	16	15	35	29	26	31	103	132	62	51	891	918	448	248
Unmarried men	636	667	20	34	15	12	78	48	27	59	73	118	57	66	904	1004	73	88
Married women	652	685	4	7	9	16	30	35	23	24	59	105	62	53	839	925	190	119
Unmarried women	671	684	17	20	23	10	46	36	18	24	68	94	54	55	893	923	152	104

Source: National time-use surveys conducted by the Survey Research Center of the University of Michigan.

[a] Labor-market participants was defined by ten or more hours of work per week.

[b] Including time at lunch.

[c] Subgroup sample sizes may not add to totals due to missing data.

Table 3.12   **Estimates of Weekly Hours at Work by Sex and Marital Status, 1965–76**

	Time Diary Estimates for Those Working[a]					
	Normal Work			Travel to Work		
	1965	1975	Percent Change	1965	1975	Percent Change
Married men	44.7	41.3	−7.6	5.0	4.5	−10.0
Unmarried men	46.0	35.2	−23.5	3.9	4.4	+12.8
All men	44.9	39.9	−11.1	4.8	4.2	−12.5
Married women	34.3	26.5	−22.7	3.2	2.3	−28.1
Unmarried women	34.9	35.6	+2.0	3.6	3.7	+2.8
All women	34.6	30.8	−11.0	3.4	2.9	−14.7

	Current Population Survey Estimates					
	Hours Worked Last Week			Participation Rates		
	1965	1975	Percent Change	1965	1975	Percent Change
Married men[b]	44.2[c]	42.9[c]	−2.9	95.5[c]	92.2[d]	−3.5
Married women[b]	34.5[c]	34.0[c]	−1.4	38.7[c]	49.0[d]	25.6
Men, 20–64 years	43.9	42.6	−3.0	94.6[c]	92.2[e]	−2.5
Women, 20–64 years	35.7	35.0	−2.0	51.7[c]	58.5[e]	13.2

Source: See table 3.11.

[a]Hours of normal work were defined to include regular work for pay outside the home or brought home, overtime, waiting or interruption during work time (for example, machine breakdown), and coffee breaks. Data are weighted using day of the week as a stratification variable and are available only for those reporting at least ten hours per week in the labor market.

[b]Married, spouse present.   [d]May.
[c]November   [e]April.

United States has been moving toward what my colleague, John Robinson, has referred to as the "post-industrious" society, with large shifts toward passive forms of leisure for reasons in addition to taxes and income-support effects. If so, this shift could be a major source of the apparent productivity decline of the last decade. What our data seem to indicate is that, as a first approximation, we are simply working less, as well as possibly working less productively. While our time-diary data show substantial declines in work hours, official statistics do not (see table 3.12), and in fact, this disparity can account for much of the recorded productivity decline (Stafford and Duncan 1980).

One more view of labor supply is that "leisure activities" and market activities are complements. The industrial revolution gave rise to interest in "hobbies" which mirror innovation and thought at work. Our time-diary data are consistent with this leisure-and-work-as-complements hypothesis. For example, craftsmen and operatives are most likely to seek out physically active recreation. Of course, it is possible that certain types of work sort out people with certain inclinations and preferences, but it is possible that leisure and work reinforce each other. If so, should we consider reverse causation?[17] That is, will a major exogenous shift to passive activities outside the workplace lead to mental capital that is less productive in the market? Perhaps. If so, we may need a labor supply-side economics to explain the decline in productivity growth and hours of market work by a more inclusive group than the working poor. A model of the type in section 3.3.2 could be used to represent the connection between leisure-time activity and the regeneration of market productivity.

Comment   Sherwin Rosen

Frank Stafford's paper is a thoughtful and wide-ranging review of income-maintenance experiments and labor supply. He begins by discussing the relationship between experiments and economic theory and concludes that experiments cannot be agnostic about matters of theory: there is an intimate connection between the two. Theories discipline thought on what questions to ask and how to ask them, and thinking of data in the context of an econometric model adds precision to the analysis and interpretation of results. But that is true whether the data come from social experiments or from "market experiments." The main virtues of social experimentation are to obtain more useful information on a particular question than is contained in available data (often collected for some other purpose) on market outcomes and to acquire superior control over variation in those exogenous variables thought to influence behavior. The better the data and experimental design, the less elaborate the model and analysis needed to answer the interesting questions. A test of any hypothesis is simultaneously a joint test of all the maintained hypotheses necessary to interpret it, and there is no way of separating the two, given the data. The less maintained the hypotheses, the better. Good experimental design can minimize potentially important intervening factors.

This line of thought suggests a trade-off between elaborate designs and

---

17. Sociologists have argued for a connection between work and leisure life-styles.

Sherwin Rosen is professor of economics, University of Chicago, and research associate, National Bureau of Economic Research.

elaborate models. Consequently, the optimum experiment will combine theorizing and design in the most economical proportions. The tighter the design around some very specific theory, the more likely are things of importance to be left out. All good theories are gross simplifications of actual behavior, and blind adherence to a specific theory can lead one wildly astray, unless of course the theory happens to be *the* correct theory. The costs of social experiments are sufficiently great that the prudent course includes some hedging. The design must be flexible enough to incorporate a wide class of influences and behavioral responses, yet not so wide that it cannot discriminate among alternative models.

The economic content of income-maintenance experiments has been greatly influenced by the neoclassical analysis of labor supply originating in the work of Paul Douglas and Lionel Robbins—the prevailing economic view on these matters in the 1960s when the possibility for experiments came to be realized. It is clear in retrospect that the simple neoclassical theory is a special case of a more general theory of time allocation, one in which Stafford's own work with time-budget data will play an important role toward further development and refinement. The neoclassical theory is fundamental, but there is a host of broader and more complex issues that must be considered. First, the marked increase in marital instability in the 1970s raised important questions about the nature of the income-support unit. Is the support unit the individual or the family, and how should the family be defined for these purposes? Whose welfare is it that we wish to change by these subsidies, and how do subsidies interact with private transfer mechanisms within and between families? Second, the nature of the choice set facing potential workers has been clarified in recent years. The many dimensions of labor supply include weeks worked, hours per day, full-time or part-time, etc., and supply responses to subsidies may differ among them. Furthermore, the nature of many employment contracts may dictate different restrictions on hours variation on a given job than between jobs, so a person's choice of labor supply may be a simultaneous choice of an employer offering the desired wage-hours package. Jobs are heterogeneous in many other dimensions. Stafford's work indicates that there is considerable variety and trend in what can be termed "on-the-job" leisure, or the intensity of work. There are a host of other factors as well, including general working conditions, opportunities for advancement, skill acquisition, and the like. How do income-maintenance schemes influence these other dimensions of choice, and how do these forces interact in determining the final distribution of welfare in society? If a given scheme was actually adopted, how would the organization of labor markets be altered to respond to the changing needs and desires of workers that are affected? The emergence of panel data (of which, perhaps, negative-income-tax experimental data are no small part) has widened the scope of labor-supply inquiry to incorporate life-cycle considerations. To what extent do we want income maintenance to subsidize transitory deviations from permanent, life-cycle earnings relative to life-cycle earnings themselves? What determines the length of working life and retirement decisions? What roles do intermittent labor-force attachment and unemployment spells play in this, and how do income-maintenance subsidies and other social-insurance programs affect this class of behavior? We have come to recognize that there are important interpersonal differences in preferences and opportunities that are known to economic agents but which cannot be observed by investigators. These differences lead to complicated selectivity issues which interact with observed behavior and which must be treated statistically by maintained assumptions on distributions of unobservables. Estimates are known to be sensitive to assumed functional forms, which cannot be verified.

These important points, some of which and more are discussed at length in Stafford's paper, apply independent of how actual-behavior data are generated. They are as valid for social experiments as for market experiments. It is a truism that so long as there is scientific progress, something of interest will be left out of any investigation. I take it as an indication of the fruitfulness of applied economics in this particular area that so many new developments have come forward in recent years and that perhaps the rate of obsolescence is higher than in other areas. The larger it is, so much the better! There is no denying that many of these factors, including the work on marital instability, variable length of horizon among experimental subjects, and localizing the experiment in a single market area, have been at least partially anticipated in the experimental design; these issues are difficult to handle in market experimental data. No doubt there is room for improvement. There is also greater hope for handling selectivity issues with experimental data. Random assignment of experimental subjects to a wide variety of treatments can overcome many thorny selection problems that simply cannot be handled except by excessively complex statistical models in nonexperimental data.

What are we to make of the fact that experimental results have been more or less similar to findings from nonexperimental data? First, the comparison is not entirely complete because most nonexperimental results have been derived from the same or very similar sets of data. Also, it is well known that estimated income effects from nonexperimental data for males typically yield unsatisfactory results, often suggesting on face value that leisure is an inferior good. And since sharp estimates of income effects are crucial in going from uncompensated to compensated behavior, which in turn is necessary for welfare analysis, the potential for improvement with experimental data is apparent. Second, that the results would be similar could not have been known in advance. Many of the nonexperimental results were arrived at first; perhaps analysts of experimental data have followed the privately optimal research stopping rule of ceasing analysis when an acceptable result was found. Perhaps further analysis going beyond existing results will change the conclusions. Third, that theories become obsolete with new findings surely does decrease the discounted future benefits of any analysis, but again that is true of both experiments and nonexperiments. If it is possible to handle some of these new factors in nonexperimental data, then the methods and extensions of maintained hypotheses that are necessary to do so can be just as well applied to experimental data too, and with more informative sources of variation added in the bargain.

It has been said that one of the main things economists have learned from social experiments is how to run experiments. To my mind that is surely a second-rate benefit because it is an awfully expensive way to learn. A superior way of learning some of the methods is to become involved in survey research at the grass-roots level. So far we as a profession have engaged in excessive division of labor with regard to microdata collection. Thinking about survey instruments themselves and how they relate to economic phenomena and economic theories is probably an area where the social rate of return is fairly large. The apparent divergence between relative private and social rates in this use of economists' time, compared to other uses, is a fact worth contemplating.

Comment   Zvi Griliches

At least three topics are covered in Stafford's excellent paper: (1) Do we need social experiments? (2) What do we know about what an NIT would do and how (where from) do we know it? and (3), the importance of "effort" and the implication of the changing uses of time on the measurement of "real" hours of work. I shall comment only on the first two.

The tone of the paper appears to question the utility of social experiments. As I see it, we need experiments for two related reasons: (1) randomization of treatment allows us to ignore a whole slew of otherwise complicating variables and considerations; (2) application of treatment makes the relevant variable "exogenous." In observational field-survey studies we are never sure how a particular X arose and whether or not the causality runs the other way, from the variables we treat as dependent to X.

Zvi Griliches is professor of economics, Harvard University, and research associate, National Bureau of Economic Research.

Surveys are also subject to the problem that little relevant information is found in the observed variation in X_{it}, either over people or over time. Consider, for example, housing prices or wage rates. In cross sections, the variation is largely due to quality differences. Over time, the "real" variation is largely common to *all* individuals or areas and is confounded with other time-series events, while purely individual variation is largely transitory or erroneous. Here is where experiments can and do help. They, in turn, are subject to serious self-selection and attrition problems, but so also are survey panel data. Good experimental design could alleviate such problems significantly.

The tone of the paper indicates that the view that experiments help is "simplistic." Is it really? Experiments turn out to be difficult, complicated, and often botched up. I am not ready to say that good, simple experiments could not be run. Most of the earlier ones were too ambitious. (Reminds me of my view about econometric research, which parallels the Downs Law of Traffic Congestion: as new data sources become available, models and the questions they ask expand to the point that average certainty [validity] of the answers remains the same—all t-ratios tend to 2.) Stafford argues that because we will want to extrapolate, we will want to fit a structural model after all, and for that we will need a wider range of variation (such as contained in surveys). I agree with Hausman and Wise that it is better to know something right in a small range, than be quite uncertain about what the wider-range relationship may actually mean. I am less worried about the extrapolation problem (similar problems arise, after all, in the analysis of survey data). I do not disagree, however, with Stafford that ultimately we want a structural theory, and hence we have to either fit it to or integrate it with the experimental results. The role of theory is threefold here: it should be guiding the experiment; it may be changed by it; and it could be changing exogenously, thereby making the experiment less interesting than was thought originally.

Ultimately Stafford concludes that theory and survey data complement experiments and help in their interpretation. I have no quarrel with that conclusion except to note that we would be less secure in our interpretation of the survey-based results if the experimental ones had not come out in the same ball park.

References

Abowd, John, and Orley Ashenfelter. 1978. Unemployment and compensating wage differentials. Paper presented at the NBER Universities Conference on Low Income Labor Markets.

Ashenfelter, Orley, and James Heckman. 1973. Estimating labor supply functions. In *Income maintenance and labor supply*. *See* Cain and Watts 1973.

Athans, Michael, and Peter L. Falb. 1966. *Optimal control: An introduction to the theory and its applications*. New York: McGraw-Hill.

Becker, Gary S. 1971. *Economics of discrimination*. 2d ed. Chicago: University of Chicago Press.

Ben-Porath, Yoram. 1967. The production of human capital and the life cycle of earnings. *Journal of Political Economy* 75 (August): 352–65.

Benus, Jacob, Jan Kmenta, and Harold Shapiro. 1976. The dynamics of household budget allocation to food expenditures. *Review of Economics and Statistics* (May): 129–38.

Bishop, John. 1980. Jobs, cash transfers, and marital instability: A review and synthesis of the evidence. Journal of Human Resources 15 (Summer): 301–34.

Blinder, Alan, and Yoram Weiss. 1976. Human capital and labor supply: A synthesis. *Journal of Political Economy* 84 (June): 449–72.

Borjas, George. 1980. The relationship between wages and weekly hours of work: the role of division bias. *Journal of Human Resources* 15 (Summer): 409–23.

Borjas, George, and James Heckman. 1979. Labor supply estimates for public policy evaluation. In *Proceedings of the thirty-first annual meeting*. Chicago: Industrial Relations Research Association.

Boskin, Michael. 1977. Social security and retirement decisions. *Economic Inquiry* 15 (January): 1–25.

————. 1967. The negative income tax and the supply of work effort. *National Tax Journal* 20: 353–67.

Brown, Murray, and Marylin Mauser. 1977. Bargaining analysis of household decisions. Paper presented at the Conference on Women in the Labor Market, Barnard College.

Burkhauser, Richard, and John Turner. 1978. A time series analysis on social security and its effect on the market wage of men at younger ages. *Journal of Political Economy* 86 (August): 701–15.

Burtless, Gary, and Jerry A. Hausman. 1978. The effect of taxation on labor supply: Evaluating the Gary Negative Income Tax Experiment. *Journal of Political Economy* 86 (no. 6): 1103–30.

Cain, Glen G., and Harold W. Watts, eds. 1973. *Income maintenance and labor supply*. New York: Academic Press.

Cogan, John. 1980. Married women labor supply: A comparison of alternative estimation procedures. In *Female labor supply: Theory and estimation*, ed. James Smith. Princeton: Princeton University Press.

Deardorff, Alan, and Frank Stafford. 1976. Compensation of cooperating factions. *Econometrica* 44 (July): 671–84.

Duncan, Greg J., and James Morgan, eds. 1977. *Five thousand American families: Patterns of economic progress.* Ann Arbor: Survey Research Center, University of Michigan.

Duncan, Gregg J., and Frank Stafford. 1980. Do union members receive compensation wage differentials? *American Economic Review* 70 (June): 355–71.

Eaton, Johnathan, and Harvey Rosen. 1980. Taxation, human capital, and uncertainty. *American Economic Review* 70 (September): 705–15.

Ehrenberg, Ronald G., and Ronald Oaxaca. 1976. Unemployment insurance, duration of unemployment, and subsequent wage gain. *American Economic Review* (December): 754–66.

Feldstein, Martin S. 1978. The effect of unemployment insurance on temporary layoff unemployment. *American Economic Review* (December): 834–46.

―――. 1976. Temporary layoffs in the theory of unemployment. *Journal of Political Economy* 84 (October): 937–57.

Fleisher, Belton, Donald Parsons, and R. D. Porter. 1973. Asset adjustment and labor supply of older workers. In *Income maintenance and labor supply*, 279–327. *See* Cain and Watts 1973.

Fraker, Thomas. 1981. The effects of social security wealth for the resolution of unemployment spells of older men. Ph.D. diss., University of Michigan.

Friedman, Milton. 1962. *Capitalism and freedom.* Chicago: University of Chicago Press.

Gerson, Janet. 1981. The allocation of time in the household: A theory of marriage and divorce. Ph.D. diss., University of Michigan.

Ghez, Gilbert, and Gary Becker. 1975. *The allocation of time and goods over the life cycle.* National Bureau of Economic Research. New York: Columbia University Press.

Greenberg, David H., and Marvin Kosters. 1973. Income guarantees and the working poor: The effect of income maintenance programs on the hours of work of male family heads. In *Income maintenance and labor supply*, 14–101. *See* Cain and Watts 1973.

Hall, Robert E. 1973. Wages, income, and hours of work in the U.S. labor force. In *Income maintenance and labor supply*, 102–62. *See* Cain and Watts 1973.

Ham, John. 1977. Rationing and the supply of labor: An econometric approach. Working paper no. 13. Industrial Relations section, Princeton University.

Hamermesh, Daniel F. 1980. Unemployment insurance and labor supply. *International Economic Review* (October): 517–27.

Hausman, Jerry A. 1981. Labor supply. In *How taxes affect economic behavior*, ed. Henry Aaron and Joe Pechman, 27–72. Washington, D.C., Brookings Institution.

Heckman, James. 1977. New evidence on the dynamics of female labor supply. Paper presented at the ASPER-DOL Conference on Women in the Labor Market, held in New York.

Hill, Martha S., and F. Thomas Juster. 1980. Constraints and complementarities in time use. Survey Research Center, University of Michigan.

Hotz, Joseph. 1978. Discussion. In *Proceedings of the thirty-first annual meeting*. Chicago: Industrial Relations Research Association.

Hutchens, Robert M. 1979. Welfare, remarriage, and marital status. *American Economic Review* 69 (June): 369–79.

Johnson, T. R., and J. H. Pencavel. 1980. Utility-based hours of work functions for husbands, wives, and single females estimated from Seattle-Denver experimental data. Research memorandum 71, Stanford Research Institute, Menlo Park, Calif.

Kalacheck, E. D., and S. Q. Raines. 1970. Labor supply of lower income workers. In *Technical Studies*, President's Commission on Income Maintenance Programs, 159–86. Washington, D.C.: GPO.

Keeley, Michael C., Philip K. Robins, Richard W. West, and Robert G. Spiegelman. 1978. The estimation of labor models using experimental data. *American Economic Review* (December): 873–87.

Leuthold, Jane H. 1978. The effect of taxation on the hours worked by married women. *Industrial and Labor Relations Review* 31: 520–26.

Lillard, Lee A. 1978. Estimation of permanent and transistory response functions in panel data: A dynamic labor supply model. *Annales de l'INSEE* 30 (no. 1): 367–94.

Lucas, Robert, and Leonard Rapping. 1970. Real wages, employment, and inflation. In *The microeconomic foundations of inflation and unemployment*. *See* Phelps 1970a.

Masters, Stanley, and Irwin Garfinkel. 1977. *Estimating the labor supply effects of income maintenance experiments*. New York: Academic Press.

Metcalf, Charles. 1973. Making inferences from controlled income maintenance experiments. *American Economic Review* 63 (June): 478–83.

Mortenson, Dale. 1977. Unemployment insurance and job search decisions. *Industrial and Labor Relations Review* 30 (July): 505–17.

———. 1970. Job search, the duration of employment and the Phillips curve. *American Economic Review* 60 (December): 847-62.

Munts, Raymond. 1970. Partial benefit schedules in unemployment insurance: Their effect on work incentive. *Journal of Human Resources* 5 (Spring): 160–76.

Nakamura, Alice, and Masao Nakamura. 1981. A comparison of the labor force behavior of married women in the United States and Canada, with special attention to the impact of income taxes. *Econometrica* 49 (March): 451–90.

Orr, Larry. 1976. Income transfers as a public good: An application to AFDC. *American Economic Review* 76 (June): 359–71.

Phelps, Edmund S., ed. 1970a. *The microeconomic foundations of inflation and unemployment.* New York: W. W. Norton.

———. 1970b. Introduction: The new microeconomics in employment and inflation theory. In *The microeconomic foundations of inflation and unemployment. See* Phelps 1970a.

Quinn, Joseph. 1977. Microeconomic determinants of early retirement; A cross-sectional view of white married men. *Journal of Human Resources* 12: 329–46.

Rees, A. 1974. Summary of results on negative income tax. *Journal of Human Resources* 9 (Spring): 158–80.

Robins, Philip K., and Nancy B. Tuma. 1977. Changes in rates of entering and leaving employment under a negative income tax program: Evidence from the Seattle and Denver Income Maintenance Experiments. Research memorandum 48, Stanford Research Institute, Menlo Park, Calif.

Robins, Philip K., and Richard W. West. 1980. Program participation and labor supply response. *Journal of Human Resources* (Fall): 524–44.

Robinson, John P. 1980. Alternative methods of measuring time use. Survey Research Center, University of Michigan.

Rosen, Sherwin, and Finis Welch. 1971. Labor supply and income redistribution. *Review of Economics and Statistics* 53: 278–82.

Rosen, Harvey. 1980. What is labor supply and do taxes affect it? *American Economic Review* 70 (May) 171–76.

———. 1976. Taxes in a labor supply model with joint-wage hours determination. *Econometrica* 44 (May): 485–507.

Ryder, Harl, Frank Stafford, and Paula Stephan. 1976. Labor, leisure, and training over the life cycle. *International Economic Review* 17 (October): 651–74.

Schultz, T. Paul. 1980. Estimating labor supply functions for married women. In *Female labor supply*, ed. James P. Smith. Princeton: Princeton University Press.

Scherer, F. M. 1976. Industrial structure, scale economies, and worker alienation. In *Essays on industrial organization in honor of Joe S. Bain*, ed. Robert F. Masson and P. David Qualls. Cambridge: Ballinger.

Spiegelman, Robert G., and K. E. Yaeger. 1980. Overview: The Seattle and Denver income maintenance experiments. *Journal of Human Resources* 15 (no. 4): 463–79.

Stafford, Frank P., and Greg Duncan. 1980. The use of time and technology by households in the United States. In *Research in labor economics*, ed. R. G. Ehrenberg, vol. 3. Greenwich, Conn.: JAI Press.

Time Use Survey. Forthcoming. In *Time Goods and Well-Being*, ed. F. Thomas Juster and Frank Stafford. Ann Arbor, Mich.: Institute for Social Research, University of Michigan.

Tobin, James. 1965. Improving the economic status of the Negro. *Daedalus* 94 (Fall): 878–98.

Varian, Hal R. 1981. Progressive taxes as social insurance. Department of Economics, University of Michigan. Typescript.

———. 1980. Redistributive taxation as social insurance. *Journal of Public Economics* 14 (August): 49–60.

Weiss, Yoram, Arden Hall, and Fred Dong. 1980. The effects of price and income on investment in schooling. *Journal of Human Resources* 15 (Fall): 611–39.

4

Macroexperiments versus Microexperiments for Health Policy

Jeffrey E. Harris

4.1 Introduction

In social *micro*experiments, the experimenter assigns treatments and gauges responses at the individual level. The response of each individual is assumed to be independent and small in comparison to the market or social system.

In social *macro*experiments, treatments are assigned at the group, community, or market level. The responses of entire social units, as well as of individuals within each unit, are the objects of interest. The responses of the individuals within each unit are correlated (Rivlin 1974; Mosteller and Mosteller 1979).

Economists and other social scientists have spent disproportionately too much effort on the design and interpretation of microexperiments. The potential value and limitations of macroexperiments have not been adequately characterized. Accordingly, we need to develop a new science of macroexperimental design and to articulate more carefully the trade-off between micro and macro designs as guides to public policy.

My argument is framed within the context of health-policy experiments. I concentrate on two policy issues: the effect of changes in health-insurance coverage on the demand for medical care and the effect of life-style intervention on the risk of coronary heart disease (CHD).

In section 4.2, I point out several problems in the design, implementa-

Jeffrey E. Harris is professor of economics, Massachusetts Institute of Technology, and research associate, National Bureau of Economic Research.

This paper was presented at the NBER Conference on Social Experimentation, Hilton Head Island, 5–7 March 1981. The work was supported by Public Health Service Research Grant no. DA–02620 and Research Career Development Award no. DA–00072. Valuable criticisms by Stephen Fortmann, Victor Fuchs, Samuel Greenhouse, Emmett Keeler, Joseph Newhouse, and Roger Sherwin are gratefully acknowledged.

145

tion, and interpretation of health-policy microexperiments. These include subject selection and attrition, anticipatory responses, Hawthorne effects, and ethical constraints on individual randomization. Although the results of microexperiments may elucidate certain mechanisms of individual behavior, they may not reveal the total, market equilibrium effects of policy alternatives.

Section 4.3 considers how macroexperiments may resolve these microexperimental difficulties. Because macroexperimentation can be less intrusive upon individuals, these experiments may avoid the potential selection and attrition biases, Hawthorne effects, and ethical constraints characteristic of microexperiments. Most important, macroexperiments can be more useful for evaluating the total market and social-system effects of policy options.

In section 4.4, I discuss two serious limitations of macroexperimentation. First, intervention at the market or community level reduces the statistical power of the experiment and, in some cases, threatens its external validity. Second, the macroexperimenter may encounter significant political and administrative obstacles to randomization.

Section 4.5 considers how these defects of macroexperimentation might be avoided. Decentralization of macroexperiments, along with experimental blocking, is suggested as a means of improving statistical power and overcoming administrative barriers to randomization. Time-series experiments, crossover designs, as well as mixtures of micro and macro designs, are considered. To resolve questions of external validity, I show how the results of different macroexperiments might be combined.

Throughout the analysis, I focus on the experience of two microexperiments—the Rand Health Insurance Study (Newhouse 1974) and the Multiple Risk Factor Intervention Trial (Multiple Risk Factor Intervention Trial Group 1976a, 1976b)—and one macroexperiment—the Stanford Heart Disease Prevention Program (Farquhar 1978). Several other macro-experiments in life-style intervention are in progress or under consideration.[1] But no bona fide macroexperiment in health insurance or in medical-care utilization has been undertaken. One goal of section 4.5 is to suggest how such experiments might be executed.

This paper is not a broad endorsement of macroexperimentation for health policy. It does not advocate the abandonment of microexperiments. Nor do I envisage a strict choice between micro and macro designs. But in many cases, precise microestimates of only one or two

1. These are the Stanford Five-City Project (Hulley and Fortmann 1980); the North Karelia Project (Puska et al. 1978); the Minnesota Heart Health Program; the Pawtucket Heart Health Program; the European Collaborative Heart Disease Prevention Project (WHO European Collaborative Group 1974; Rose et al. 1980); and the Pennsylvania County Health Improvement Program (Stolley 1980).

parameters of a problem do not justify our plunging into full-scale policies. Less precise macroassessments of the total impact of contemplated policies may then be warranted.

4.2 Problems with Microexperiments

First, I set forth the background of two microexperiments in health policy.

4.2.1 The Multiple Risk Factor Intervention Trial (MRFIT)

Epidemiologists have repeatedly shown that high blood pressure, elevated blood cholesterol, and cigarette smoking are independent, powerful predictors of an individual's risk of fatal and nonfatal events of coronary heart disease (Truett, Cornfield, and Kannel 1967). Men and women who spontaneously quit smoking incur a lower risk of subsequent coronary events than continuing smokers (Friedman et al. 1981). These findings have been derived from the natural histories of various study populations (for example, residents of Framingham, Massachusetts). To assess the causal nature of such predictive relationships, and to gauge the reversibility of the disease process, it would be logical to attempt to reverse each of the above risk factors in a randomized experiment.

Separate clinical trials have been instituted to lower blood cholesterol, to treat hypertension, and to induce smoking cessation (Davis and Havlik 1977; Hypertension Detection and Follow-up Program Cooperative Group 1979a, 1979b; Rose and Hamilton 1978). The difficulty with such single-factor experiments is that participation in the trial is a total experience (Syme 1978). An experiment may be designed to test the isolated effect to lowering blood pressure. But when subjects are instructed to take antihypertensive medications, and possibly to restrict salt and caloric intake and increase physical activity, they inevitably modify dietary fat intake, smoking, and other aspects of behavior.

The Multiple Risk Factor Intervention Trial (Kuller et al. 1980; MRFIT Group 1976a, 1976b, 1977; Sherwin, Sexton, and Dischinger 1979) recognized this limitation of single-factor trials. The protocol was designed to test the hypothesis that lowering serum cholesterol by diet, reducing high blood pressure by diet and drugs, and cessation of cigarette smoking, *in combination*, would result in a reduced risk of death from CHD. Men aged thirty-five to fifty-seven, who displayed various combinations of cigarette smoking, elevated blood pressure, and cholesterol, but who displayed no initial evidence of CHD, were to be followed for six years. After initial screening of 361,661 subjects during 1974–76, a total of 12,866 subjects were randomly assigned either to a program of special intervention (SI) directed toward these risk factors or to their usual source of medical care (UC). The experiment is being conducted at

MRFIT clinics in twenty-two sites across the country and is scheduled for completion in early 1982.

4.2.2   The Rand Health Insurance Study (HIS)

The responsiveness of medical-care demand to price is an important factor in the design of health insurance and the control of rising medical expenditures. Price elasticities of demand for medical services have been estimated from a variety of data sources. But the main source of price variation in these nonexperimental data is the terms of insurance coverage. Since consumers select their insurance on the basis of health status, income, family composition, and other factors affecting demand, such estimates could be seriously misleading.

The Rand Health Insurance Study (Manning et al. 1981; Manning, Newhouse, and Ware 1982; Morris 1979; Morris, Newhouse, and Archibald 1980; Newhouse 1974; Newhouse et al. 1979) was designed to over come this limitation. A sample of approximately 8,000 individuals in 2,823 families was enrolled in six sites across the country. Families were enrolled in one of fourteen different HIS insurance plans for either three or five years. These plans ranged from free care, to 95 percent coinsurance below a maximum dollar expenditure, to assignment in a prepaid group practice. Low-income families were over sampled. Persons eligible for Medicare, heads of households sixty-one years of age and older at the time of enrollment, members of the military, and the institutionalized population were excluded. Enrollment of subjects at the Dayton, Ohio site was completed in 1975, while enrollment at the Georgetown County, South Carolina site was completed in 1979. In addition to analysis of the effects of various insurance plans on medical care demand, the effects of coverage on health status (Brook et al. 1979; Ware et al. 1980), certain administrative aspects of health insurance, and the effects of HMO care are under study.

Both MRFIT and HIS can be legitimately called second-generation social experiments. Their designers took advantage of considerable prior experience in clinical trials and social experimentation. Nevertheless, these microexperiments exhibit important difficulties in design, execution, and interpretation. These difficulties will now be considered.

4.2.3   Subject Selection and Other Pre-Experimental Biases

In MRFIT, subjects were initially screened, primarily at work sites, by a series of medical examinations (Kuller et al. 1980). Those eligible at the first screening on the basis of blood pressure, cholesterol, and smoking habits were invited to a second, more detailed medical screening, at which time the purpose and duration of the study were explained. For those who returned for the third and final screening, informed consent was obtained and then randomization was performed. Since the trial was aimed at men with high CHD risk, and since the experiment could not be blinded, potential subjects were necessarily informed of their medical status during the screening process.

It is reasonable to suspect that the initial volunteers in this experiment were highly motivated and therefore more susceptible to intervention than the general population. Of those subjects initially eligible by risk-factor criteria, about 30 percent declined to participate. Some of them merely refused to consider quitting smoking. It is also hard to imagine that the screening process itself had little effect on subjects' behavior and attitudes. Among those subjects who were ultimately randomized, mean diastolic blood pressure declined by about 10mm Hg from the first to the final screening examination, while the fraction of smokers declined by about 5 percent. Comparable changes were observed in blood cholesterol. These results may reflect changes in measurement methods between screening exams or statistical regression to the mean. Nevertheless, the evidence suggests that the pre-experimental phase constituted a form of life-style intervention.

The planners of MRFIT screened for subjects with high CHD risks in order to increase the statistical power of the experiment (MRFIT Group 1977).[2] But this practice is not without its problems. Blood pressure, cholesterol, and smoking are undoubtedly influenced by such factors as diet, stress, physical activity, socioeconomic status, family history, occupation, and peer pressure, many of which are difficult to measure. These additional, unmeasured variables also affect how subjects' CHD rates respond to experimental intervention. Pre-experimental screening on the basis of blood pressure, cholesterol, and smoking can produce a population of subjects that is highly unrepresentative with respect to the unmeasured variables. Some men who qualify for this study will be former quitters who have returned to the habit as a result of, say, transient job-related stress. Others will be light smokers who have transient elevations in blood pressure due to, say, excessive salt use or weight gain. Still others will be inveterate heavy smokers. Although the experiment would still yield an unbiased estimate of the effect of special intervention among those patients who qualified, it is not clear how the estimated experimental effect relates to the overall population response. This difficulty applies not only to experimental responses in risk factors, but also to the effect of intervention on CHD incidence. It is compounded further if the additional, unmeasured variables affect subject attrition during the experiment.

2. Selection was actually based on "modifiable risk," which is not necessarily synonymous with "high risk." This modifiable-risk score was based on a multiple logistic model of CHD risk, estimated from the Framingham study data (Truett, Cornfield, and Kannel 1967), in combination with educated guesses about differential success rates in reducing risk factors.

In the Health Insurance Study, the experimenters randomly sampled dwelling units and conducted initial interviews in order to ascertain the occupants' ages, incomes, and other data pertinent to eligibility. A base-line interview was administered to eligible families in order to elicit information about prior insurance status. Following verification of the insurance information, families were selected, assigned to the various plans, and contacted for an enrollment interview (Newhouse 1974; Morris 1979; Morris, Newhouse, and Archibald 1980). If the assigned plan represented less extensive insurance than the subjects had prior to entry, then the experimenters offered them a compensating incentive payment, in fixed installments, but unconditional upon subsequent medical-care consumption. Consent to participate in the study was elicited *after* these steps had been taken. Among families who completed base-line interviews and were assigned to treatments, 11 percent refused the enrollment interview. Of those who agreed to the enrollment interview, 27 percent refused the offer to enroll.

The HIS incentive payment scheme was intended to ensure that subjects in all treatment groups were no worse off financially by participating in the experiment. At worst, such payments were supposed to have a small income effect on demand. Nevertheless, with refusal rates in excess of 25 percent, it is worth inquiring whether prior assignment to a plan could have affected the decision to participate in the experiment. Those families assigned to the high coinsurance plans were more likely to receive incentive payments. In these families, the decision to participate should depend more heavily upon attitudes toward risk, expectations about subsequent health-care utilization, and other unmeasured variables. In fact, families who expect to make substantial use of medical care will be more likely to refuse to participate in the high coinsurance plans. It is at least arguable that these phenomena will result in an overly optimistic estimate of the effect of cost sharing on the medical-care use.

In both MRFIT and HIS, data have been collected on the characteristics of those subjects who refused to participate at the various pre-experimental stages, at least beyond the initial screening. It may thus be possible to assess some of the determinants of the decision to participate and to correct for potential nonparticipation biases. But the determinants of the decision to participate, it must be recognized, are not easily measured. So long as such intangibles play an important role, potential nonparticipation biases cannot be completely excluded. Moreover, replenishment of nonparticipants on the basis of observed characteristics, as suggested by Morris, Newhouse, and Archibald (1980), could be inappropriate.

4.2.4   Subject-Attrition Biases

Since MRFIT and HIS are still in progress, little information on attrition rates has been published. In the Health Insurance Study, the three-year cumulative attrition rates for the free and nonfree plans have been 4 percent and 8 percent, respectively. In the MRFIT experiment, vital status has thus far been ascertainable for almost all of the participants. But the ascertainment of other morbid end points, such as nonfatal heart attacks, has been more difficult. Detection of these morbid events (by evidence on periodic electrocardiograms) required that subjects return for repeated checkups and examinations. At the end of the second year of the study, 6 percent of the special-intervention group and 7.2 percent of the usual-care group had missed their annual examinations. These proportions were 8 and 9 percent, respectively, by the fourth year. Among the SI participants, 16.3 percent had missed their biannual interim visits by the fourth year. The extent to which nonreporting subjects experienced a higher incidence of nonfatal morbid events is unclear.

It must be emphasized that subject attrition does not merely erode the statistical power of an experiment. Those who drop out may be least susceptible to the contemplated intervention. Certain imperfect covariates of the decision to drop out can be measured. But any attempt to correct for unmeasured determinants requires a model of the distribution of these determinants. The interpretation of the experimental effect may then be very sensitive to unverifiable assumptions about the parametric form of such a model (Harris 1982; Hausman and Wise, chap. 5 of this volume). In microexperiments, the only foolproof remedy for attrition bias is to keep subjects from dropping out altogether.

4.2.5   Hawthorne Effects and Anticipatory Responses

The subject's knowledge of his treatment assignment raises some serious problems for the MRFIT experiment. Although the usual-care subject does not receive the benefits of group sessions, counseling, behavioral therapy, and dietary instruction, he and his physician are informed of his risk status. Moreover, subjects in the UC group are asked, as in the SI group, to return for periodic visits and examinations. Highly motivated subjects who consent to randomization, but who end up in the UC group, may nevertheless alter their behavior. This phenomenon will reduce the contrast between UC and SI interventions and diminish the power of the experiment.

Preliminary reports from MRFIT (Sherwin, Sexton, and Dischinger 1979; Kuller et al. 1980; Schoenberger 1981) in fact show improvements in risk-factor scores for both SI and UC groups. After four years, SI men exhibited an 11 mm Hg drop in diastolic blood pressure, a 19 mg/dl drop in serum cholesterol, and a 41 percent smoking-cessation rate. UC men showed a 6 mm Hg drop in diastolic blood pressure, an 11 mg/dl drop in serum cholesterol, and a 23 percent smoking-cessation rate. Among SI men, 56 percent were being treated with antihypertensive drugs, compared to 41 percent in the UC group. These improvements could reflect further regression toward the mean or trends in behavior independent of the experiment. But the motivating effect of the experiment itself can hardly be excluded.

MRFIT experimenters recognize that many years may be required before the observed changes in risk factors are manifested in reduced CHD rates. In that case, the long-term mortality results will hinge critically on subjects' behavior after the termination of formal life-style intervention. Perhaps the UC men, who received dramatic attention only in the pre-experimental period and who were forced to take responsibility for their behavior from the start, will display greater long-run improvements. By contrast, if SI subjects become dependent upon the experiment itself, then discontinuation of formal intervention could lead to higher relapse rates (Syme 1978).

The planners of the HIS have made special efforts to detect instrumentation artifacts and anticipatory responses (Newhouse et al. 1979). Participants' incentives to file insurance claims might depend on the amount of reimbursement. Hence, the plan assigment could affect subjects' reporting of medical-care utilization. To avoid this interaction between treatment and measurement of response, a system of weekly reminders to file claims was used. But the reminders themselves were also found to affect reporting. Therefore, a subexperiment involving biweekly probes was instituted. Since intrusive questionnaires and health reports could also affect subject desires to seek medical care, the sequence of examinations was similarly varied in a subexperiment. For the prepaid-care group, moreover, a set of "controls on controls" was employed, with no instrumentation at all. To ascertain whether certain subjects would earmark the incentive payments solely for medical care, the schedule of incentive payments and bonuses was also varied. In order to detect possible anticipatory responses to the beginning and end of the study, the experimenters plan to follow the three-year intervention group for an additional two years. They also plan to be watchful of initial declines in price elasticity after the onset of the experiment, followed by increases in price sensitivity as the end of the experiment approaches, followed by postexperimental responses to intraexperimental price changes (Arrow 1975).

It is difficult at this stage to see how all these instrumentation and anticipation artifacts can be estimated precisely. The issue here is not so much the separate, main effect of each form of instrumentation, but its interaction with treatment effects. There are too many interactions of instrumentation, treatment, and subject anticipation to test all of them satisfactorily. It is not completely clear how information on such artifacts can be easily incorporated into the final results.

4.2.6 Ethical Constraints

In the Multiple Risk Factor Intervention Trial, ethical considerations dictated that subjects with initial diastolic blood pressures above 114 mm

Hg be excluded from the study. Unfortunately, this form of sample truncation leads to difficulties similar to those encountered at the other end of the risk-factor scale. Thus, those individuals with previously undetected, severe hypertension may be derived from a population least motivated to seek routine care. These persons may have life-styles or other unmeasured characteristics that counteract or reduce any salutory effects of risk-factor reduction.

Even if a high-risk subject is eligible by screening criteria, ethical considerations dictate that treatment cannot be completely withheld. Hence, MRFIT does not compare treatment and nontreatment, but intensive intervention with "usual care." The usual care is not even average care, since the men randomized to the UC group have already undergone pre-experimental "treatment." Moreover, the planners of the experiment felt compelled to tell UC subjects that they were at high risk, including which risk factors were implicated (Kuller et al. 1980).

4.2.7 Interpretation of Treatment Effects

The design of MRFIT explicitly recognizes that people do not change their CHD risk factors one at a time. But its interpretation is still complicated by concomitant changes in dimensions of behavior other than the three risk factors. Subjects who are asked to change the saturated-fat content of their diet may also be influenced to increase their physical activity, which may in turn affect cardiac status. Men involved in a smoking-cessation group may alter their responses to stress, which could in turn affect cholesterol levels. Among SI subjects, in fact, nonsmokers and men who had quit smoking had the greatest improvements in serum cholesterol (Kuller et al. 1980, table 8). This makes it difficult to assess whether the effect of intervention resulted from changes in diet, serum-cholesterol levels, or other factors (Syme 1978). Furthermore, the methods of life-style intervention may vary considerably across the twenty-two clinical centers in MRFIT. Within a specific MRFIT clinic, treatments are further adapted to the idiosyncracies of the experimental subject. Even if we regard special intervention as a homogeneous entity, usual care remains ill defined. In the final analysis, if CHD rates improve with intervention in MRFIT, it may be difficult to know exactly what was responsible.

To be sure, one might attempt to elucidate the details of the experimental effect by specifying a response model. Thus, the Health Insurance Study was designed to estimate contrasts between the effects of different plans (e.g., the 95 percent coinsurance group versus the free-care group, or the prepaid-care group versus the remaining fee-for-service groups). But as early HIS data came in, the experimenters found the distribution of health-care expenditures to be highly asymmetric, with a discrete atom at zero expenditures and a fat right-hand tail (Manning et al. 1981; Manning, Newhouse, and Ware 1982). To perform statistical tests of treatment effects, they therefore proposed a multiple-stage response model, involving the decision to seek care and expenditures conditional upon that decision. In addition to expenditures, health status was considered an important outcome measure. But health status could be both a determinant and a consequence of medical-care utilization (Brook et al. 1979; Ware et al. 1980). These considerations led the experimenters to some interesting, but even more complicated structural models of the experimental response. No doubt with further structural specifications, price elasticities and the parameters of response to deductibles and exclusions might also be estimated. I do not wish to denigrate these sophisticated efforts, but it should be pointed out that the conclusions derived from detailed-response surface models may be very sensitive to the structural specification assumed by the analyst. As discussed in several other papers in this volume, such models are far removed from the classical ideal of the one-way analysis of variance.

4.2.8   Relevance of the Results to Policy Options

Even if MRFIT clearly demonstrates a reduction in CHD risk, its special intervention does not necessarily correspond to a viable policy option. For one thing, widespread intervention at the individual level is expensive. Although employment-based health and fitness programs have become more prevalent, they may be quite different from the specialized research environments of the MRFIT clinical centers. Moreover, changes in life-style are likely to involve social learning, the diffusion of information, the changing of norms, and other phenomena that render individuals' responses interdependent. It is not clear that MRFIT captures these phenomena (Farquhar 1978; Kasl 1978; Syme 1978). Finally, such microexperiments reveal little about the effects of mobilizing voluntary health agencies, public restrictions on smoking, or the use of the mass media. Thus, MRFIT may reveal that CHD rates can be reversed. It may also offer some confirmation of the causal effects of risk factors. But it will offer much less information on the magnitudes of treatment effects in the general population. We could still be far from an operational public policy for preventing coronary heart disease.

The Health Insurance Study was designed primarily to be a *demand* experiment. Except for comparative analysis of responses at sites with different supply conditions, no attempt was made to assess the *supply* response to an insurance-induced increase in demand. Nor were the market-equilibrium effects of changes in coverage at issue. Yet the supply response to changes in insurance coverage is a critical factor in the recent rapid rise of health-care expenditures in this country (Feldstein 1977; Harris 1979, 1980; Newhouse 1978). Even after the HIS results are complete, policy makers contemplating changes in insurance coverage will still be uncertain about the effects of reimbursement on hospital behavior, the consequences of insurance subsidy for technological change, or the effect of extensive insurance on competitive-market discipline.

The HIS, to be sure, focuses to a great extent on ambulatory-care demand. If the supply of ambulatory care were relatively elastic, and if the supply response of the ambulatory-care sector were independent of the remainder of the health-care sector, then the results of the experiment may offer a more complete picture of the ambulatory-care market response. Even so, the behavior of the elderly population, who consume a substantial and growing fraction of health-care costs, is not assessed in HIS. The decision to exclude the Medicare-eligible population from HIS was based on practical concerns about pre-experimental and experimental logistics. And a case can be made that experiment on elderly responses to insurance ought to be designed very differently. But if young and old demand from the same suppliers, then changes in the coverage of the under-sixty-five population could affect the price and access to care of the elderly. What is more, the redistributive effects of changes in insurance may be quite different in the market than within the confines of the microexperiment. At the very least, the proper application of the Health Insurance Study results to policy decisions necessitates the use of other nonexperimental data.

4.3 Possible Macroexperimental Remedies

I now set forth the background of an illustrative macroexperiment.

4.3.1 The Stanford Heart Disease
Prevention Program (SHDPP)

From 1972 to 1975, the Stanford Heart Disease Prevention Program (Farquhar 1978; Farquhar et al. 1977; Meyer et al. 1980; Stern et al. 1976) conducted a field experiment in three California communities, each with a population of approximately 15,000. The objective of this pathbreaking study was to develop methods for modifying CHD risk that would be generally applicable to other community settings. Previous research had suggested that mass media campaigns directed at large populations could effectively transmit information, alter some attitudes, and produce small shifts in behavior such as influencing consumer product choice. But the effect of the media on more complex behavior was poorly characterized.

The planners of SHDPP therefore attempted a factorial experiment in which the combined effect of mass media and individualized intervention was assessed. From pre-experimentally surveyed populations in all three towns, they drew a subsample of men and women, aged thirty-five to fifty-nine, at high risk for CHD on the basis of cigarette smoking, blood pressure, and cholesterol level. In two towns (Watsonville and Gilroy,

Calif.), an extensive media campaign was conducted. In Watsonville only, two-thirds of the high-risk subjects were randomly assigned to individualized intervention, while the remaining third served as the media-only control. In the third town (Tracy, Calif.), no intervention was performed. Most of the reported results of this experiment have been derived from annual follow-up surveys of the original pre-experimental samples and the high-risk subsamples in the three towns.

Since the trial was to be coordinated from a single research center, intervention was restricted only to two towns. Although the assignment to individualized intervention in Watsonville was performed randomly, the allocation of media-based treatments was nonrandom. Although the three towns were geographically isolated, the overlapping television signals of Watsonville and Gilroy dictated that these two towns be assigned to media intervention.

4.3.2   Longitudinal versus Cross-Sectional Sampling

The planners of the SHDPP experiment relied upon longitudinal observations from a cohort of pre-experimentally screened subjects. Changes in CHD mortality statistics in each community over four years would have been too small to distinguish a treatment effect. Accordingly, a longitudinal sample may have appeared most appropriate to ascertain changes over time in behavior and knowledge of risk factors. Because media intervention was not randomly assigned, it may have seemed logical to use serial observations on many variables to bolster the claim that an observed effect was causal. But reliance on a cohort of pre-experimentally screened subjects leaves the experimental results wide open to many of the criticisms of microexperimentation, including selection artifacts, attrition biases, and Hawthorne effects.

Of the entire pre-experimental sample of 2,151 subjects in the three towns, only 1,204 actually completed all three follow-up surveys. The great fraction of those who failed to complete the study actively refused to participate or later dropped out (Stern et al. 1976, table 1; Maccoby et al. 1977, table 1). Among the 381 high-risk subjects who completed the baseline survey and who had not moved or died, 75 had dropped out after two years (Maccoby et al. 1977, table 2). By three years, the attrition rates among eligible high-risk subjects varied from 22 to 33 percent of eligible subjects across towns (Meyer et al. 1980, table 2). The average dietary cholesterol and saturated-fat intake, smoking prevalence and intensity, and systolic and diastolic blood pressures generally showed improvements over time in both experimental and control groups (Meyer et al. 1980, table 4). After three years, the only striking finding was that the subjects given both media exposure and individualized instruction had quit smoking at a higher rate than the other groups. Relative weight and blood pressure showed no difference, while the differential changes in cholesterol were only suggestive. In view of these results, it is not unreasonable to suspect that the ultimate participants in SHDPP were highly motivated, that subject attrition was biased, favoring a positive treatment effect, and that many subjects were aware of the presence of an experiment.

These difficulties, however, should not be inherent to macroexperiments. Since the treatments are applied at the market or community level, there is no compelling reason why the responses in each unit should be obtained from a cohort. Sufficiently large, independent cross-sectional samples could be used to assess end points within each macro-unit. Since all of the residents in a community are subject to the same treatment, it matters little if different residents are sampled pre- and postexperimentally. Even in the case of certain morbid events of CHD, repeated cross-sectional samples of health-care providers could serve as a reasonable substitute for longitudinal samples. To be sure, these procedures sacrifice precision. But they avoid the biases engendered by subjects' decisions to participate and remain in a cohort, as well as their awareness of participation in an experiment.[3]

It is arguable that this trade-off between bias and precision does not differ from that encountered in microexperimentation. Thus, the experimenter who does not screen on risk factors or other dependent variables sacrifices statistical power. Overcoming this loss of precision requires more subjects, which in turn increases the cost of the experiment. However, the cost of increasing the size of repeated cross-sectional surveys within communities may be far less than the cost of including additional subjects in a longitudinal microexperiment, with all its follow-up interviews, diaries, and logs.

The advantage of repeated cross-sectional samples in macroexperiments is that individual subjects are less likely to be aware of the experiment. In fact it may be possible to perform blinded experiments, or at least blinded controls.[4] Even if some subjects became aware of experimentation, their incentives to avoid or anticipate the treatment may be weaker than in a microexperiment, where subjects can make decisions to participate separately from other economic choices. Thus, in a macroexperiment, an individual will have less incentive to leave a community merely to avoid certain media messages. So long as a different cross section is sampled on each round, refusals to respond are much less severe a problem. Of course, it is possible for an entire community to be aware of the presence of the experiment. But it is hardly clear that this is so undesirable. If the institution of an experimental policy causes antic-

3. In the Stanford Five-City Project, the Pawtucket Heart Health Program, and the Minnesota Heart Health Program, a mixture of cohort and cross-sectional sampling is being used.

4. A blind-control community is planned for the Pawtucket Heart Health Program.

ipatory emigration, or compensatory changes in local laws, or mass protests, that would appear to be a result worth knowing.

Repeated cross-sectional sampling in macroexperiments may further avoid ethical problems inherent in individual randomization. This is because the controls in a macroexperiment are "faceless," and the lives at stake are not specifically identified. To be sure, any subject found during sampling to be at high risk must still be informed of his condition and referred appropriately. However, so long as the experimenter samples from independent cross sections, and so long as the samples are not large in comparison to the population of the community, these ethical obligations should not materially affect the results. It is arguable that imposing involuntary participation on the citizens of a community is itself unethical (Hulley and Fortmann 1980), but I do not see this objection as insurmountable.

4.3.3   Costs of Macroexperimentation

Macroexperiments may incur lower costs of instrumentation, but the more difficult question is the costs of treatment. In a microexperiment, only those individuals who are recruited and sampled undergo treatment. In a macroexperiment, everyone in a community receives the treatment, even if his experimental response is not measured.

Certain types of macroexperiments, such as those involving price subsidies in large communities, are undoubtedly very expensive. But in many instances macroexperimental intervention may exhibit significant economies of scale. This applies especially to the use of mass media in SHDPP and related experiments, where the marginal cost of exposing an additional person to a health message is near zero.

4.3.4   Relevance of Macroexperimentation

Despite its problems of instrumentation, the SHDPP media experiment had one salient advantage over clinical trials such as MRFIT. The experimental treatment—that is, the use of mass media to transmit health information, to alter preferences, and possibly to change behavior—corresponded to a genuine policy option. The microexperiment may have revealed little about the social and behavioral mechanisms underlying the response to media intervention (Leventhal et al. 1980), but the elucidation of mechanisms should not be the objective of macroexperimentation. The main idea is to observe the effect of a contemplated policy in an experimental setting that closely approximates the environment in which the policy is to be applied.

The logical response, of course, is to ask whether the "black box" results of a macroexperiment are really relevant to the policy under consideration. Even if SHDPP and its progeny experiments should demonstrate an effect of media intervention on coronary risk factors and rates, how do we know that media intervention will succeed in other communities? To this and related questions I now turn.

4.4   More Problems with Macroexperiments

4.4.1   The Confounding of Treatment Effects and Site Effects

My most serious concern about the Stanford three-city trial is the experimenters' assessment of the number of independent observations in their sample. In the early scientific reports on this study, the authors assumed that the number of independent observations equalled the total number of sampled subjects in the three communities. This assumption would be valid if applied only to the Watsonville microexperiment in which subjects were individually randomized. But for the mass media macroexperiments, there were really only three independent observations.

Confusion over the number of degrees of freedom in macroexperiments has been widespread. In fact, the issue appears to have been resolved, broached all over again, and then settled several times in the literature. Yet biostatisticians continue to propose formulas for appropriate sample size in community trials as if the individual were the unit of randomization (Gillum, Williams, and Sondik 1980).

The confusion derives in part from the view that outcome measurement in community-prevention trials is merely a form of cluster sampling (Cornfield 1978; Gillum, Williams, and Sondik 1980). If the experimenter wishes to estimate, say, CHD death rates, then sampling by community, rather than by individuals, will increase the variance of estimated population rates. The increase in variance would be inversely related to the degree of homogeneity of death rates within communities and directly related to the extent of heterogeneity between communities. Hence, if the experimenter could select relatively homogeneous intervention sites, the loss of efficiency would appear to be minimal. But this view ignores the fact that an experiment has been conducted and must be interpreted. The real issue is that in the interpretation of the results, the "site effects" are confounded with the "treatment effects."

Consider the following example. Suppose that community A is chosen for a media campaign and community B is selected as control. Suppose further that we could randomly allocate N subjects each to live in these two towns. Each subject, it is assumed, belongs to a homogeneous population with respect to pre-experimental risk of CHD. How should we interpret the results of the media campaign? If we believed that the two communities were merely artificial vessels for separating experimental from control groups and that within each community there was no intercorrelation of subject responses, then we have 2N observations on the two treatments. But if the billboard density in a community affects the frequency of messages, or the ideology of the local television station owner affects the prominence of health-related commercials, or if the configuration of voluntary agencies affects opinion leadership, or if social networks permit greater diffusion of information, or if subjects' responses depend on their conformity with others, or if subjects' changes in dietary habits depend on food prices in a community, then we no longer have 2N independent observations. Even if we could randomly assign subjects to communities A and B, the results could be quite different if town B were instead chosen for intervention and town A were instead chosen for the control. Moreover, it would not help to assess the pre-experimental variance of death rates between and within communities. By construction, these variances would all be zero. The issue is not pre-experimental death rates, but the responses of death rates to the intervention.

To be sure, site effects are common in microexperiments, such as MRFIT, where the size of the experiment dictates the deployment of multiple clinical centers. But the situation in microexperiments is considerably different because randomization of subjects takes place within each site. Hence, site effects can be distinguished from treatment effects, and site-treatment interactions can be tested.

The literature on clinical trials is replete with tests of site effects and site-treatment interactions (e.g., hospital effects in the National Halothane Study, clinical-center effects in the University Group Diabetes Program trial of insulin or oral hypoglycemic agents versus placebo). Hopefully, in the analysis of the final results of MRFIT, treatment successes at particular clinical centers will receive scrutiny. But in pure macroexperiments, there is no crossover of treatments within a community. The site effects are fully nested within the treatments. Sampling more subjects at each site will diminish the variance of the estimated death rate within each site, but it will not affect the precision of these site-treatment interactions. In fact, if we have only two treatments and two sites, there are no degrees of freedom to disentangle these treatment-site interactions. Only more sites will solve this difficulty.

4.4.2 External Validity

When the experimenter tests for site-treatment interactions, he is asking whether any specific characteristic of a market or community could be uniquely responsible for, say, an observed effect of media campaigns. If he samples enough communities, he can distinguish between a general media effect, applicable to all sites, and media effects that are merely idiosyncratic for certain communities. But then how does the experimenter know that the selected sites constitute a representative sample of these idiosyncracies? What would be the effect of media intervention in communities where a single, large employer also started his own employee health program, or where a national manufacturer test marketed a new, low-cholesterol product? If relatively small towns were selected, as in SHDPP, what would the results tell us about the effects of intervention in large cities? Would they be relevant to macroexperiments on work groups or domiciliary institutions (Rose et al. 1980; Sherwin 1978; WHO European Collaborative Group 1974)?

So long as the site-treatment interactions are regarded as random effects, the experimenter is obligated to choose judiciously experimental sites that are representative of the environment in which the policy is to be instituted. I recognize that even in macroexperiments, one ought to select sites that are not wholly unrepresentative. It is thus worth inquiring whether the communities selected for HIS possess doctors, hospitals, medical standards, and institutions that are typical of the United States. And I have already inquired whether the clinical centers in MRFIT are representative of programs of individualized intervention throughout the country. But it seems to me that the burden on macroexperiments is much greater.

4.4.3   Randomization of Macrounits

Many of the proponents of community-based intervention trials regard randomization as an impractical ideal. There are just too many administrative political obstacles. Unfortunately, I see virtually no way out of the requirement that experimental sites, once selected, must be allocated randomly to treatments. I acknowledge numerous instances where evidence from nonrandomized studies has proved convincing. But in those cases, the analysis has hinged on a paucity of plausible rival explanations for the observed difference between treatment and control groups (Campbell and Stanley 1966). But in macroexperimentation, there is likely to be an abundance of rival explanations. It is not hard to imagine that a town with its own television station or health-conscious opinion leaders will be more willing to undergo a media campaign. Such a community may be more susceptible to the effects of such an intervention.

4.5   Toward a Science of Macroexperimentation

Despite substantial advances in design, execution, and interpretation, microexperiments still have serious and possibly inherent difficulties. Individuals make nonrandom decisions to participate or drop out of the experiment. They may be influenced by the instrumentation process. Even in the absence of these difficulties, microexperiments do not necessarily test real policy options. Macroexperimentation, on the other hand, may avoid some of these problems. But convincing macroexperiments require many observations at the community or market level. Moreover, political and administrative factors may dictate nonrandom selection of communities, with its attendant difficulties. And there is always uncertainty whether the observed effect of treatment in a sample of communities was not due to idiosyncratic, unrepresentative characteristics of the experimental sites.

We are thus faced with a serious dilemma. Should we perform a microexperiment, optimistic that instrumentation artifacts will not arise, and thankful to learn something about one aspect of a complicated policy problem? Or should we plunge ahead with a "sloppy" macroexperiment, with all of its difficulties of interpretation and generalization?

4.5.1   Decentralized Macroexperiments

Because SHDPP was to be coordinated by a single research center, the experiment was restricted to only three towns. Once these three were selected, random assignment to media exposure was made impossible by overlapping television signals. But it is worth speculating what experimental design might have arisen from a multi-center trial. If the Stanford group had been one of many research centers, couldn't they have selected a pair of towns, both of which had nonoverlapping television signals? Why couldn't treatment be randomly assigned between the two towns? Why couldn't the Stanford city-pair be one block in a larger matched-pair experiment?

My point here is that many of the most serious difficulties of macroexperiments may result from overcentralization. So long as we could allocate pairs of comparable sites (or perhaps larger subsets) to individual experimental blocks, the execution of each block could be the responsibility of a separate research center. Within each block, randomization may be more feasible. Increasing the statistical power of the experiment, and perhaps its external validity, means increasing the number of blocks.

Such a design is not entirely speculative. In fact, the WHO European Collaborative Group (1974; Rose et al. 1980) has been conducting a macroexperiment in CHD prevention in twelve pairs of factories in various cities. These factories (or in some cases occupational units within factories) were recruited into the trial before random assignment to treatment or control. The factory pairs were matched as far as possible by age, geographical area, and the nature of the industry. The subjects include all male employees aged forty to fifty-nine years, not merely those at high risk. This design unfortunately involves longitudinal follow-up of cohorts. Hence, it may be susceptible to participation biases, selective employee turnover, and Hawthorne effects. But it illustrates the possibility of randomization within blocked pairs of macro-units.

One might object that only small units, such as factories and domiciliary institutions, are susceptible to randomization (Sherwin 1978). Larger political entities will merely balk at the uncertain prospect of receiving the less desirable assignment. But it is hardly clear to me that this state of affairs is inevitable. For one thing, the possibility of randomization among matched pairs may be more palatable politically than random drawings from a larger population of sites. In some cases where the eligible sites are political subdivisions under the governance of a higher authority, the possibility of site self-selection may not be so serious. In fact, several macroexperiments in cancer screening, in which census tracts, townships, or counties are the relevant sites, have already been proposed (Apostolides and Henderson 1977). Moreover, in cases where communities or organizations have already received some type of government grant or benefit, the continued receipt of that benefit could be made the incentive for participation in the experiment. In cases where various communities apply for grants to become demonstration sites for a particular innovation, the awards process could be broken down into two stages. A subset of deserving, eligible sites would first be chosen. Among eligible sites, treatment and control assignments could then be made. It is remarkable to me how often government agencies and other grantors first make the awards to the most deserving sites and then ponder how a comparable set of control sites is to be chosen from the losers for the purpose of project evaluation.

When intervention at a large number of sites is managed by one research or administrative group, the inevitable consequence is a rationing of limited intervention effort to a few sites. In extreme cases, many of the so-called intervention sites do not receive any intervention because the research team has merely lost control of the project. Administrative decentralization of macroexperiments could allay some of these problems. Moreover, some degree of blinding may be possible. At the least, a research team responsible for intervention in one block of sites need not know the progress of the experiment in other blocks.

4.5.2   Time-Series Experiments and Crossover Designs

The possibility that communities or other macro-units could serve as their own controls has not been adequately explored. Admittedly, any comparison over time is susceptible to confounding interpretations. Experimental responses take some time to be completed. What appears to be the effect of a cross-over may actually be a transient from earlier intervention (Morris, Newhouse, and Archibald 1980). If the macroexperiment is not blinded, then the effects of crossover could be confused with anticipatory responses or other Hawthorne effects. Nevertheless, there is a variety of familiar devices for detecting time-varying responses.

Although these devices have been derived from microexperiments, they could at least be tried in the macrosetting.

For example, in the case of a matched-pair design, the treatment and control communities could reverse their assignments later in the experiment. The timing of this reversal need not be scheduled in advance, or at least known to the experimental units. Stopping short of complete crossover, I could also envisage folding-back designs. We could begin by a series of observations on communities in which no intervention is instituted. Thereafter, one or more of the communities becomes a treatment site. In sequence, the remaining communities receive the intervention. Again, the sequence and schedule of assignment could be random and unknown to the experimental units. If all of the units are destined ultimately to receive the intervention, randomization with respect to the sequence and timing of the intervention may not present so many political or administrative obstacles. Such folding back designs may be particularly useful when the endpoints are subject to habit formation and thus difficult to change in short intervention intervals.

4.5.3   Mixed Macro and Micro Designs

In some cases, a mixture of micro and macro designs might enhance the power of the experiment. Such cases arise when the interventions at the individual and site levels are qualitatively similar.

In the SHDPP trial, a subexperiment of individual intervention was performed within Watsonville, a town receiving media intervention. This subexperiment was designed to test the interaction between the two types of experimental treatments. Unfortunately, the investigators were unable to conduct an identical subexperiment in Tracy, the town receiving no media intervention. But even if a full factorial design had been undertaken, the two types of treatment were qualitatively different, so that only their crude interaction could be profitably investigated.

In other cases, however, both interventions could be close enough to conform to a simple response model. Suppose, for example, that the experimenter wishes to investigate the effects of varying employer contributions to employee health-insurance premiums. Since changes in employee benefits are typically performed at the level of the firm, a macroexperiment would be appropriate, with various firms corresponding to different macro sites. But within each firm, employer contributions could be further varied among employees. Such an experiment could offer considerable insight into firm-specific and employee-specific responses to changes in employee premium subsidies.

4.5.4   Combining Macroexperiments

A potential significant advantage of macroexperimental blocking is its ability to enhance the external validity of the experiment. Within each block, experimental sites might possess similar characteristics, but between blocks the site characteristics could vary considerably. In community-based life-style intervention, it would be especially informative for blocks to vary with respect to the size, climate, age structure, sex, racial, and ethnic composition of their member communities.

A number of independent community-based life-style-intervention trials are already in progress in this country. Taken together, these trials might be considered a single macroexperiment with multiple blocks. The difficulty with this interpretation, however, is that the method of intervention may vary considerably from one block to the next. We thus cannot easily distinguish between a block effect and a block-treatment interaction. If some community trials show significant effects of life-style intervention and others do not, it will be unclear whether the discrepancies resulted from differences in the type of media intervention across trials, or differences in the susceptibility of communities to media messages. The results of different trials could be combined only if we had some prior information on the relationship between types of media intervention employed.

Some recent theoretical work on combining diverse experiments might be usefully applied to this problem (DuMouchel and Harris 1983). A complete exposition is necessarily beyond the scope of the present paper. But the main idea is to specify formally a structural relationship between the treatment effects in each community trial. For example, the magnitude of the effect on CHD rates might depend on the extent of electronic-media intervention, the duration of intervention, or the recruitment of voluntary agencies. A model of the treatment effect that relates these characteristics is then superimposed upon the results of each trial. The main issue in the application of such a technique is the degree to which life-style intervention in each trial was independent of the characteristics of the communities under observation. For example, if the experimenters in a particular trial resorted to scientifically oriented media messages because the target communities were highly educated, it may be impossible to distinguish between the treatment effect of media content and the role of educational background in a community's response.

4.5.5 Competition Experiments, Regulation Experiments, and Deregulation Experiments

Reduction of the tax subsidy on health-insurance coverage, elimination of barriers to entry for prepaid health-care providers, and enhancement of consumer choice of health-insurance plans have been proposed to control rising health-care expenditures. Virtually all of the evidence supporting the efficacy of these interventions is nonexperimental. Our policy makers could, of course, take the available data as sufficient cause to plunge ahead with a full-scale policy. But the correct course, it seems to me, is to assess some of these innovations experimentally before taking such a precipitous step. I have already hinted how several large employers in a number of different cities might serve as sites for experimental changes in employee health-insurance benefits. Perhaps several distinct divisions of the same large corporation could form an experimental block. Community-based experiments, in which the effects on market competition are observed, are also conceivable.

Regulatory controls on health-care expenditures have also been suggested. Although various innovative forms of hospital reimbursement have been tried, most of the so-called reimbursement experiments have really been uncontrolled demonstration projects. In view of the substantial likelihood that hospitals subject to those novel controls have been selected in a biased manner, it is hard to know exactly what significance these projects should have for future policy decisions. It is difficult for me to see why the experimenters have not blocked participating hospitals according to, say, size, teaching status, or range of facilities, and then randomly assigned the novel form of reimbursement within each block.

One variant of the fold-back design discussed above is the deregulation experiment. In this case, the experimental treatment is the removal of an intervention already in place. The sequence and timing of deregulation at various sites is the critical control variable. This type of design may be particularly useful when the value of a regulatory program is in question. Even if our policy makers deem that physician-peer review schemes or health-planning agencies are to be discontinued, it would be valuable to learn something about the effects of these policies during their demise.

4.6   Conclusions

This paper can be easily criticized for its lack of balance. I have sought out the most subtle crack in microexperiments, yet I am willing to cover large faults in macroexperiments with hopeful speculation.

The plain truth is that macroexperiments in public policy—or at least corrupted versions of macroexperiments—are far more prevalent than the microexperiments to which social scientists have devoted so much attention. It is not too soon to develop some meaningful strategies for effective macroexperimentation.

4.7   Epilogue, 1981–84

After this paper was written (spring 1981), the main results of the Multiple Risk Factor Intervention Trial were published (MRFIT Group 1982). Although CHD deaths in the special-intervention group were 7 percent less than in the usual-care group, the difference was not statistically significant. One reason for the weak results was the unexpectedly low death rate of the usual-care group—40 percent lower than expected. The usual-care subjects apparently benefitted from the information about their high CHD risk and the provision to their physicians of original and follow-up medical data.

Although both the experimental and control groups showed declines in blood pressure, cholesterol and cigarette use, nevertheless the experiment was singularly successful in achieving much greater smoking cessation in the SI group than in the UC group (figure 1 and table 2 in MRFIT Group 1982; also, Ockene et al. 1982). Among men who were smokers at initial screening, however, mortality differences between the SI and UC groups were modest (table 5 in MRFIT Group 1982). Yet among all subjects (both SI and UC) who smoked at the time of entry, those persons known to have quit smoking in the first study year had considerably lower subsequent death rates than those known to have continued smoking (table 9 in MRFIT Group 1982). A plausible interpretation is that smokers who missed their first year follow-up visit had much higher subsequent death rates than those smokers who reported their status. Moreover, the mortality differential between those who missed follow-up visits and those who returned was more marked for the SI subjects. Thus, special intervention was apparently more effective than usual care in producing attrition among the really sick people. Those SI subjects who remained in the intervention program had lower CHD mortality, but not much lower than those nonattriters in the UC group.

After the current paper was written, the Stanford Heart Disease Prevention Project published a reanalysis of the three-city data (Williams et al. 1981). The new analysis acknowledged that the communities, and not the individual subjects, could be the experimental units. For such endpoints as cholesterol and blood pressure, the authors computed mean values for each of the three towns and for each of the four years of the study. The slopes derived from linear trend regressions on each town were then compared. By stacking together the slope estimations in a single regression, the authors were able to make a few statistically significant inferences, but the results still had far less precision than those previously reported.

After this paper was written, the Rand group published a number of "interim results" of its Health Insurance Study. Such results were based on about 40 percent of the total person years that are ultimately available for analysis (Keeler et al. 1982; Newhouse et al. 1982; Duan et al. 1983). In comparison to free care, copayment for medical services was found to reduce the number of ambulatory visits and the number of hospitalizations among adults, but not the cost per hospital stay. When health-care use was aggregated into episodes of illness, copayment was found to reduce the number of episodes but not the cost per episode.

The interpretation of the Rand findings is not obvious. More than two-thirds of hospitalized subjects incurred expenses that exceeded the maximum expenditure for even the highest copayment plans. Hence, most hospitalized patients faced marginal coinsurance rates that were effectively zero. An alternative explanation is that patients with full coverage were hospitalized with less serious and thus less costly illnesses. Or perhaps patients have little or no influence on the disposition of care once they have sought treatment. In any case, these findings highlight the study's limited focus on the demand side of the medical-cost problem. The continuing rise in medical expenditures reflects increases in the costs per hospital stay and no doubt the costs per episode of illness. On the demand side, these critical variables may to be unaffected by realistic changes in coverage. But what about the supply side?

Statistical analysis of the HIS results has not been so simple. The pattern of health-care expenses for each of the plans included a substantial fraction with zero claims. The distribution of positive expenditures showed a long right-hand tail caused by rare, very large claims. Thus, confidence intervals derived from the conventional normality assumption were quite large. To improve precision, the Rand investigators devised a four-equation regression model to assess the effects of the experimental plans. In the first probit equation, the probability of medical use depended on plan dummy variables and various covariates (for example, physician visits predicted from 1971 national data based on the age and sex of each subject). In a second probit equation, the probability of hospital expenditures conditional on use of care depended on additional interaction effects between age and plan that the Rand authors discovered to be important. In a third regression equation, the logarithm of expenditures among those with only outpatient use had a variance component for intrafamily effects. In the fourth regression equation, the logarithm of expenditures among those with inpatient care did not depend on dummy variables for individual plans. Because of large outliers, the latter equation was estimated by a robust weighted regression method. To correct for the bias in transforming the predicted mean expenditures from the log scale back to the arithmetic scale, a new nonparametric estimate was developed. The standard errors for the transformed means were then estimated from first-order approximations (Duan et al. 1983). The authors have acknowledged that predicted expenditures by plan (and their confidence intervals) are highly model-dependent and that there is the danger of overfitting the data. Much to their credit, they have performed some interesting tests for such overfitting on a subsample of the interim data. But they do concede with appropriate caution that later analysis of the full experiment may lead to further modeling changes as more data are accumulated at the far right tail of the expenditure distribution.

In retrospect, my paper glossed over certain problems of macroexperimentation that deserved more careful scrunity.

First, I did not address what types of policy interventions are accessible to macroexperimental analysis. The media campaigns of SHDPP were obviously suited to community-wide study. But many policy interventions are aimed at small, diffusely scattered populations of eligible persons. How, for example, might we assess a proposed plan for insurance coverage of a particular medical intervention such as organ transplantation or hospice care for terminal illness? Here, we need to be more creative in defining appropriate macroexperimental units, such as transplantation centers or individual hospices.

Second, I merely suggested without strong supporting evidence that macroexperimentation might be more immune to the Hawthorne effects, selection and attrition biases, and other artifacts that have plagued microstudies. Certainly, if we sampled towns with pre-experimentally high childhood leukemia rates and then in half of them compelled residents to drink only bottled water, we might very well see leukemia rates fall (by regression to the mean) or maybe a large confounding population exodus. But for more realistic cases, it is a serious empirical question whether such artifacts will be significant. In MRFIT, to be sure, we might know enough about intertemporal variation in an individual's serum cholesterol levels to correct for potential regression to the mean and pre-experimental selection bias. But it is not obvious that comparable data on intertemporal variation in site characteristics would be so scarce.

Third, I acknowledge that repeated, independent cross sections would result in much less precise intrasite estimates than might be afforded by cohort sampling. But I avoided asking exactly how much precision might be lost by the use of such cross sections. Certainly, if the endpoint under consideration displayed extremely high intertemporal correlations among individuals, the required sample sizes might be an order of magnitude larger. But it is not obvious that the cost of such cross-sectional sampling will be so much larger.

Fourth, I was too cavalier about the generalizability of macroexperimental results. The success of a macroexperimental study of the use of electronic media in health promotion might depend, say, upon which celebrities gave testimonials. The effects of changes in tax treatment of health insurance among various experimental corporate sites might depend, say, upon the relations between organized labor and top management. The effects of alteration of physician payment for hospital-based care might depend, say, upon the facilities available at the site hospitals. Such uncertainties are inherent in any form of public policy evaluation. Macroexperimentation, however, may be better equipped to overcome such challenges to external validity.

Fifth, I did not meet the challenge of designing a macroexperiment analogous to the HIS. The difficulty I encountered here is that a health-insurance macroexperiment would end up asking questions quite different from those asked in the Rand study. Do changes in insurance coverage affect the rate of introduction of new techniques into a market, or the rate of entry of hospitals, prepaid plans or other providers? Would expansion of coverage result in various health-care rationing schemes, including queues, triage, or more regulation? To be sure, observed changes in entry into experimental communities (from nonexperimental areas) might not mimic the responses to a nationally available insurance system. It may take considerably longer for suppliers' responses to changes in insurance to reach long-run equilibrium. Still, the questions are too important to be ignored.

Finally, wasn't I just kidding myself about the real costs of macroexperimentation? Wouldn't large-scale interventions entail enormous administrative and treatment expenses? I think not. We are constantly instituting new demonstration projects and innovations in the health-care arena without careful advanced planning as to the ultimate evaluation of such efforts. The genuine costs of macroexperiments lie in the additional resources required to look forward as well as back.

Comment   Paul B. Ginsburg

Jeffrey Harris's stimulating paper argues that we have had an imbalance between social microexperiments and social macroexperiments. Drawing upon the experience of experimentation in the health area, he shows that microexperiments have had serious problems that would be difficult to correct, while the problems with macroexperiments tend to be more amenable to solution through clever experimental design.

The paper describes clearly the seriousness of some of the following obstacles to the validity of microexperiments: 1) biases in the selection of subjects and attrition, 2) anticipatory responses and Hawthorne effects, 3) ethical restraints on randomization, and 4) interdependence among individuals.

It then discusses how macroexperiments can avoid these problems. For example, macroexperiments can study market equilibria, thus recording the effects of interdependencies among individuals. By not requiring individual volunteers, selection biases are eliminated. The nature of intervention in macroexperiments also avoids many ethical constraints,

Paul B. Ginsburg is a deputy assistant director, Human Resources Division, Congressional Budget Office.

such as the need to inform control-group participants of the presence of medical conditions and the value of conventional treatments.

Nevertheless, macroexperiments do have some serious disadvantages. One is reduced statistical power. Harris points out that the relevant number of observations in a macroexperiment is the number of sites, not the size of the affected population. Given the inability to control other determinants of the outcome in question, inferences from a handful of sites have limited statistical power. Another problem is the administrative and political obstacles to randomization.

Harris's paper is a valuable one. His critiques of microexperiments are clearly presented and convincing. Rather than simply listing theoretical problems, he makes a careful case about their importance for validity. His ideas for overcoming some of the problems in macroexperiments are good ones that will benefit social experiments.

While I agree with many of the points that Harris makes, I am somewhat uncomfortable with his characterization of the choice as one between a microexperiment or a macroexperiment. I wonder how frequently both options are practically available and are the first and second choices. A more common choice is between an experiment and collection of nonexperimental data. With the Health Insurance Study, for example, I would expect those most critical of the problems encountered by it to advocate increased collection of nonexperimental data rather than a macroexperiment with national health insurance. The latter would be quite expensive, and its limited time period would lead us to question whether full-fledged market effects are being observed. Indeed, the nonexperimental alternative to the Rand Experiment was actually performed, funded by a different agency in the Department of Health and Human Services. The National Medical Care Expenditure Survey, sponsored by the National Center for Health Services Research and the National Center for Health Statistics took a substantial step forward from previous health-care surveys by employing periodic interviews and obtaining direct information from insurers, employers, and medical providers to supplement that obtained from the respondent.

Often the choice of micro- versus macroexperiments is dictated by the nature of the proposed intervention. Since SHDPP used mass media as the intervention, no choice between a micro- or macroexperiment existed. When an intervention specific to individuals is the object of study, there is a theoretical choice, but expense often renders the macro version unrealistic.

I am in agreement with Harris that creativity on the part of researchers can yield a great deal of macroexperimental analysis. Government is frequently initiating (and more currently terminating) programs. Budgetary, administrative, and political constraints often require that programs be phased in or phased out. Participation in the design of this process by researchers could tremendously increase its potential generation of evaluative information.

One program of this sort that I am familiar with is the Professional Standards Review Organization (PSRO) program, which reviews the appropriateness of medical services delivered to Medicare and Medicaid patients. The program was phased in by funding as many local volunteer organizations as the federal budget would permit. While the willingness of a local physicians' group to participate was important to the workings of the program, randomization among the volunteers could have been performed, even if it resulted in some delay in implementation.

Now the program is being phased out. The Department of Health and Human Services is selecting for defunding those agencies it feels are least effective. Since ability to distinguish between those more effective than others is limited, a larger list of the least effective organizations could be developed and randomization performed on this list to choose which ones to defund.

Harris's idea for getting information from demonstrations is a good one. He is correct that the manner in which organizations are chosen for demonstrations prevents useful inferences, but that randomization among the volunteers could provide meaningful information.

The suggestions concerning social experiments for competition in the financing and delivery of health care are interesting. A true macroexperiment, involving selecting certain markets for changes in tax policies and changes in Medicare reimbursement, is probably not feasible. But an experiment would be feasible and useful to test employees' responses to a choice of insurance plans, which is perhaps the link in the competition model that the least is known about. The experimenter could probably even simulate tax-free rebates without changing the tax law by making payments to offset taxes due. I do not know whether such an experiment would be characterized as micro or macro. Clearly it has elements of both. Its results would be far more useful than those reported by employers initiating such programs on their own.

Comment   Lawrence L. Orr

Choosing between Macroexperiments and Microexperiments

Jeffrey Harris argues that "economists and other social scientists . . . have spent disproportionately too much effort on the design and interpretation

Lawrence L. Orr is director, Office of Technical Analysis, A.S.P.E.R., U.S. Department of Labor.

of microexperiments" and suggests that greater attention should be given to the potential use of macroexperiments. He defines microexperiments as those in which "the experimenter assigns treatments and gauges responses at the level of the individual," whereas "in social macroexperiments, treatments are assigned at the group, community, or market level." While Harris is careful to assure us that "this paper is not a broad endorsement of macroexperiments" and "does not advocate the abandonment of microexperiments," the theme of the paper is that microexperiments are subject to a long list of inherent defects that, one gathers, render confident interpretation of the results almost impossible, whereas the (much shorter list of) shortcomings of macroexperiments are remediable through clever design.

On the basis of my own experience with both types of experimental research,[1] I find both Harris's indictment of microexperiments and his enthusiasm for macroexperiments seriously overdrawn. Perhaps more fundamentally, I think that he has not posed the central question in the most useful way: The real question is not which type of experiment is "better" in some absolute sense, but which is more appropriate to the problem at hand.

Harris and I appear to have fundamentally different views of the role of experiments in the policy process. Harris appears to take as his starting point a single well-defined program (or, at most, a few) of unknown efficacy; the role of the experiment is to provide a comprehensive, holistic evaluation of this program or programs, so that the policy maker can make a simple go/no go, adopt/reject decision.

This approach leads him naturally to what I would term "black box" experiments, applied to whole populations with or without experimental variations, relatively simple aggregate-outcome measures, and little or no analysis of underlying response behavior. In contrast, I tend to assume that the policy maker starts with a whole range of program options that can be characterized by a finite set of policy parameters (tax rates, subsidy levels, staff/client ratios, etc.). The function of the experiment, then, is to provide measures of the response to these policy parameters that will enable the policy maker to select that combination, or those levels, of policy instruments that achieve the "best" outcomes, i.e., to design the program. This paradigm leads me naturally to experiments with many variations and extensive analysis of micro data in order to estimate individual response functions.

1. In recent years, I have had some involvement in the design, execution, and/or analysis of the four income-maintenance experiments conducted by OEO and HEW, HUD's housing-allowance experiments, the OEO/HEW health-insurance experiment, HEW's experiments in AFDC administration and disability insurance, and DOL's Employment Opportunity Pilot Projects and (the stillborn) Positive Adjustment Assistance Demonstrations. All except the DOL projects were (primarily) microexperiments; the DOL projects fit Harris's definition of macroexperiments.

This latter view of the role of experiments seems to me in keeping with the way we treat most other research—we seldom expect individual nonexperimental research projects to render global assessments of major policy initiatives—but I will concede that there is a nontrivial set of policy questions for which the black box experiment is appropriate. As I have already suggested, the trick is to figure out which policy issues are in that set.

To do that, though, one must have a full appreciation for the relative strengths and weaknesses of the two modes of experimentation. Therefore, in what follows, I will first discuss briefly the methodological issues raised in the paper with respect to microexperiments and some of the problems of doing macroexperiments, before attempting to lay out a general set of criteria for choosing between the two in addressing any particular policy questions.

I should note at the outset that much of my experience with experimentation is in nonhealth areas and that therefore many of the examples and counterexamples in what follows relate to nonhealth interventions. The issues raised by Harris, however, are primarily methodological ones that cut across substantive research areas, so the actual subject matter under investigation is often of secondary importance to the argument. If one is to argue from example—and it appears that in many cases that is the best we can do at this stage of development of the art of experimentation—it seems to me that more examples are preferable to less.

There is no question that a number of serious methodological problems are encountered in designing and interpreting microexperiments; most of them are listed in this paper. But it should be recognized that many of these problems are not peculiar to microexperimentation; they apply with equal force to many other types of empirical research, including macroexperiments. Thus, for example, the problems of misreporting, interview refusal, attrition, and Hawthorne effects are really problems of longitudinal survey research. Any researcher doing nonexperimental statistical analysis of the Current Population Survey or the Health Interview Survey faces these same problems, although it is my observation that nonexperimental researchers are much less likely than experimenters to recognize or attempt to deal with them. Moreover, these problems will also afflict any macroexperiment that relies on surveys for its data base (as Harris himself notes).

Some of the problems posed by Harris—for example, the necessity of using "detailed-response surface models" for analysis and the constraints imposed by ethical considerations—are inherent in the problem being addressed, not in the experimental methodology. It seems self-evident that sorting out the causal relationships among health-insurance coverage, consumption of medical care, and health status is an exceedingly complex endeavor that is likely to require complex analytical models, however the research data is generated. Likewise, if it is unethical to provide (or withhold) a particular treatment to a randomly selected individual in a microexperiment, it is hard for me to conceive that it is ethical to do so to a group or entire community in a macroexperiment.

There are, of course, limitations that are inherent in microexperimentation itself. Microexperiments are inevitably of relatively short duration and therefore may not reveal long-run, steady-state responses. This characteristic is, of course, shared by macroexperiments. If the likelihood of bias in a particular application seems serious, the researcher might be well advised to consider some nonexperimental data source, such as observations on "natural experiments" or data from ongoing programs, instead of—or in addition to—experimentation. Likewise, so long as participation in microexperiments is voluntary, selection bias is an ever-present danger. As I argue below, however, closely analogous problems exist in macroexperiments. Selection bias is, of course, endemic in nonexperimental data.

Perhaps the most fundamental criticism raised by Harris—and the point on which we disagree most strongly—is the relevance of microexperiments to policy. In the context of the Multiple Risk Factor Intervention Trial, he argues that the treatment "does not necessarily correspond to a viable policy option." This is so, he argues, because intervention at the individual level is expensive; public policies are more likely to take the form of organizational, educational, or regulatory efforts aimed at diffusing information or changing behavior in the community at large. I certainly agree that MRFIT will not predict the outcome of those policies. If the objective was to learn what effect, say, a particular mass media educational campaign would have on aggregate rates of coronary heart disease in the community, then by all means that is the policy that should have been tested, and it could probably only be tested with a macroexperiment. The fact that the researchers did not do so indicates that either that was not their objective or that they showed poor judgment in their choice of research strategy; it does not strike me as an indictment of microexperimentation per se, beyond the rather obvious point that no single methodology is applicable to all problems. It does seem useful (in some cases) to carefully test treatments that represent a stronger intervention than could be replicated nationally, in order to establish an upper bound on the effects that can reasonably be expected from a particular type of policy. I have no way of knowing whether that was part of the motivation for MRFIT.

Harris levels a similar criticism at the Health Insurance Study. As he indicates, that experiment was designed primarily to estimate the effects of alternative levels and forms of cost sharing on the demand for medical care. Thus, he argues, it excludes a variety of institutional and supply-side responses that might have an important effect on outcomes in a national program, and therefore will not be able to directly predict those outcomes. I certainly would not quarrel with that characterization of the experiment, nor would its other designers. But I don't particularly regard that as a serious criticism either of the methodology or of the experiment itself. No single project can address all aspects of a complex, multi–billion dollar national program, and the Health Insurance Experiment is no exception. It was never intended to directly predict the utilization outcomes under any particular national health-insurance plan. Rather, it was intended to fill a gaping hole in our knowledge about underlying consumer behavior in the health sector. It was recognized from the beginning that demand-side information would have to be combined with whatever analyses are possible of institutional and supply-side response to derive national estimates of costs and utilization; but it is equally true that no reasonable estimates of national outcomes can be produced without the demand-side information that will be produced by the experiment. In short, this criticism is a perfect illustration of my fundamental disagreement with Harris over whether experiments should attempt holistic replication of complex policies or should simply attempt to generate reliable information on one or more—presumably important—pieces of the policy design problem.

Harris's discussion of macroexperiments is much more sanguine, although he does acknowledge some of the problems posed by this type of experiment. He notes, for example, that since the basic unit of observation in a macroexperiment is an entire group or community, the feasible sample size (i.e., number of communities) and representativeness may be severely limited, and that confounding of site and treatment effects may be a serious problem. It may also be difficult to randomize groups or communities to treatment and control status because of administrative or political considerations. Finally, he concedes that attempts to measure outcomes with longitudinal, individual-level survey data will be subject to many of the problems encountered in microexperiments and suggests that repeated cross-sectional surveys be conducted instead. His discussion of these issues seriously underestimates their likely severity, however, and is overly sanguine about their proposed remedies. It also omits some of the more serious difficulties of mounting rigorous macroexperiments.

Many of the problems of macroexperiments flow from the sheer size of the natural observational units. Where the unit of observation is an entire market, for example, these projects can be extremely expensive. The original planning budgets for HUD's housing-allowance supply experiment (two housing markets) and DOL's Employment Opportunity Pilot Projects (fifteen labor markets) were each on the order of $400 million. That is considerably more than the budgets of all the income-maintenance experiments, the health-insurance experiment, and the housing-allowance demand experiment (all microexperiments) combined. The high cost of "saturating" an entire market leads, of course, to severe limits on the number of observations. It also tends to favor the selection of small markets and, for many purposes, virtually precludes selecting cities like New York, Los Angeles, or Chicago, thereby jeopardizing the representativeness of the sample.

The constraints on budget and sample size can be severe even with units of observation much smaller than an entire market. The Labor Department recently hired two contractors to prepare alternative designs for a set of demonstrations of employment and training services for workers disemployed in plant closings. One contractor estimated that the optimal number of plants required to disentangle plant effects from individual responses was 133; the other contractor (using different assumptions) arrived at an optimal sample size of about 1,000 plants. The DOL budget for the project was $50 million—about the cost of a "typical" microexperiment. That budget would have supported a sample of at most 50 plants, even if the sample were heavily skewed toward atypically small plants.

The sample-size constraint not only affects the statistical precision of the results, it also severely restricts the number of treatment options that can be tested. In the Employment Opportunity Pilot Projects, for example, an initial list of seven "planned variations" of the basic program was ultimately reduced to two, after long and painful deliberation, on the grounds that more variations within a fifteen-site project would jeopardize the chance of learning anything reliable about either the variations or the basic program itself. Even in the plant-closing demonstrations, with a potential sample of as many as fifty plants, both design contractors agreed that it would be risky to try more than five or six different treatments unless randomization within plants (i.e., embedding microexperiments within the macroexperiment) was allowed. In both of these cases, there were literally dozens or even hundreds of treatment levels and combinations that were of policy interest and very little ability to use the treatments actually tested to interpolate or extrapolate to options not tested.

These projects illustrate vividly the problem of black box experiments mentioned earlier. In projects like these, where only a small fraction of a large number of potential policy options can be implemented, the experimenter is in the almost impossible position of trying to predict which policy options will be relevant as much as ten years in the future, when the project has been completed and the data analyzed. In the light of the recent dramatic policy shifts at the federal level, this task seems almost hopeless. The Employment Opportunity Pilot Projects, for example, were focused heavily on public-service employment when they were initiated in 1979; in March 1981, President Reagan terminated all federal support for public-service employment. By way of contrast, the treatments in the Health Insurance Experiment span the entire range of policy options in one important dimension of health-financing policy.

Perhaps the most serious problem arising out of the scale of macroexperiments is the difficulty of control and administration. It is not only that the number and size of sites required for valid inference presents a serious span-of-control problem—although that is certainly the case. The scale of these projects will often require that they be implemented by the regular-program bureaucracy. The experimenters' objectives will conflict in important ways with the objectives of regular-program operators, and it will be exceedingly difficult to ensure that even those few treatments selected for testing are actually implemented as intended. The monitors of DOL's Employment Opportunity Pilot Projects faced a steady stream of resistance and requests for exceptions to federal guidelines from the CETA prime sponsors running the project. Often program operators simply ignored the guidelines when they departed from normal practice or were in conflict with the operators' concept of what was best for the client, or for their own agency. One of the planned variations in the Employment Opportunity Pilot Projects was a set of employment subsidies designed to encourage placement of AFDC recipients in private-sector jobs. It was only after this subexperiment was well underway that the DOL monitors discovered that the only clients being referred to the project from the welfare agency were the rejects and failures from WIN's own placement activities. Needless to say, this had a major impact on the project's placement rate—the principal outcome measure—although it did wonders for WIN's placement rate.

The scale and visibility of macroexperiments also makes them extremely vulnerable to a variety of political pressures. The Minnesota Work Equity Project, for example, became embroiled in political controversy that delayed its implementation for nearly a year and had serious adverse effects on its ultimate design and implementation. The Employment Opportunity Pilot Projects, with an annual budget of $100 to $200 million, was an obvious target for federal budget cutters throughout its brief life. In 1980, the project was seriously scaled back in midcourse as part of President Carter's budget-balancing effort, and in 1981 it was prematurely terminated by the new administration. In contrast, the Health Insurance Study, with an annual budget less than one-tenth as large, escaped the budget cutters' ax on both occasions.

A final limitation of macroexperiments, not discussed by Harris, is closely analogous to the selectivity problem posed by voluntary participation in macroexperiments. Participation in macroexperiments is, after all, also voluntary—both at the site and individual levels. The experience with site selection for experiments and demonstrations is no more encouraging than the individual take-up rates in microexperiments. In the

Food Stamp Workfare Demonstrations, for example, a national solicitation netted a total of seven volunteer sites—six rural counties and one urban county where the food stamp caseload is allegedly heavily composed of "beach bums." In both the Health Insurance Study and the Employment Opportunities Pilot Projects, the experimenters first selected sites and then approached the local authorities, attempting to elicit their approval and/or cooperation. In both cases, exactly one-seventh of the sites approached either refused or failed to cooperate to such a degree that a program was never initiated.

The issue of individual participation and selectivity bias is somewhat more subtle in macroexperiments than in microexperiments, but no less real or important. In any intervention that relies for its effect on any positive action on the part of individuals, the extent of individual participation—whether it be enrollment in a program, application for benefits, or simply response to a mass media educational campaign—will be heavily dependent on the level of program outreach. The level and effectiveness of outreach efforts are exceedingly difficult to control in most cases, and the resulting participation rates can vary widely; I have seen participation rates anywhere from 1 or 2 percent to 40 or 50 percent in response to what appear to be comparable outreach efforts. The individuals who respond to outreach directed toward the general population are, of course, just as self-selected as the randomly selected individuals who agree to participate in a microexperiment. Indeed, since participation rates are likely to be much lower in a macroexperiment, the potential for selectivity bias seems more serious. If one had confidence that the experimental outreach and participation would be replicated in a national program (or in another site), this potential bias would not be a problem, since the experimental outcomes would then be unbiased predictors of national-program outcomes. But that seems a heroic assumption, given the idiosyncratic nature of local outreach activities and the extreme variation in resulting participation rates.

While I do not believe that macroexperiments avoid the selectivity-bias problem, I do feel that one of the advantages of macroexperiments is their potential for measuring, if only crudely, participation rates. For the reasons just discussed, participation rates in a macroexperiment are likely to be an imprecise predictor of national rates, but participation can't be predicted at all from a microexperiment because the outreach method is highly artificial. And participation rates are a very important determinant of program cost and/or effectiveness.

Harris suggests several methodological approaches to mitigate the shortcomings of macroexperiments. I agree that steps could be taken to improve the methodological rigor of such projects. I am more skeptical than Harris, however, as to the practicality and likely effectiveness of some of his suggestions.

I heartily endorse, for example, the suggestion of random selection of treatment and comparison sites from matched pairs. I am much more dubious about the possibility of "crossover and fold-back designs" in which the timing and sequence of program start-up and termination are "random and unknown to the experimental units." In most cases projects like these require extensive prior negotiation and planning with local officials or agencies; it would often be virtually impossible—and possibly unethical—to keep such crucial information from the local personnel.

On the other hand, Harris's suggestion of mixed macro and micro designs is quite appealing. In fact, the design of the Employment Opportunity Pilot Projects included two microexperiments embedded within the overall macroexperiment. Unfortunately, the results of that effort were not entirely encouraging, largely because the microexperiments, like the macroexperiment itself, were administered by the regular program operators; the challenge of implementing random assignment and multiple treatments proved to be a difficult one for the program operators. I have already described the problems encountered in sample referral from WIN to the employment-subsidy experiment; the other experiment-within-the-experiment, involving alternative job-search assistance techniques, had such difficulty establishing an effective outreach effort that the results were virtually useless, and ultimately the experiment was abandoned.

The suggestion that the results of many independent macroexperiments could be combined is less appealing, even in principle. My office has just completed a survey of about a dozen experiments and demonstrations in job-search assistance, all of which were modeled on a single, apparently successful, project. While we did not attempt any rigorous pooling of data or results, it quickly became clear that the diversity of treatment design, data collection, outcome definition, and sample selection in these projects almost defied description, let alone formal modeling. I am doubtful that the task would be any easier in most other cases.

Finally, Harris suggests that many of the problems of data collection could be avoided by using repeated cross-sectional surveys, rather than longitudinal surveys. While there is some validity to this suggestion, the precision of the estimates of treatment effects could suffer substantially because of individual variation. Moreover, contrary to his assertion, repeated cross sections might be much more expensive in many cases than longitudinal surveys. If the population of interest is a subset of the general population (e.g., poor people, sick people, or program eligibles) a large number of screening interviews may be required to identify each useful observation. In a longitudinal survey, this screening operation need only be performed once; in repeated cross sections it would have to be done for each successive wave. In the Employment Opportunity Pilot Projects, for example, approximately fifteen screening interviews with a random sample of the general population were required for each program eligible identified.

Taking all of the strengths and weaknesses of both experimental modes into account, I would propose the following general criteria for deciding which experimental method is appropriate for a particular policy issue.

1. *Policy interest.* If the objective is to measure the overall efficacy of a single program or small number of programs, macroexperimentation may be more appropriate; if the objective is to estimate behavioral responses to a wide range of program variants, microexperimentation is indicated. Policy interest in estimation of participation rates also favors macroexperimentation.

2. *Nature of the treatment.* The nature of the treatment will occasionally dictate one mode of experimentation. For example, educational campaigns that rely on mass media could not be implemented in a micro-experiment. On the other hand, treatments that require complicated explanations or interactions with participants—such as "buying out" an existing health-insurance plan—may be better implemented in a microexperiment.

3. *Nature of the response.* Macroexperimentation may be indicated if interactions among individuals in the group or community are thought to have an important effect on the response to the treatment. Purely individualistic responses can be measured in either mode of experiment.

4. *Administrative considerations.* The scale and objectives of macroexperiments will usually dictate that they be administered through existing institutions and organizations. Careful thought must be given to whether that is possible in a experimental context. Span-of-control problems, competing institutional objectives, ingrained organizational behavior, and garden-variety start-up problems may seriously compromise implementation of the treatment in a short-duration experiment. On the other hand, microexperiments will be even more difficult to run through existing institutions because of the multiplicity and complexity of treatments; they will usually require a special administrative structure under the direct control of the experimenters. The degree to which this arrangement realistically replicates the administrative structure of a permanent program, and how critical the difference is to the outcomes of interest, must be carefully assessed.

5. *Statistical considerations.* The estimates of treatment effect are likely to be more precise and unbiased in a microexperiment, because of the problems of cost, sample size, selectivity bias, administrative control, and lack of a true control group in macroexperiments. These potential disadvantages must be analyzed and weighed against whatever other factors favor macroexperimentation.

References

Arrow, Kenneth J. 1975. *Two notes on inferring long-run behavior from social experiments*. Rand Report P–5546. Santa Monica: Rand Corporation.

Apostolides, Aristide, and Maureen Henderson. 1977. Evaluation of cancer screening programs: Parallels with clinical trials. *Cancer 39*: 1179–85.

Brook, Robert H., John E. Ware, Jr., Allyson Davies-Avery, et al. 1979. *Conceptualization and measurement of health for adults in the health insurance study: Vol. 7, overview*. Rand Report R–1987/8–HEW. Santa Monica: Rand Corporation.

Campbell, Donald T., and Julian C. Stanley. 1966. *Experimental and Quasi-Experimental Designs for Research*. Chicago: Rand McNally.

Cornfield, Jerome. 1978. Randomization by group: A formal analysis. *American Journal of Epidemiology 108*: 100–102.

Davis, C. E., and R. J. Havlik. 1977. Clinical trials of lipid lowering and coronary artery disease prevention. In *Hyperlipidemia: Diagnosis and therapy*, ed., B. M. Rifkind and R. I. Levy. New York: Grune and Stratton.

Duan, Naihua, Willard G. Manning, Carl N. Morris, and Joseph Newhouse. 1983. A comparison of alternative models of the demand for medical care. *Journal of Business and Economic Statistics 1*: 115–26.

DuMouchel, William H., and Jeffrey E. Harris. 1983. Bayes and empirical Bayes methods for combining the results of cancer studies in humans and other species (with discussion). *Journal of the American Statistical Association 78*: 293–315.

Farquhar, John W. 1978. The community-based model of life-style intervention trials. *American Journal of Epidemiology 108*: 103–11.

Farquhar, John W., Nathan Maccoby, Peter D. Wood, et al. 1977. Community education for cardiovascular health. *Lancet 1*: 1192–95.

Feldstein, Martin S. 1977. Quality change and the demand for hospital care. *Econometrica 45*: 1681–702.

Friedman, Gary D., Diana B. Petitti, Richard D. Bawol, and A. B. Siegelaub. 1981. Mortality in cigarette smokers and quitters. *New England Journal of Medicine 304*: 1407–10.

Gillum, Richard F., Paul T. Williams, and Edward Sondik. 1980. Some considerations for the planning of total-community prevention trials: When is sample size adequate? *Journal of Community Health 5*: 270–78.

Harris, Jeffrey E. 1982. Prenatal medical care and infant mortality. In *Economic Aspects of Health*, ed. V. Fuchs. Chicago: University of Chicago Press.

————. 1980. Commentary. *National Health Insurance: What now? What later? What never?*, ed. M. Pauly. Washington, D.C.: American Enterprise Institute.

————. 1979. The aggregate coinsurance rate and the supply of innovations in the hospital sector. Department of Economics working paper, Massachusetts Institute of Technology.

Hulley, Stephen B., and Stephen F. Fortman. 1980. Clinical trials of changing behavior to prevent cardiovascular disease. In *Perspectives in behavioral medicine*, ed. S. M. Weiss. New York: Academic Press.

Hypertension Detection and Follow-up Program Cooperative Group. 1979a. Five-year findings of the hypertension detection follow-up program: I. Reduction in mortality of persons with high blood pressure, including mild hypertension. *Journal of the American Medical Association* 242: 2562–71.

Hypertension Detection and Follow-up Program Cooperative Group. 1979b. Five-year findings of the hypertension detection follow-up program: II. Mortality by race, sex, and age. *Journal of the American Medical Association* 242: 2572–77.

Kasl, Stanislav V. 1980. Cardiovascular risk reduction in a community setting: Some comments. *Journal of Consulting and Clinical Psychology* 48: 143–49.

————. 1978. A social-psychological perspective on successful community control of high blood pressure: A review. *Journal of Behavioral Medicine* 1: 347–81.

Keeler, Emmett B., John E. Rolph, Naihua Duan, et al. 1982. *The demand for episodes of medical treatment: Interim results from the Health Insurance Experiment*. Rand Report R–2829–HHS. Santa Monica: Rand Corporation.

Kuller, Lewis, James Neaton, Arlene Caggiula, and Lorita Falvo-Gerard. 1980. Primary prevention of heart attacks: The multiple risk factor intervention trial. *American Journal of Epidemiology* 112: 185–99.

Leventhal, Howard, Martin A. Safer, Paul D. Cleary and Mary Gutman. 1980. Cardiovascular risk modification by community-based programs for life-style change: Comments on the Stanford study. *Journal of Consulting and Clinical Psychology* 48: 150–58.

Maccoby, Nathan, John W. Farquhar, Peter D. Wood, and Janet Alexander. 1977. Reducing the risk of cardiovascular disease: Effects of a community-based campaign on knowledge and behavior. *Journal of Community Health* 3: 100–114.

Manning, Willard G., Jr., Carl N. Morris, Joseph P. Newhouse, et al. 1981. A two part model of the demand for medical care: Preliminary results from the Health Insurance Study. In *Health, economics, and health economics*, ed. J. van der Gaag and M. Perlman. Amsterdam: North Holland.

Manning, Willard G., Jr., Joseph P. Newhouse, and John E. Ware, Jr. 1982. The status of health in demand estimation: Beyond excellent, good, fair, and poor. In *Economic Aspects of Health*, ed. V. Fuchs. Chicago: University of Chicago Press.

Meyer, Anthony J., Joyce D. Nash, Alfred L. McAlister, Nathan Maccoby, and John W. Farquhar. 1980. Skills training in a cardiovascular health education campaign. *Journal of Consulting and Clinical Psychology* 48: 129–42.

Morris, Carl. 1979. A finite selection model for experimental design of the Health Insurance Study. *Journal of Econometrics* 11: 43–61.

Morris, Carl N., Joseph P. Newhouse, and Rae W. Archibald. 1980. *On the theory and practice of obtaining unbiased and efficient samples in social surveys*. Rand Report R–2173–HEW. Santa Monica: Rand Corporation.

Mosteller, Fred, and Gail Mosteller. 1979. New statistical methods in public policy: Part I, experimentation. *Journal of Contemporary Business* 8: 79–92.

Multiple Risk Factor Intervention Trial Group 1982. Multiple risk factor intervention trial: Risk factor changes and mortality results. *Journal of the American Medical Association* 248: 1465–77.

———. 1977. Statistical design considerations in the NHLBI Multiple Risk Factor Intervention Trial. *Journal of Chronic Diseases* 30: 261–75.

———. 1976a. The Multiple Risk Factor Intervention Trial (MRFIT). *Journal of the American Medical Association* 235: 825–27.

———. 1976b. The Multiple Risk Factor Intervention Trial. *Annals of the New York Academy of Medicine* 304: 293–308.

Newhouse, Joseph P. 1978. *The erosion of the medical marketplace*. Rand Report R–2141. Santa Monica: Rand Corporation.

———. 1974. A design for a health insurance experiment. *Inquiry* 2: 5–27.

Newhouse, Joseph P., Willard G. Manning, Carl N. Morris, et al. 1982. *Some interim results from a controlled trial of cost sharing in health insurance*. Rand Report R–2847–HHS. Santa Monica: Rand Corporation.

Newhouse, Joseph P., Kent H. Marquis, Carl N. Morris, Charles E. Phelps, and William H. Rogers. 1979. Measurement issues in the second generation of social experiments: The Health Insurance Study. *Journal of Econometrics* 11: 117–29.

Ockene, Judith K., Norman Hymowitz, Mary Sexton, and Steven K. Broste. 1982. Comparison of patterns of smoking behavior change among smokers in the Multiple Risk Factor Intervention Trial. *Preventive Medicine* 11: 621–38.

Puska, P., J. Tuomilehto, A. Nissinen, et al. 1978. Changing the cardiovascular risk in an entire community: The North Karelia project. Paper presented at the International Symposium on Primary Prevention in Early Childhood of Atherosclerotic and Hypertensive Diseases, Chicago, Ill.

Rivlin, Alice. 1974. Allocating resources for policy research: How can experiments be more useful? *American Economic Review Papers and Proceedings* 64: 346–54.

Rose, Geoffrey, and R. J. S. Hamilton. 1978. A randomised controlled trial of the effect on middle-aged men of advice to stop smoking. *Journal of Epidemiology and Community Health* 32: 275–81.

Rose, Geoffrey, R. F. Heller, Hugh T. Pedoe, and D. G. S. Christie. 1980. Heart disease prevention project: A randomized controlled trial in industry. *British Medical Journal* 280: 747–51.

Schoenberger, James A. 1981. The Multiple Risk Factor Intervention Trial. Presentation at American Heart Association meetings, Washington, D.C.

Sherwin, Roger. 1978. Controlled trials of the diet-heart hypothesis: Some comments on the experimental unit. *American Journal of Epidemiology* 108: 92–99.

Sherwin, Roger, Mary Sexton, and Patricia Dischinger. 1979. The Multiple Risk Factor Intervention Trial of the primary prevention of coronary heart disease: Risk factor changes after two years. Paper presented at the Seventh Asian Pacific Congress of Cardiology, Bangkok.

Stern, Michael P., John W. Farquhar, Nathan Maccoby, and Susan H. Russell. 1976. Results of a two-year health education campaign on dietary behavior: The Stanford three community study. *Circulation* 54: 826–33.

Strolley, Paul D. 1980. Epidemiologic studies of coronary heart disease: Two approaches. *American Journal of Epidemiology* 112: 217–24.

Syme, S. Leonard. 1978. Life style intervention in clinic-based trials. *American Journal of Epidemiology* 108: 87–91.

Truett, J., J. Cornfield, and W. Kannel. 1967. Multivariate analysis of the risk of coronary heart disease in Framingham. *Journal of Chronic Diseases* 20: 511–24.

Ware, John E., Jr., Robert H. Brook, Allyson Davies-Avery, et al. 1980. *Conceptualization and measurement of health for adults in the health insurance study: Vol. 1, model of health and methodology.* Rand Report R–1987/1–HEW. Santa Monica: Rand Corporation.

WHO European Collaborative Group. 1974. An international controlled trial in the multifactorial prevention of coronary heart disease. *International Journal of Epidemiology* 3: 219–24.

Williams, Paul T., Stephen P. Fortmann, John W. Farquhar, Ann Varady, and Susan Mellan. 1981. A comparison of statistical methods for evaluating risk factor changes in community-based studies: An example from the Stanford three-community study. *Journal of Chronic Diseases* 34: 565–71.

5 Technical Problems in Social Experimentation: Cost versus Ease of Analysis

Jerry A. Hausman and David A. Wise

Over the past decade, a major portion of empirical economic research has been based on what have come to be known as social experiments. Primary examples include a series of income-maintenance experiments, a housing-allowance demand experiment, several electricity-pricing experiments, and a health-insurance experiment. Much of our discussion in this paper is motivated by the income-maintenance experiments but it draws from our experience with the housing-allowance and electricity experiments as well.

The goal of this paper is to set forth general guidelines that we believe would enhance the usefulness of future social experiments and to suggest ways of correcting for their inherent limitations. Our conclusion and results can be summarized briefly.

Although the major motivation for an experiment is to overcome the inherent limitations of structural econometric models, in many instances the experimental designs have subverted this motivation. The primary advantages of randomized controlled experiments were often lost. In particular, in large measure it was impossible to estimate an experimental effect using straightforward analysis-of-variance methods, as a standard experimental design would suggest. Rather, a careful analysis of the results often required complicated structural models based on strong model-specification assumptions, the necessity for which an experiment should be designed to obviate. Section 5.1 provides a simple explanation of this goal and is intended to motivate the remainder of the paper.

Jerry A. Hausman is professor of economics, Massachusetts Institute of Technology, and research associate, National Bureau of Economic Research. David A. Wise is John F. Stambaugh Professor of Political Economy, John F. Kennedy School of Government, Harvard University, and research associate, National Bureau of Economic Research.

The major complication for the analysis of the experiments was induced by an endogenous-sample-selection and treatment-assignment procedure that selected the experimental participants and assigned them to control versus treatment groups partly on the basis of an outcome variable whose change the experiments were intended to measure. To overcome at the time of the experimental results' analysis the complications caused by the endogenous sample selection and treatment assignment required rather complex statistical techniques and detracted greatly from the simplicity we believe should be a goal of experimental designs.

We propose that to overcome these difficulties, an experimental design should as nearly as possible allow analysis based on a simple analysis-of-variance model. This would mean that sample selection and treatment assignment should be based on randomization and that stratification on response variables should be avoided.

Although complexities attendant to endogenous stratification can be avoided, there are inherent limitations of the experiments that cannot be. Two major ones are self-determination of participation and self-selection out through attrition. But these problems, we believe, can be corrected for with relative ease if endogenous stratification is eliminated.

Finally, we propose that as a guiding principle, the experiments should have as a first priority the precise estimation of a single or a small number of treatment effects. The experiments to date have in general been hampered by a large number of treatments together with small sample sizes so that no single treatment could be estimated accurately.

Following the motivation in section 5.1, we have elaborated in section 5.2 these several general guidelines that we believe would enhance the effectiveness of future experiments. The problem of endogenous stratification and a way of avoiding it are set forth in section 5.3. A method of correcting for the inherent self-selection problems of social experiments is suggested in section 5.4.

5.1   Unbiased Estimates, Structural Models, and Randomization

Obtaining unbiased estimates is the major motivation for a large portion of econometric theory and for the application of econometric techniques in empirical analysis. Econometricians generally have in mind a model of the form

(1) $$Y = f(X, \epsilon),$$

where X represents measured and ϵ unmeasured determinants of Y. The goal is to estimate the effects of the elements of X on Y. A common specification of f in equation (1) is

(2) $$Y = X\beta + \epsilon,$$

where β is a vector of parameters to be estimated, with each element of β measuring the effect on Y of a unit change in the corresponding element of X.

The guiding principle for econometricians is that simple estimation techniques (e.g., least squares) will yield unbiased estimates of β if X is uncorrelated with ϵ. "Unbiased" is understood to mean and is indeed defined to mean an unbiased estimate of the "causal" effect of X on Y—the understood definition of β in much, but not all, of econometric analysis. But although the principle is demonstrably true in theory, it is often difficult to approximate in practice and its existence impossible to verify without reservation. Nonetheless, the goal remains.

To move toward it, econometricians use two general modes of reasoning. One is economic theory that restricts the function form of f, although usually only within broad bounds. The other is statistical theory that in large part prescribes methods to correct for correlation between X and ϵ, and thus obtaining unbiased estimates of β. The combination of economic and statistical theory often leads—at least in the abstract—to specification and estimation of structural models. Structural models can be thought of as those in which the parameters have a causal interpretation, with the concomitant property that if unbiased estimates of them are obtained they also could be given a causal interpretation. But although theoretical prescription of models and their empirical estimation can restrict the form of f, they can do so only within limits. The estimates must be interpreted within the constraints implicit in the assumptions that underlie them. In particular, it is usually not possible to know for sure that X is uncorrelated with ϵ, or if not, that corrections have been made for correlations that exist.

A response to this dilemma is to choose selected values of X in such a way that they are by design uncorrelated with other determinants of Y, thus allowing unbiased estimation of the corresponding values of β. This technique is randomization, and it is most often employed within the context of a randomized controlled experiment. For purposes of exposition we shall henceforth use as an example an estimation of the effects of income-maintenance plans—taxes and guarantees—on earnings.

Suppose that the plan is T, called the treatment, and that earnings depend on T, on other measured variables X, and on unmeasured determinants ϵ according to

$$(3) \qquad Y = \beta_1 T + f(X, \epsilon) \, .$$

If individuals (more often families) are chosen at random from the population and assigned values of T, in large samples T will be uncorrelated with ϵ and with X as well. Then simple least-squares analysis-of-variance estimation of the model

$$(4) \qquad Y = \beta_1 T + \eta \, ,$$

where η is equal to f and treated as a disturbance term in this model, will yield unbiased estimates of β.

The primary motivation for this approach is to circumvent the uncertainties inherent in the assumptions of structural econometric models by constructing T in such a way that it is uncorrelated with other determinants of Y, thus by construction assuring unbiased estimation of β_1.

We have set forth these possibly oversimplified ideas to serve as background and motivation for our subsequent discussion. In particular, it is important to keep in mind the motivation for randomized controlled experiments. Although in the large social experiments we believe it is impossible to create the theoretical paradigm of such an experiment, the paradigm should serve as a guide to their designs as well as to the analysis of their results—much as the theoretical goal of Xs uncorrelated with error terms serves as a guide to empirical analysis based on nonexperimental data. We shall argue, for example, that the use of complex structural models to analyze the data from social experiments, or experimental designs that require such models or depend in large part on structural-model assumptions, are often in contradiction to the primary motivation for the experiments and thus subvert their intent; they are often inconsistent with the raison d'être of experiments. We will elaborate on this and other general propositions in the next section.

5.2 General Goals and Guiding Propositions

With the powerful advantage of hindsight, and aided by our part in the analysis of social experiments to date, we shall set forth several propositions that will enhance the value of future experiments. To do this we will explain what we believe to be the major inherent limitations of such experiments. The primary ones are self-determination of experimental participation and self-determination of withdrawal from the experiment. These limitations can be corrected for, and some suggestions for doing so are contained in the following sections. Other design characteristics of the experiments to date unnecessarily complicate their analysis and in particular make it much more difficult to correct for their inherent limitations. The primary design feature of this type is stratification on endogenous variables. We will address this question first, then turn to a discussion of inherent limitations, and then address other principles that we believe should guide future experimental designs.

5.2.1 Stratification on Endogenous Variables

As described in the previous section, the reason for an experiment is, by randomization, to eliminate correlation between the treatment variable and other determinants of the response variable that is under study. In each of the income-maintenance experiments, however, the experimental sample was selected in part on the basis of the dependent variable, and the assignment to treatment versus control group was based in part on the dependent variable as well. In general, the group eligible for selection—based on family status, race, age of family head, etc.—was stratified on the basis of income (and other variables), and persons were selected from within the strata. In the New Jersey experiment, persons with incomes greater than 1.5 times the poverty level were excluded altogether. In the other experiments, the stratification on income was less complete, but as a result a bit more complicated. Assignment to control versus treatment group was also based in part on income. Whether the outcome of interest is income or hours worked, which is a component of income, such a procedure induces correlation between right-hand variables, including the treatment effect, and unmeasured determinants of income. Thus it is not straightforward to obtain unbiased estimates of treatment effects using simple analysis-of-variance or -covariance techniques.

Theoretically, an elaborate analysis of variance procedure that allowed for estimation of separate treatment effects within each strata would yield unbiased estimates. But because the strata were so numerous, the treatments so many, and the sample sizes relatively small, this method of analysis was impractical because reasonably precise estimates of treatment effects could not be obtained. Thus to correct for endogenous stratification and treatment assignment required rather complicated models (Hausman and Wise 1977, 1979, 1980).

Analysis of experimental results based on such techniques has at least two major shortcomings. First, it is relatively complicated—requiring nonlinear maximum-likelihood estimation for example. This is a shortcoming in itself, but seems especially troublesome in the context of an experiment one of whose major advantages presumably is simplicity. Second, and more important, it necessitates the imposition of functional-form constraints. The models proposed by Hausman and Wise are generally structural in spirit, and in particular require distributional assumptions against which the results may not be robust. To correct for endogenous stratification, for example, requires analysis based on truncated distributions in which the distribution assumed is necessarily a key component. Since the primary advantage of an experiment presumably is to lessen or avoid the necessity for such assumptions, it seems contradictory to design experiments whose effects cannot be evaluated accurately without them.

The elimination of stratification on endogenous variables would avoid this source of complication. The most straightforward procedure would be to randomly select an experimental group from the population and randomly assign these selected to control or treatment status, without consideration of income or other endogenous variables. Two major objections to such a procedure are cost and political feasibility. Indeed the two are not unrelated. Most seriously considered income-support programs are intended to guarantee a minimum income to families who would otherwise have relatively low incomes. And presumably it is primarily this group whose labor supply and earnings would be affected by the plan. Nonetheless, it has been difficult to obtain funds for experimental programs that guaranteed support for higher-income families, even though under most plans payments to this group would be small, since their earnings would be unlikely to fall below the "breakeven" point at which payments are zero. In addition, if it is important to obtain a "good" estimate of the effect of the program on low-income families, then it is necessary to have a large enough number of low-income families to do so. Of course a large random sample from the population would also provide a large number of low-income families, but larger sample sizes increase the cost of the experiment.

We do not present numbers on the marginal cost of an additional experimental family. Preliminary investigation, however, suggests that it is small relative to the fixed costs of running an experiment. Suppose that, for whatever reason, it is not feasible to select a random sample from the population. We propose in this case that the sample be as random as possible. That is, randomly select persons with incomes below a given level, without endogenous stratification within this group. But what should be the measure of income that determines eligibility?

We have proposed in section 5.3—after a more detailed description of the endogenous stratification problem—a method for selecting the experimental group, based on predicted income, in such a way that the stratification is not endogenous.

5.2.2 Inherent Limitations on Random Sample Selection

We have argued that endogenous stratification procedures unduly complicate the analysis of experimental results and that procedures that avoid such stratification would be preferable. Nonetheless, there are inherent limitations on randomization in social experiments. It is surely impossible to attain the theoretical paradigm of a randomized controlled experiment. There are at least two major reason for this problem, both involving individual self-selection.

One reason is that persons cannot in general be made to participate in an experiment if selected by a random procedure. Some of those randomly selected will participate while others will not. If the individual-participation decision is related to the effect that the treatment would have on individuals, then the estimated treatment effect will be a biased estimate of the effect to be expected if the treatment were instituted as a program applying to the entire population.

The 1954 Salk-vaccine experiment provides a good example of this effect. There were two primary versions of the experimental design. In the "placebo control" areas, children who agreed to be inoculated (or, more accurately, whose parents agreed to the inoculation) were randomly assigned to the vaccine group or to the placebo group. In the "observed control" area, second-grade children who agreed to inoculation received the vaccine, while first and third graders served as the control group. Selected results are shown in table 5.1.

Children in the placebo control areas who were not inoculated contracted polio at a rate of 54 per 100,000. The comparable figure for children who participated in the experiment was 81, the rate for those who participated and received the placebo. Similarly in the observed control areas, second-grade children who were not inoculated had a substantially lower rate (53), than the rate for the control group (61). Thus apparently children who were more likely to contract polio, and thus more likely to be helped by the vaccine, were more likely to participate in the experiment. This tends to exaggerate the effect of the vaccine. For example, one might conclude on the basis of the vaccinated and control groups in the observed control areas that the vaccine reduced the rate from 61 to 34. But apparently the rate for all children would have been less than 61 without the vaccine. It is of course apparent from this data that the vaccine was effective, regardless of this uncertainty about the magnitude of the effect. But if the effect had been less clear, this self-determination of participation could have led to considerable uncertainty about desirability of universal inoculation.

A similar effect was apparent in the recent housing-allowance-demand experiment. Because of the nature of the primary experimental allowance, many families could benefit under the allowance plan only if they

Table 5.1   Reported Cases of Poliomyelitis

Study Group	Study Population	All Reported Cases per 100,000
Placebo control areas		
Vaccinated	200,745	41
Placebo	201,229	81
Not inoculated	338,778	54
Observed control areas		
Vaccinated	221,998	34
Controls	725,173	61
Second graders not inoculated	123,605	53

Source: (Meier 1978, table 2, p. 11).

were willing to move. It seems apparent from subsequent analysis that of low-income renters who were asked to participate in the experiment, those who were less adverse to moving were more likely to participate in the experiment (see Venti and Wise 1982). Thus the estimated experimental effect tended to exaggerate the increase in rent that would be induced by the allowance where it applied to all low-income renters.

We have suggested in section 5.4 a procedure that we believe could be used to correct for this potential bias, assuming that the self-selection cannot be avoided.

The other form of self-selection is attrition from the experimental sample, once a sample has been selected. Again, the problem is that determinants of dropping out may be related to the experimental response that would otherwise be observed. For example, persons who are not affected by the treatment, possibly because they have high incomes for example, may be more likely to drop out than those who are affected and thus receive higher payments. This is the problem addressed by Hausman and Wise (1979).

If the experimental design is not complicated by endogenous stratification and assignment, then correction for self-determination of participation and attrition would be relatively simple. Indeed correction for both simultaneously is quite feasible, and this approach is taken in section 5.4. Such a correction, however, is much more complicated if the experimental design is also complicated by endogenous stratification and assignment. This reinforces the proposal that such stratification be avoided in favor of random sampling. Then analysis of experimental results can address complications that are unavoidable without having to devote extraordinary effort to correct for complications induced by the experimental design.

5.2.3   Additional Concerns

A characteristic of experiments to date has been a rather large number of treatments. The income-maintenance experiments, for example, entailed several treatments defined by different combinations of income-guarantee levels and tax rates. In none of the experiments, however, were the sample sizes large enough to obtain precise estimates of the effects of any particular treatment. Thus analysts generally resorted to estimation of a single effect that did not distinguish the various treatments, or they assumed a structural model that allowed interpolation across individuals assigned to different treatments. The more the latter procedure was followed, the less consistent the analysis was with the motivation for an experiment. That is, it subverted the major goal of using random selection and treatment assignment to circumvent the inherent limitations of hypothesized structural models.

Thus it seems to us that priorities should be ordered in such a way that the primary goals of an experiment are met first. The first goal we propose should be the estimation of an experimental effect for *a* treatment. Then additional treatments should be added only if each additional one can also be estimated with precision. The proposition is that precise estimation of the effect of single treatment or the effects of a few treatments is to be preferred to imprecise estimates of many. This we propose should be done in such a way that simple analysis of covariance estimates of treatment effects may be obtained, subject to the limitations on randomization discussed above and detailed more fully below. Thus we would propose an evaluation model of the form

$$Y = \alpha_1 T_1 + \alpha_2 T_2 + \ldots + \alpha_k T_k + X\beta + \epsilon,$$

where the α_k are treatment effects. We propose an analysis-of-covariance model because our research (Hausman and Wise 1979) has suggested that the use of exogenous control variables, represented by X, reduces the effect of attrition on estimated experimental effects; we presume that it would be likely to reduce the effect of self-determination of participation as well.

The reader will note the absence of a structural parameterization that attempts, for example, to describe income and substitution effects. This is because we believe that simple precise estimates of a few effects will be more readily understood by most observers and will thus carry more weight in the decision-making process. In addition, if, for policy purposes, it is desirable to estimate the effects of possible programs not described by treatments, then interpolations can be made between estimated treatment effects. If the experimental treatments are at the bounds of possible programs, then of course this calculation is easier. Although it can be argued that structural models are necessary to make interpolations, we believe that for almost any situation we can think of, the simplicity of, say, linear interpolations far outweigh the possible advantages of interpolations based on a structural model. At the same time, the spirit of the experiment is maintained.

If the experiment is to inform the policy-making process, we believe that a single number that can be supported can be more confidently relied on than more complex analysis. That the labor-supply effect of a known treatment is 16 percent and not 2 percent, for example, is much more important than whether the effect of a plan close to the treatment is 16 percent or 17 percent.

This is not to say that experimental data should not be used to estimate structural econometric models. These data can of course be used like other survey data for this purpose. But the experiment should be thought of in the first instance as a way to obtain accurate estimates of the effects of particular programs. Structural models with parameters estimated on survey data could also be used to make such estimates. (Presumably this would be done to a considerable extent before an experiment were undertaken, if for no other reason than to help to inform the choice of experimental treatment or treatments.) In this sense, the experiment could be thought of as checking the accuracy of predictions based on analysis of survey data. That is, the experiments should be designed to provide a selected number of points "on" the response surface, defined for example by tax rate and guarantee levels. It is rather straightforward to check for example the degree to which alternative structural models fit these "known" points on the response surface. In short, an experiment should be used to avoid the inherent limitations of structural models in providing accurate estimates of the effects of specified programs. The major advantage of experiments should not be lost sight of in an effort to estimate models that will predict the result of any plan. A lack of confidence in such estimates is the motivation for the experiments. To use the experimental data only to provide more such estimates, or to set up the experiments in such a way that only such estimates are possible, is to travel to Rome to buy canned peas.

5.3 Endogenous Sampling and Stratification

As discussed in the introduction above, a major feature of classical experimental design is that it leads to a simple analysis-of-variance (ANOVA) model that minimizes the number of maintained assumptions implicit in the interpretation of parameter estimates. That is, the analysis is "model free" in two important aspects: (1) In the simplest cases a main-effects ANOVA specification is adequate. Questions about the need to include, for example, further right-hand variables—as in much of econometric and statistical analysis—do not arise. Correct randomization assures that disturbance terms have expectation equal to zero. Also, questions of functional form are absent because each experimental-treatment effect is measured by a parameter. (2) Distributional assumptions are kept to a minimum in estimation. While distributions of test statistics are certainly used in inference, asymptotic theory may provide a reasonably good approximation in many cases. Classical experimental design together with ANOVA offer the opportunity either to eliminate or to decrease greatly a major problem that arises in econometric studies based on observational, i.e., nonexperimental data.[1]

Yet in many of the social experiments the classical approach has not been followed. Given a limited experimental budget and a "target

---

1. We do not mean to disregard important problems that still remain. Questions of interactions may still arise, for example.

population," the designers of the experiments, in concentrating sample selection on that part of the population most likely to be affected by the treatment policy, induced endogenous sample selection and treatment assignment. The presence of endogenous sampling complicates the analysis of the experiment greatly and thus limits our ability to treat other problems that arise, in particular, sample self-selection and attrition. And possibly as important, it typically forces the analyst to maintain distributional assumptions about the random variables under study. These distributional assumptions are not innocuous even in large samples. Significant empirical departures from these assumptions may lead to large biases in estimation of experimental effects (e.g., Goldberger 1980). Most importantly, if the endogenous sampling is ignored in the analysis, extremely large biases may result in estimated experimental effects. In this section we will present three examples of endogenous sampling as well as techniques developed to eliminate the problems that it creates. We then propose an alternative approach that attempts to choose selectively from the target population without inducing endogenous sample selection.

The problems associated with endogenous sampling occur because a pre-experimental endogenous variable is used in sample selection and in treatment assignment. The effect on the estimated treatment effect arises because of correlation between unmeasured determinants of the response variable in the experimental and pre-experimental periods. These time effects have often been ignored in the experimental designs.[2] We shall illustrate the problem within the context of an ANOVA framework, which when generalized to a random-effects specification, allows for serial correlation. We consider a single-period experiment with one period of pre-experimental data.

(5)
$$Y_{it} = u_t + \beta_j T_{jt} + \mu_i + \eta_{it};$$

$$t = 1,2; \ j = 1, \ldots, J.$$

$$E\mu_i = E\eta_{it} = 0; \ V(\mu_i) = \sigma_\mu^2;$$

$$V(\eta_{it}) = \sigma_\eta^2; \ \rho = \frac{\sigma_\mu^2}{\sigma_\eta^2 + \sigma_\mu^2}.$$

We have decomposed the disturbance term into a permanent individual component μ_i, and another component η_{it} assumed independent across time periods.[3] The indicator variable T_{jt} is 1 if the individual is receiving the experimental treatment j in period t and zero otherwise. Time effects are absorbed into the constant terms u_t. The importance of the individual

---

2. For a further discussion of time effects in experimental design, see Hausman (1980).
3. Of course with only two periods, this assumption is only a normalization.

component μ_i is given by the correlation ρ between the disturbance term in the two time periods. Such correlations often exceed .5 in econometric studies.

Suppose that the expected cost of an experimental treatment varies across individuals and treatments as a function of Y_{i1}. Designers of experiments have for this reason used Y_{i1} in sample selection and in treatment assignment. Because of the presence of μ_i in both periods, the endogenous sampling and treatment assignment based on pre-experimental data carries over to the experimental period as well. A simple example will help to make the point clear. Suppose we have two experimental treatments called generous (G) and not-generous (NG). The G treatment is expected to cost more for "high Y" individuals because of an expected percentage reduction in work effort. Therefore, the designer forms two groups of individuals based on Y_{i1}. Low Y_1 individuals are assigned either the G plan or control status; the high Y_1 individuals receive either the NG plan or control status. But when we use ANOVA to analyze the experimental results we see from equation (5) that $E(\mu_i \mid T_{jt}) \neq 0$. Thus, our estimates are biased for the population since we have not accounted for the presence of individual effects that persist over time. Since it is unlikely in most economic and social experiments that ρ is near zero, substantial biases may arise from endogenous sample designs.

We shall now consider three experimental designs in which endogenous sampling was used. In the New Jersey Negative Income Tax Experiment any individual whose pre-experimental income exceeded 1.5 times the government-set poverty limit was excluded from the sample. This sample truncation was used because the major effect of an NIT program was expected to be seen on low-income individuals and families. A simple rule was thus used to make the sample resemble the target population. Suppose a model like equation (5) is used to analyze the effects on hours worked. Suppose also that individuals' earnings are low in period one either because they have low μ or because η_1 is negative even though μ is positive. Low μ people with positive η_1 have been excluded from the sample. The analyst must maintain the assumption that the effect on hours worked for the sample combination of low μ and high μ people (with negative η) will represent the total population response. This assumption appears unlikely to hold true because we might well expect the behavioral response to differ among the low μ and high μ people. In other words, if we were to change the sample truncation point from 1.5 times the poverty limit to another level, the estimated experimental effect would be likely to change as well.

In the Connecticut Time-of-Day Electricity Demonstration (TOD; 1977), the sample was grouped into quintiles on the basis of electricity usage in the year prior to the demonstration. Then households in the upper quintiles were disproportionately sampled since the electric utility correctly thought that their reaction to the introduction of time-of-day electricity rates would have the largest effects on system revenues.

In the Seattle-Denver Income Maintenance Experiment, (SIME-DIME), the Conlisk-Watts framework was used for treatment assignment. It allowed the expected cost of an experimental treatment c_j for treatment T_j to vary with "normal income," which in practice was closely related to pre-experimental income. Consider the Conlisk-Watts framework in the regression form.

(6) $Y = X\beta + \epsilon$;

$X_j = (0, \ldots, 0, 1, 0, \ldots, 0); j = 1, J$;

$E\epsilon = 0$;

$V(\epsilon) = \sigma^2 I$.

Here X_1 denotes the control observations and $j = 2, \ldots,$ J denotes the $J - 1$ experimental treatments and normal-income classifications. The Conlisk-Watts design uses as an optimization criterion the minimization of the variance of linear function $P\hat{\beta}$ of the estimated coefficients, subject to a budget constraint. We want to choose $n_j, j = 1,$ J (the number of individuals in a given row of the design matrix) in an optimal manner. Let $D = P'P$. The complete problem is an integer programming problem with a convex objective function subject to linear constraints.

(7) $\min q(n_1, \ldots, n_m) = \text{tr}[D \sum_{j=1}^{J} n_j x_j' x_j)^{-1}]$,

$n_j \geq 0$ for all j .

For large $N = \Sigma n_j$ a suitable approximation is to treat the n_j as continuous and to round off the results to the nearest integer. To estimate the experimental effects in each class via the contrasts, $\hat{\beta}_j - \hat{\beta}_1$, the appropriate P matrix is an $(m - 1) \times m$ matrix with the first column -1s and each of the remaining columns all zeroes and a single 1. Thus $P_j = [-1, 0, \ldots,$ $0, 1, \ldots, 0]$. We solve equation (7) to find

(8) $n_1 = C \dfrac{((J - 1)/c_1)^{\frac{1}{2}}}{E}$,

$n_j = C(c_j^{-\frac{1}{2}} E^{-1})$,

$E = [(J - 1)c_1 + \sum_{j=2}^{J} c_j]^{\frac{1}{2}}$.

The optimal design thus increases the probability of inclusion in the sample for low c_j individuals. But since c_j is a function of pre-experimental income, we see that $E(\mu_i | X_j) \neq 0$ which will lead to bias in the estimation of experimental effects.

We do not want to give the erroneous impression that endogenous sampling destroys the possibility of experimental analysis. In fact, we have written several papers addressing the problem (Hausman and Wise 1976, 1977, 1980, 1981). And endogenous sampling can reduce the cost of an experiment considerably.[4] But we emphasize the model functional form and distributional assumptions that endogenous sampling requires.

To illustrate the nature of these assumptions, we consider again the three examples, and for each we discuss possible model specifications.

1. *Sample truncation*. In Hausman and Wise 1976 and 1977, models to correct for sample truncation are developed. The approach taken assumes that the earnings conditional on personal attributes are distributed log normal. A two-period model is necessary since sample truncation was performed on the pre-experimental data. But since the correlation of the disturbances across years (ρ in equation 5) is not zero, truncation on pre-experimental data will affect the analysis of the experimental results. Therefore, we define a model of the form

$$(9) \qquad y_{it} = Z_{it}\gamma + \epsilon_{it}; \quad t = 1, 2; \quad \epsilon_{it} = \mu_i + \eta_{it};$$

with the usual stochastic assumptions. We assume that $f(y_{i1}, y_{i2} | Z_{i1}, Z_{i2})$ is bivariate normal. The Z_{it}s include experimental treatments as well as individual characteristics. Then the likelihood can be written

$$(10) \qquad L = \prod_{i=1}^{N} f(y_{1i}, y_{2i}) = \prod_{i=1}^{N} \frac{\widetilde{\phi}(y_{1i}, y_{2i})}{\Phi[(L_i - Z_{1i}\beta)/\sigma]},$$

where $\widetilde{\phi}$ is the bivariate normal density and Φ is the univariate normal distribution. For the New Jersey NIT experiment we estimate $\hat{\rho} = .85$, which demonstrates the potential importance of correcting for truncation. The log normal is a convenient distribution that leads to a likelihood function that is quite tractable using modern computers. Still, if the choice of log normal is not correct, it represents a specification error.

An even more difficult problem arises if we want to analyze hours rather than earnings. Since truncation takes place on earnings we must analyze hours and wages jointly, and the four-equation model that results leads to a likelihood function considerably more complicated than equation (10) (Hausman and Wise 1976, 432). Furthermore, given the identity between earnings and the product of wages and hours, we must now assume that both wages and hours are distributed log normally. Almost no other assumptions lead to a tractable likelihood function, even though

---

4. Manski and McFadden (1981) consider a similar question in attempting to minimize sample-survey costs in a discrete-choice-model framework.

some evidence exists that hours might be better represented by a conditional normal distribution.[5] And lastly, because of the complications induced in the likelihood function by truncation, our ability to handle other problems, like sample attrition or taxation, are limited. Thus the analysis has been greatly complicated by what seems to be a reasonable design criterion, concentrating on the target population of the proposed policy.

2. *Stratification on the endogenous variables.* To keep the analysis simple we here assume that income has been grouped into two intervals, even though in the Gary NIT experiment as well as the Connecticut TOD demonstration quintiles were used. Assume that below some level L, an unknown proportion of a random sample of the population is sampled, P_1, and above L, a proportion P_2.[6] Then the density function is

(11)
$$h(y) = \begin{cases} \dfrac{P_1 \cdot f(y)}{P_1 \cdot Pr[y \leq L] + P_2 \cdot Pr[y > L]}, & \text{if } y \leq L \\[3mm] \dfrac{P_2 \cdot f(y)}{P_1 \cdot Pr[y \leq L] + P_2 \cdot Pr[y > L]}, & \text{if } y > L, \end{cases}$$

where f is the normal-density function $N(Z\beta, \sigma^2)$. Only the ratio $P = P_2/P_1$ can be identified. Therefore, we divide through the expressions in equation (11) by P_1. Again using normality assumption for y, and assuming N_1 persons with $y \leq L$ and N_2 with $y > 1$, the log likelihood function is

(12)
$$L = \sum_{i=1}^{N_1} \ln f(y_i) - \sum_{i=1}^{N_1} \ln [\Phi_i + P(1 - \Phi_i)]$$

$$+ \sum_{i=1}^{N_2} \ln P + \sum_{i=1}^{N_2} \ln f(y_i) - \sum_{i=1}^{N_2} \ln [\Phi_i + P(1 - \Phi_i)]$$

$$= \sum_{i=1}^{N} \ln f(y_i) - \sum_{i=1}^{N} \ln (P + (1 - P)\Phi_i) + N_2 \ln P,$$

where $\Phi_1 = \Phi [(L - Z_i\beta)]$. Again, a maintained distributional assumption is necessary and a rather complicated maximum-likelihood problem is presented. Furthermore, when we want to do a two-period analysis or consider other problems, our ability to do so is limited by the rapidly increasing complications induced by the stratification on the endogenous variable.

3. *Treatment assignment using an endogenous variable.* Our last example is the SIME-DIME NIT experimental design. Here seven income

---

5. The opportunity to do any type of nonparametric analysis is severely limited here because we do not have observations on the part of the sample that was truncated.

6. If P_1 and P_2 are known, the analysis can be simplified somewhat. See Hausman and Wise (1981).

intervals, called "E-levels," were used to define rows in the Conlisk-Watts design framework of equations (6)–(18). The costs c_j were then derived as a function of E-level. The expected cost of a treatment was presumed to rise with E-level because it was assumed that tax revenues would decline and that NIT payments would increase. The result was that no one in the highest E-level interval was assigned treatment status; all were assigned to be controls where, of course, the cost does not grow with E-level. Furthermore, in general, persons with higher E-levels were more likely to be assigned to experimental treatments with more generous support levels. Thus, treatment assignment was based on an endogenous variable—pre-experimental income—which was highly correlated with the response variable during the experiment.

Treatment assignment using endogenous variables does not in theory prevent the use of ANOVA in the analysis phase of an experiment. What is needed, however, is an elaborate specification allowing a separate β in equation (5) for each E-level and treatment or control assignment. But in the SIME-DIME experiment, for example, including manpower treatments, there would be $J = 59$ columns in the X matrix. In fact, if full ANOVA were done without deleting higher-order interactions as did the design model, J would exceed 200. Thus even for the comparatively large sample sizes as in the SIME-DIME, we cannot hope to obtain precise estimates of experimental effects. And when other factors such as race and city are added to the analysis, full ANOVA estimation becomes hopeless. Thus we are left with estimating ANOVA specifications with many fewer parameters than the experimental design requires. One approach is to enter E-level as a right-hand-side variable in linear form. But we immediately lose the model-free aspect of ANOVA since correctness of functional form becomes an issue. In fact, a linear specification of E-level is not totally appropriate since it does not remove all correlation between the treatment variable and the stochastic disturbance.

Again, a model of treatment assignment can be constructed, as specified by Hausman and Wise 1980. But since treatment assignment is a zero-one outcome, a probit model (or logit model) is required along with the necessary distributional assumptions. An additional complication arises here because we must specify the partly unknown model of treatment assignment correctly.[7] Thus, both distributional assumptions and functional-form assumptions are required for model estimation. The resulting likelihood function used in estimation is even more complicated than equations (10) and (12). And as emphasized above, additional complications like sample attrition are almost impossible to treat jointly with the sample-assignment issues.

---

7. The unknown aspect arises because there does not exist a straightforward model for assignment of E-level. Part of the assignment procedure involved qualitative judgments.

A simple solution exists to these design and analysis problems. Randomize over pre-experimental income. Then problems of endogenous assignment or stratification do not occur, so ANOVA specifications again are appropriate. But in making such a choice, we give up the notion of a target population; so the precision of our analysis for a particular group may decrease, given size and experimental budget. Or to state the problem in an alternative manner, for a given level of precision in estimation, the necessary budget for an experiment might increase substantially.

An alternative approach is to stratify on exogenous variables only and to approximate the goals of endogenous stratification by using predicted values of the endogenous variable.[8]

We shall consider the first example, sample truncation, since the issues can be seen quite clearly. Figure 5.1 represents the density of earnings with a truncation point T.[9] Suppose our aim is to sample people in the area of the distribution marked I. Now instead of using pre-experimental income with its associated problems, consider the use of "exogenous" income stratification, based on income predicted on the basis of exogenous variables, say from the regression equation

(13) $$\hat{Y}_i = Z_i \delta + \epsilon_i,$$

where the prediction is

$$\hat{Y}_i = Z_i \delta = Z_i \delta + Z(Z'Z)^{-1} Z' \epsilon.$$

Note that ϵ_i still enters the last term through the product $Z_i' \epsilon_i$. But for a sample of size N this term is of order $1/N$, so it quite rapidly disappears as the sample becomes large. The variables included in Z_i would be education, training, union membership, age, etc. We could then base truncation, so problems that arise from the individual effect $\mu_i = \epsilon_{it} - \eta_{it}$ being present in both periods no longer occur.

If the covariance between y_i and $\hat{y}_i$ were very high, we would have solved the problem. Then the predicted value would do almost as well as the actual endogenous variable. But for log earnings the R^2 of the regression is around .25; multiple correlation coefficients in the range of .25 to .60 are quite common for many cross-sectional regressions in econometrics. Thus, if we use $\hat{y}_i < F$ as the truncation point, we expect on average to do about 1.2 as well as pure random sampling in selecting $y_i < L$.

While this is an improvement, we might do even better by choosing a point $k < L$ as our sample truncation point. Perhaps a useful approach to

8. This approach was employed in the design of a survey for electricity use in Vermont by Hausman and Trimble (1981).

9. We are assuming a common truncation point, although in the NIT experiment it depended on family size, which partly defines the poverty limit. But we can add varying truncation points to our analysis with no added complications.

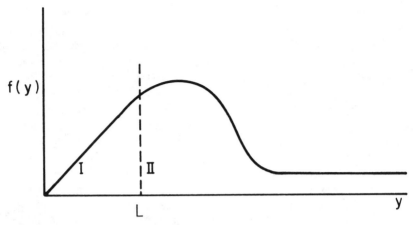

Fig. 5.1   Selection based on an exogenous variable.

the choice of k can be constructed as follows. Assume the benefit to estimation of the experimental effect has expected value of the form $V(y_i) = \beta / (y_i - \bar{y})^2$. That is, we expect to learn little about labor-supply response from low-income or high-income individuals. On the other hand, cost is expected to grow linearly with income $c(y_i) = cy_i$. Suppose we want to solve for the optimum truncation point k, given our knowledge that since we are using predicted income $\hat{y}_i$, the actual $y_i = \hat{y}_i + \epsilon_i$ will differ. The optimization problem is

$$(14) \qquad \max_{k} \beta/(y_i - \bar{y})^2, \quad \text{s.t. } \Sigma cy_1 \leq C, \quad \hat{y}_i = y_i - \epsilon i \leq k.$$

We solve the corresponding expected value problem

$$(15) \qquad \max_{k} L = E(\beta/(\hat{y}_i + \epsilon_i - \bar{y})^2) + \lambda_1 E(C - \Sigma c(\hat{y}_i + \epsilon_i))$$
$$+ \lambda_2(k - \hat{y}_i).$$

The form of the solution can be seen by assuming that the variable has been transformed to make the residuals approximately normal and that we center the data to set $\bar{y} = 0$. Then we choose k to

$$(16) \qquad \max_{k} L' = \beta / \left[\mathrm{var}(\hat{y}_i) + 1 - \frac{\left(\frac{k}{\sigma}\right)\phi\left(\frac{k}{\sigma}\right)}{\Phi\left(\frac{k}{\sigma}\right)} - \left(\frac{\phi\left(\frac{k}{\sigma}\right)}{\Phi\left(\frac{k}{\sigma}\right)}\right)^2 \right]$$

$$+ \lambda\left(C - c\,\Sigma\hat{y}_i - \sigma\left(\frac{\phi\left(\frac{k}{\sigma}\right)}{\Phi\left(\frac{k}{\sigma}\right)}\right)\right),$$

where σ is the standard deviation of the residual distribution. The first-order conditions of equation (16) are straightforward, and the problem can be solved straightforwardly on a computer since the constraint will be satisfied with equality and all the functions are monotonic in k. In this problem the gains over random sampling increase as the variance of the residuals decreases, so y_i and $\hat{y}_i$ are more highly correlated as we would expect. If the correlation becomes very small, we will be quite close to random sampling. But in many cases random sampling may be preferable to endogenous sampling, which as we have attempted to show, can lead to difficult problems in the analysis phase of an experiment.

5.4 Self-Determination of Participation and Attrition

We have addressed in the previous sections a problem largely induced by experimental design, a problem that should be avoided. In this section we will address a major potential problem that cannot in general be avoided but that can be corrected for without undue complication, as long as it is not accompanied by induced endogenous stratification.

Suppose it were possible to select a random sample of families from the population, or from a subset of the population (say with predicted income below a certain level). Of the families selected at random, some, when asked to participate in the experiment, will do so, while others will elect not to participate. Even though a random sample is identified, those who choose to participate may not represent a random sample. In experiments to date no systematic record has been kept of who, when asked, participates and who does not. Thus it has not been possible to identify systematic differences (and in particular unmeasured ones) between those who participate and those who do not; of course, if differences existed, there has been no way to correct for them. In the income-maintenance experiments, for example, a procedure like the following was used. Each experiment was conducted within a single city or a small number of cities. All families within the city or within some section of the city were canvassed to locate those with a few predetermined characteristics. In these experiments, income, race, age of family head, and number of dependents were attributes that determined eligibility. Those who were found to meet the eligibility criteria were asked to enroll in the experiment. Of those who did enroll, some were assigned to a treatment group and others to a control group. It is the enrollment decision that concerns us here.

Suppose that instead of using a procedure like the above, we were to begin with an external source of data on families. The U.S. census is a logical choice. Census data provide information on family income, race, one or two parents in a family, education of family head, number of dependents, etc. Suppose that the known family attributes are represented by a vector of characteristics X. From families surveyed by the Census Bureau, a random sample could be chosen.

For simplicity, suppose the goal is to estimate a single-treatment effect. Ideally we would like to randomly assign part of this randomly selected sample to a control group and others to the treatment group. Then after some time period, we would like to compare controls and experimentals, with Y the outcome of interest, using a simple analysis of variance model of the form

$$(17) \qquad Y_i = \beta_0 + \beta_1 T_i + \epsilon_i,$$

where T_i is an indicator variable with the value 1 for experimentals and 0 for controls.

But suppose not all of the random sample agrees to participate. Suppose participation depends on X and a random disturbance term η in the following way:

$$(18) \qquad P_i = X_i \alpha + \eta_i,$$

where P_i is an unobserved index variable with the property that individual i agrees to participate if $P_i > 0$. If Y_i and P_i are jointly normal with correlation coefficient ρ, and η is normalized to have variance 1, we know that the expected value of Y_i, given that individual i enrolls is given by

$$(19) \qquad E(Y_i \mid P_i > 0) = \beta_0 + \beta_1 T_i + \rho_{\epsilon\eta}\sigma_\epsilon \frac{\phi(X_i\alpha)}{\Phi[X_i\alpha]}.$$

Suppose that β_1 is estimated by least squares using the sample of participants and ignoring the last term in equation (3). Let the inverse Mills ratio $\phi(\cdot)/\Phi[\cdot]$ be represented by M_i. According to standard excluded-variable arguments, if M is correlated with T, the least-squares estimate of β_1 will be biased. As the sample of participants becomes large, the least-squares estimate goes to

$$(20) \qquad \beta_1 + \rho_{MT}\rho_{\epsilon\eta}\rho_\epsilon \frac{\sigma_M}{\sigma_T},$$

where ρ_{MT} is the correlation between M and T. If the treatment indicator T, however, is assigned randomly, then it will be uncorrelated with X and thus with M which is a function of X. Under these simple assumptions, the least-squares estimate of the treatment effect will be consistent, as long as the assignment to control versus treatment groups is random. Each participant could be randomly assigned, or each of those in the census sample could be randomly assigned prior to enrollment, as long as at the time of enrollment, prospective participants did not know their assignment.

But the model as set out above hides by omission a potential major source of self-selection bias. Suppose that if the treatment were given to all persons in the population, the responses would vary among them. It is clear that this is indeed the case (even after controlling for measured family characteristics). It seems plausible that the decision to participate will depend on the potential response. For example, it is often hypothesized that persons whose behavior is most likely to be affected will be most likely to participate, even though they do not know prior to enrollment whether they will be in the treatment or in the control group. This is the essence of the examples given in section 1.2.2.

The idea may be represented by a random-effects model of the form

(21) $$Y_i = \beta_0 + (\beta_1 + b_i)T_i + \epsilon_i = \beta_0 + \beta_1 T_i + b_i T_i + \epsilon_i ,$$

where from the perspective of the analyst, b is random with mean 0. Using (21), the expected value of Y_i among participants is given by

(22) $$E(Y_i \mid P_i > 0) = \beta_0 + \beta_1 T_i + (\rho_{b\eta}\sigma_b T_i + \rho_{\epsilon\eta}\sigma_\epsilon)\frac{\phi(\cdot)}{\Phi[\cdot]}.$$

In this case, it is clear that the least term will be correlated with T_i, and a least-squares estimate of β_1 would be biased.

Joint maximum-likelihood estimation of (18) and (21), however, could be used to obtain a consistent estimate of β_1. The procedure is similar to the one proposed by Hausman and Wise (1979), except that the equations pertain to the response variables and participation, rather than to the response variable and attrition. In this case, there are two possible outcomes: Individual i doesn't participate with probability,

(23) $$1 - \Phi[X_i\alpha], = P_{1i} ,$$

or individual i participates with response Y_i, with likelihood

(24)
$$\Phi\left[\frac{X_i\alpha + \dfrac{\rho_{\eta b}\sigma_b T_i + \rho_{\epsilon\eta}\sigma_\epsilon}{\sigma_b^2 T_i^2 + \sigma_\epsilon^2}\cdot(Y_i - \beta_0 - \beta_1 T)}{\left(1 - \left(\dfrac{\rho_{\eta b}\sigma_b T + \rho_{\epsilon\eta}\sigma_\epsilon}{\sqrt{\sigma_b^2 T_i^2 + \sigma_\epsilon^2}}\right)^2\right)^{1/2}}\right]$$

$$\cdot \frac{1}{\left(\sigma_b^2 T_i^2 + \sigma_\epsilon^2\right)^{1/2}}\cdot\phi\left(\frac{Y_i - \beta_0 - \beta_1 T}{\left(\sigma_b^2 T_i^2 + \sigma_\epsilon^2\right)}\right) = P_{2i} .$$

The likelihood function

(25) $$L = \sum_{i=1}^{N_1} \ln P_{1i} + \sum_{i=1}^{N_2} \ln P_{2i}$$

can easily be maximized to obtain estimates of β along with the other parameters of the model.

The other component of self-selection that seems unavoidable in social experiments is attrition. Some participants will inevitably drop out of the experiment before the treatment response is measured. To take advantage of individual specific characteristics that persist over time, it is advantageous to observe participants for some period of time before the treatment becomes effective. This will lead to four equations of the form

$$(26) \qquad P_i = X_i\alpha + \epsilon_{1i},$$
$$Y_{1i} = X_{1i}\delta + \epsilon_{2i},$$
$$Y_{2i} = X_{2i}\delta + \beta_1 T + \epsilon_{3i},$$
$$A_i = X_i\gamma + \epsilon_{4i},$$

Where Y_1 pertains to the response variable before the treatment period, Y_2 to the response variable during the experimental period, and A is an unobserved indicator variable with the property that individual i leaves the experiment, if $A_i < 0$. This system of equations can also be estimated readily with available maximum-likelihood techniques (see Venti and Wise 1981).

Comment   John Conlisk

Endogenous stratification is the main issue discussed by Hausman and Wise. I have little to say about it because they have said things well. Regarding endogenous stratification that can be avoided, as when negative-tax experimenters stratify on actual pre-experiment earnings rather than on an exogenous earnings-capacity measure, the Hausman and Wise advice is very simple: Don't do it. In my view, the advice is feasible and very important—-perhaps the best message of the conference. Regarding endogenous stratification that cannot be avoided, as when subjects self-select through nonparticipation or attrition, Hausman and Wise describe the applicable statistical techniques.

In addition to analyzing endogenous stratification, Hausman and Wise devote substantial attention to other design issues. This other material is less clear and less well developed. Roughly speaking, Hausman and Wise advocate the simplest kind of classical design—a fully randomized design intended for a one-way analysis of variance (ANOVA). I have a long comment about the randomization advice, a shorter comment about the ANOVA advice, and a short concluding comment.

Randomization

Consider the kind of textbook example associated with a classical ANOVA design. Suppose a large number of planting boxes are to be

John Conlisk is professor of economics, University of California, San Diego.

soiled, seeded, cultivated, harvested, and measured in a uniform manner. Some of the boxes, however, are to be selected at random for application of a chemical whose effect the experimenter wishes to estimate. If we think of the plants in a given box as analogous to a family in a social experiment, what complications to the example would we add to make it more like the social experiment? Here are some possibilities.

Suppose that the plants are at substantial and different stages of maturity when the experiment begins, that the number of plants per box and the sizes of boxes vary, that the soil and other nutritional history varies, that the experimenter is allowed to apply the chemical and measure the effect over only a short duration, that the cost per box varies greatly, and that plant biology leads us to expect interaction between the treatment (the chemical) and the covariates (plant age, box size, and so on). If plants could walk out on the experimenter, we could add self-selection to the list of horrors.

Before the conference, my reading of the Hausman and Wise advice was that, despite the complications just listed, the experimenter should stick to the simple strategy of full randomization—that is, no use should be made of the exogenous covariate information in assigning boxes to treatment. My intuition balked at this notion because it sounded like throwing away information. Why not use the covariates at the design stage, especially covariates expected to interact with the treatment? At the conference, however, I was told that this was a misreading of the Hausman and Wise paper. They did not object to categorizing the boxes into strata, or blocks, according to the exogenous covariates. The advice was merely that there should be full randomization of treatment assignment within a given stratum. This advice, however, leaves me puzzled. If a stratum is defined broadly, so that the covariates have a substantial range within the stratum (especially covariates expected to interact with treatment), my original question remains. Is there no use to be made of these covariates in assigning boxes to treatment? If a stratum is defined narrowly so that important covariates are essentially held fixed within a stratum, then the estimated treatment effect may be so stratum-specific that nothing important can be learned without experimenting at several different strata. In this case, the design advice is thoroughly incomplete without a discussion of strata selection and data pooling.

Whatever the truth about Hausman and Wise's meaning, the issues need clarification. To address the issues more formally, consider a version of Hausman and Wise's equation (3), plus an interaction effect.

(1) $$Y = \beta_1 T(1 + \beta_2 Z)^{-1} + \beta_3 Z + \beta_4 X + \epsilon.$$

Here T is the treatment variable; X and Z are scalar exogenous variables. Consider first the case $\beta_2 = \beta_3 = 0$. Then Z drops out, and the model becomes like the one Hausman and Wise use to make the following case for randomization. For a sizable sample, random assignment of subjects to levels of T leaves T independent of X and ϵ; hence the treatment effect $\delta Y / \delta T = \beta_1$ can be estimated from a simple regression of Y on T. No serious assumptions about X and ϵ need be made; indeed no data on X are needed. X can be viewed as an extraneous nuisance variable whose potential for creating econometric problems is neutralized by randomization.

Now consider the case of $\beta_2 > 0$ and $\beta_4 = 0$. Here X disappears and the exogenous variable to contend with is Z. The treatment effect

$$\delta Y / \delta T = \beta_1 (1 + \beta_2 Z)^{-1}$$

is a function of Z; for a reason given below, $\delta Y / \delta T$ is constructed to go to zero as Z gets large (hence the nonlinearity is β_2). Since $\delta Y / \delta T$ depends on Z, then Z is not simply a nuisance variable. Rather it is a central part of the object of study. It is not surprising that the case for randomization unravels when it is Z rather than X at issue. Random assignment of subjects to treatment levels makes T independent of Z and ϵ, but this independence does not buy much. It does not buy off the need for Z data, nor does it neutralize econometric problems caused by Z. For example, measurement error in Z or correlation of Z with ϵ will, through the algebraic interaction of Z and T, prevent consistent regression estimation of the treatment parameters β_1 and β_2. That is, randomization will not prevent the need for strong assumptions about Z and ϵ.

It is thus important to ask whether the exogenous variables in a social experiment are more like X or more like Z. To be concrete, consider a negative-tax interpretation of equation (1). Suppose the response variable Y is an earnings variable (perhaps in logs); suppose T is a guarantee level (with the negative-tax break-even point fixed and suppressed); and suppose the major exogenous variable is some measure of earnings capacity (perhaps constructed as the predicted value from a regression of pre-experiment earnings on schooling, age, and other exogenous variables). Since we expect the treatment effect to decline toward zero as earnings capacity gets to and beyond the break-even income, earnings capacity acts like Z in the treatment effect

$$\delta Y / \delta T = \beta_1 (1 + \beta_2 Z)^{-1}.$$

That is, earnings capacity is better represented by Z than by X in equation (1). From the viewpoint of economic behavior, the difference is crucial. To omit the interaction between treatment T and earnings capacity Z would be to assume that a negative tax has the same expected influence on a surgeon as on an unskilled laborer. More generally, to omit the interaction would be to assume that an agent's expected response to an economic stimulus is independent of his economic circumstance. Suppose then that Z represents earnings capacity and that X represents some other exogenous variable. It appears to me that all the social experiments involve important exogenous variables that, like Z in equation (1), interact with treatments. Since the potential of Z for creating econometric problems cannot be neutralized by randomization, how should we interpret the Hausman and Wise advice about randomization? There seem to be two cases.

Case 1

Perhaps Hausman and Wise are merely saying that, at a fixed value of Z, one should randomize so as to neutralize the potential nuisances of X and ϵ. That is, define a stratum by a fixed value $Z = Z_0$ (in practice, a narrow range for Z), randomize within the stratum, and estimate the stratum-specific treatment effect

$$(\delta Y / \delta T)_0 = \beta_1 (1 + \beta_2 Z_0)^{-1}$$

by a simple regression of Y on T. If this is the advice, it appears to be perfectly logical, but not very helpful. The hard design problems are in dealing with Z. Is knowledge of the treatment effect at a single Z value enough information to justify the experiment? Probably not. Then how many Z values (how many strata) should be chosen, and what should they be? Will continuity of response across Z values be assumed, as in equation (1), to lay a foundation for data pooling across strata? If so, then the standard sort of assumptions about Z (independence of ϵ and so on) must be made, despite Hausman and Wise's desire to avoid them. If continuity in Z is not assumed, as Hausman and Wise would probably advise, then each stratum is in effect a separate experiment; and the multiplicity of experiments fragments the effective budget and sample for each.

Case 2

Perhaps Hausman and Wise are advising not just randomization at a given Z, but rather randomization across the full range of Z, either in the population or at least up to some sizeable truncation point. Advocacy of such "full" randomization is the way their paper clearly reads to me, despite discussion at the conference. As noted above, however, the independence of T and Z resulting from full randomization will not prevent the need for data on Z or the need for assumptions about Z (such as independence of ϵ). This absence of a positive case for full randomization should be coupled with the presence of a negative case. Let $C(T,Z)$ be the expected cost of one observation at treatment level T for a subject with earnings capacity Z. The form of $C(T,Z)$ may be such that cost efficiency in design leads to a correlation between T and Z. In addition, if a continuous-response function is assumed, as in equation (1), efficient exploitation of the geometric placement of available (T,Z) points may lead to designs with correlation between T and Z.

In summary, Hausman and Wise have argued that proper randomization will lead to simple designs and a much reduced need for econometric structure. Their argument is not convincing, primarily because it neglects interactions between treatments and exogenous variables. Such interactions are typically central to the behavior studied in social experiments. When these interactions, along with cost and geometric considerations, are accounted for, I see no reason to suppose that a good design will be the sort of simple design Hausman and Wise have in mind, nor do I see a useful way to substitute simple rules of thumb (like randomization and ANOVA response functions) for a full-blown, optimal design analysis specific to the context at hand.

Response Functional Form

The issue here is the disagreement between designers who favor some sort of continuous response function and those who favor an ANOVA response function (a separate parameter for every point on the response function considered). In the many discussions I have heard about the response-functional-form issue, I have never heard anyone claim that true response functions are likely to be other than continuous and fairly smooth. For example, Hausman and Wise remark in the paper that they are willing to estimate unknown points on a response surface by linear interpolation between known points. People's reluctance to impose continuity of response seems to be based on the fear that the only way to do it is to make a commitment to some specific functional form, and thus to risk an inaccurate outcome if the specific functional form is wrong.

This reasoning, in my opinion, is incorrect. It is possible to impose continuity and a degree of smoothness in a way that is robust to a great variety of specific functional forms (see Conlisk 1973). Handled properly, continuity of response is not to be thought of as an assumption in the same league with, say, normality of residuals. Residual normality is a very strong assumption which nearly everyone would have doubts about; it is understandable that Hausman and Wise wish to avoid a normality assumption when they can. Response continuity, however, is a relatively weak assumption which everyone believes in; it is not so understandable why Hausman and Wise wish to avoid it. The advantage of a response-continuity assumption is greater design efficiency. If an optimal design model is "told" that response information gathered at one design point is partially transferable to adjacent design points, then the model can pick and choose among design points and can thereby get more out of the given design budget.

In the design phase of the New Jersey experiment, there was a disagreement between the Mathematica group, which favored an ANOVA response function, and the University of Wisconsin group, which favored response-continuity assumptions. On this issue, Hausman and Wise are a curious cross, having the Mathematica assumptions and the Wisconsin conclusions.

The New Jersey design involved nine combinations of negative-tax parameters at each of three earnings-capacity levels—a total of twenty-seven treatments. Under the response-continuity assumptions favored by the Wisconsin group, the optimal design model (used by both groups) led to a concentration of observations at many fewer than twenty-seven treatments. The design model in effect advised the designers to observe the response at a few well-chosen treatments and to infer the response at other treatments by fitting a response function. Under the ANOVA assumption favored by the Mathematica group, the design model led to a more even distribution of observations across all twenty-seven treatments; all treatments have to be handled separately when there is no response continuity.

The Hausman and Wise advice might be paraphrased as follows: By all means, assume an ANOVA response function (the Mathematica assumption); continuity of response would be uncomfortably restrictive. However, to promote precision, keep the number of treatments small; one can always interpolate to other treatments at the experiment's end (the Wisconsin conclusion). Is this more like the Mathematica position or more like the Wisconsin position? The answer, I think, is unclear until Hausman and Wise complete their advice by describing how they would choose their small number of treatments. If their choice depended in part on the ultimate interpolations that data users would surely make, then I would view them as assuming response continuity without admitting it. If their choice ignored this ultimate use of the data, I would wonder why.

Conclusion

The Hausman and Wise analysis of endogenous stratification is well grounded in formal models presented in this paper and in their other papers. The major piece of design advice, to avoid endogenous stratification when possible, is persuasive and important.

The remaining design advice, in my opinion, is not well grounded in formal models; the arguments strike me as overly casual. Examples: The advice to randomize and the simple model to support that advice are of little use until the central issue of treatment–covariate interaction is formally handled. The advice to avoid restrictive assumptions is of little use without a robustness analysis to help distinguish weak from strong assumptions. The advice to keep the number of treatments reasonably small is of little use without a model, involving a cost constraint, that defines reasonable smallness. Explicit in the paper's subtitle ("Cost versus Ease of Analysis") and implicit in much of the discussion are trade-offs forced by the need to limit costs; but no formal model of the trade-offs is presented. The advice to avoid response-continuity assumptions, but to interpolate at the experiment's end, has a flavor of self-contradiction that calls for a design model to sort out the logic. A final example: Having emphasized that nonparticipation and attrition will create a problem in the data analysis, Hausman and Wise argue that this problem is an additional reason to stick to a simple classical design. But why should a particular problem in the data argue for a design developed in contexts not involving that problem? What is needed is an extension of design theory to handle nonparticipation and attrition in an explicit way.

Comment

Figure 5.1 describes the process of social experimentation as a series of transitions. First, the population is screened to form a subject pool. Some subjects are rejected because they fail to meet the screening criteria; others are accepted but balk and refuse to participate. Second, there may be a period of pre-experimental observation which results in some subjects being rejected and others dropping out. The retained subjects form the experimental subject pool. This completes the pre-experimental phase of the study, labeled I on the diagram. Third, the experimental subject pool is assigned treatments. The result, after further attrition, is a set of complete observations. Fourth, the experimental data are used to estimate a model of the effects of treatment. Population statistics may provide information required to compensate for refusals and attritals. Fifth, the estimated model is used to draw policy conclusions. Population statistics may be useful for correcting or augmenting statistics for the set of complete experimental observations.

Associated with the transitions in this diagram are probabilities conditioned on previous events. The likelihood of complete observations is a product of these probabilities. The analyst maintains hypotheses that place these probabilities in suitable parametric families. Then the model can be estimated by the method of maximum likelihood or the method of moments.

Design decisions are the choice of *sample frame*, which determines screening probabilities, and the choice of *experimental design*, which determines the conditional distribution of treatments. Factors in the design decision are (1) cost, (2) technical or political feasibility, and (3) the simplicity and precision of the statistical model. Given an objective function of these factors, one can in principle chose an optimal design.

Hausman and Wise have drawn four main conclusions on the design of social experiments. First, it is desirable to analyze the effects of treatments with a simple ANOVA model embodying a minimum of structural

Daniel L. McFadden is professor of economics, Massachusetts Institute of Technology.

assumptions. Second, employment of an ANOVA requires an exogenous sample frame and random treatment assignment. Third, if cost constraints or technical/political constraints make a random sample frame infeasible, then exogenous stratification on predicted endogenous variables is preferable to endogenous stratification. Fourth, the problems of balking and attrition can be handled by straightforward methods for random designs, but are greatly complicated by endogenous designs. I will comment on each of these conclusions in turn.

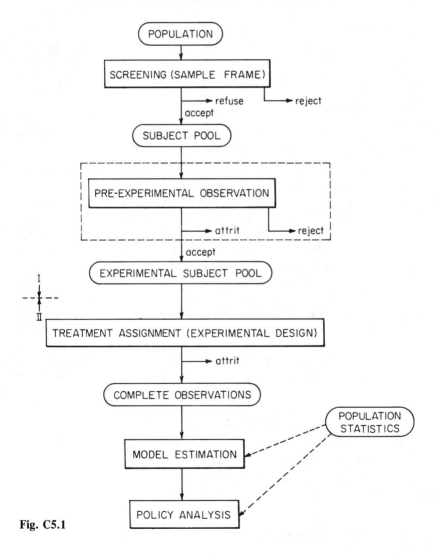

SOCIAL EXPERIMERIMENTAL DESIGN

Fig. C5.1

An ANOVA Model Is Desirable

I heartily endorse the criterion of designing experiments so that a simple, direct, robust statistical model like ANOVA can be used. The authors go on to argue that policy questions can be answered best by measuring the effects of a few treatments precisely and using simple linear interpolation between treatments. There are several objections to this view. First, some cases exist where policy is clearly focused on the response surface rather than on specific treatments—an example is the interest in cross-price elasticities in electric time-of-day pricing experiments. ANOVA with linear interpolation can be viewed as one way of fitting a response surface. Another way is higher-order interpolation, or splines. A third way is a traditional structural model, with maintained structural hypotheses providing the smoothing. What is best in this range depends on the application. A final comment concerns the authors' concentration on first-order treatment effects: Second-order interactions of treatments with concomitant variables such as age and education may also be of strong policy interest—economy may require some structural hypotheses in specifying these interactions.

ANOVA Models Require an Exogenous Sample Frame and Random Treatment Assignment

Hausman and Wise do not distinguish carefully the screening phase of an experiment from the treatment-assignment phase. When this distinction is made, it is clear that the key to the use of the ANOVA model is random treatment assignment, conditioned on the experimental subject pool. This is true no matter what sample frame is used to obtain the experimental subject pool. Random treatment assignment creates a "cordon sanitaire" which isolates the effects of endogenous sampling, balks, and pre-experimental attrition.

This observation has several important implications. First, the value of random treatment assignment should be emphasized. This method permits estimation of treatment and interaction effects by simple ANOVA or COVA methods with minimal structural assumptions and isolates sample biases introduced by endogenous sampling, balks, and attrition.

Second, with random treatment assignment, there is no need to require exogenous sampling. Then endogenous sampling may be a useful tool for reducing experiment cost and meeting technical and political constraints. One loses only simple consistent estimators of main and concomitant variable effects, which are unlikely to be important for policy analysis. (See note at end of "Comment.")

Exogenous Stratification on Predicted Endogenous Variables Is Preferable to Endogenous Stratification

Ceteris paribus, exogenous stratification leads to simpler and more precise estimators than endogenous stratification and is the method of choice. The Hausman-Wise suggestion of using an exogenous surrogate for endogenous sampling is a good one. There are two caveats. First, the cost economies from endogenous stratification may not be obtainable using a surrogate. For example, in a study of locational choice, the primary economies in sampling come from actual geographical stratification. Even a good surrogate for actual location requires a different, more costly, method of contacting subjects.

Second, the whole issue of exogenous versus endogenous stratification becomes blurred when the experiment is used for different policy purposes. For example, exogenous stratification, by location in an experiment on the effects of housing subsidies on consumption patterns, becomes endogenous when location decisions are a subject of policy questions.

Problems of Balking and Attrition Have
Straightforward Solutions for Random Sample Frames,
but Are Greatly Complicated by Endogenous Designs

The above discussion emphasizes that random treatment assignment isolates biases introduced by balking and attrition in the pre-experimental phase. This simplification is both substantial and desirable. It does not require an exogenous sample frame.

Even with random treatment assignment, attrition in the experimental phase can introduce bias, due to $E(T\epsilon \mid$ complete observation$) \neq 0$. With maintained structural hypotheses, this bias can be corrected by maximum-likelihood methods of the sort outlined by Hausman and Wise. Alternative methods are to estimate

$$Y = \mu + T\alpha + (T \times X)\gamma$$
$$+ X\beta + E(\epsilon \mid \text{complete observation}) + \eta$$

by NLLS or a multi-step Amemiya-Heckman procedure, or to introduce regressors spanning $E(\epsilon \mid$ complete observation$)$. All these methods tend to be distribution-specific, with the last method being least so. If the sample frame is endogenous or there are pre-experimental balks or attrition, then the conditional distribution of ϵ will be more complex and will be influenced by the structure of these effects, as the authors claim. The difference is quantitative, but not qualitative, in the complexity of model specification and estimation. Since pre-experimental balks or attrition force this problem even for exogenous sample frames, I do not consider this a strong argument against endogenous sampling.

Balking and attrition are potential sources of severe bias in social experiments and require careful treatment. It is worthwhile to attempt to correct these biases, even at the cost of additional structural hypotheses and the loss of simple ANOVA methods. I believe the focus of further research on social experimental methodology should be on robust methods for correcting self-selection biases.

Note

COVA Model: $Y = \mu + T\alpha + X\beta + (T \otimes X)\gamma + \epsilon$.

T = Treatment-dummy vector
X = Commitment variables
$T \otimes X$ = Second-order interactions
μ = Main effect
α = Treatment effects
β = Concomitant variable effects
γ = Interaction effects

Endogenous sample frame and/or endogenous refusal or attrition $=> E(\epsilon \mid X$, experimental sample pool) $\neq 0$.

Random treatment assignment $=> E(T \mid X, \epsilon) = 0$.

RESULTS:

1. Random treatment assignment $=>$ treatment and interaction effects can be estimated consistently from the regression $Y = \mu + T\alpha + (T \otimes X)\gamma + \eta$, or treatment effects alone from the regression $Y = \mu + T\alpha + \eta$.

2. Exogenous determination of the experimental sample pool, i.e., $E(\epsilon \mid X$, experimental sample pool) $= 0$, and exogenous treatment assignment $=>$ treatment, concomitant variable, and interaction effects can be estimated consistently from the regression $Y = \mu + T\alpha + X\beta + (T \otimes X)\gamma + \epsilon$.

References

Conlisk, John. 1973. Choice of response functional form in designing subsidy experiments. *Econometrica* 41: 643–56.

Goldberger, Arthur. 1980. Abnormal selection. University of Wisconsin. Mimeo.

Hausman, Jerry A. 1980. The effects of time in economic experiments. Presented at the World Econometrics Society conference, Aix-en-Provence.

Hausman, Jerry A., and J. Trimble. 1981. Sample design consideration for the Vermont TOD use survey. *Journal of Public Use Data* 9.

Hausman, Jerry A., and David A. Wise. 1981. Stratification on endogenous variables and estimation: The Gary income maintenance experiment. In *Structural analysis of discrete data: With econometric applications*, ed. Charles Manski and Daniel McFadden. Cambridge: MIT Press.

———. 1980. Earnings effects, sample selection, and treatment assignment in the Seattle-Denver income maintenance experiment. Working paper.

———. 1979. Attrition bias in experimental and panel data: The Gary income maintenance experiment. *Econometrica* 47: 455–73.

————. 1977. Social experimentation, truncated distributions, and efficient estimation. *Econometrica* 45: 319–39.

————. 1976. The evaluation of results from truncated samples: The New Jersey negative income tax experiment. *Annals of Economic and Social Measurement* 5: 421–45.

Manski, Charles, and Daniel McFadden. 1981. Alternative estimators and sample designs for discrete choice analysis. In *Structural analysis of discrete data: With econometric applications. See* Hausman and Wise 1981.

Meier, Paul. 1978. The biggest public experiment ever: The trial of the Salk poliomyelitis vaccine. In *Statistics: A guide to the unknown,* ed. Judith M. Tanur, et al, 2d ed. San Francisco: Holden-Day.

Venti, Steven F., and David A. Wise. 1982. Moving and housing expenditure: Transaction costs and disequilibrium. NBER Working Paper no. 735.

————. 1981. Individual attributes and self-selection of higher education: College attendance versus college completion. *Journal of Public Economics,* forthcoming. (Also Test scores and self-selection, NBER Working Paper no. 709.)

6   Toward Evaluating the Cost-Effectiveness of Medical and Social Experiments

Frederick Mosteller
Milton C. Weinstein

6.1 Introduction

6.1.1 Why Evaluate Medical Experiments?

Although the life expectancy of the U.S. population seems finally to be lengthening, after a prolonged period during which not much improvement was seen (U.S. Department of Health and Human Services 1980), the nation has been increasingly concerned about costs of health care (Fuchs 1974; Hiatt 1975). One possible response to this concern is an accelerated strategy for evaluating the efficacy of medical practices, with the hope that identifying those practices that are not efficacious will lead to their abandonment and, therefore, to substantial savings in health care resources (Cochrane 1972). Undeniably, some medical practices, though costly, may not be efficacious; others may never have had their efficacy evaluated. Often-cited examples are tonsillectomy and adenoidectomy—procedures whose appropriateness has raised doubts for decades, yet only recently has rigorous evaluation of their benefits begun. The Office of Technology Assessment reviewed a substantial number of diagnostic, preventive, and therapeutic practices in several areas of medicine and found that few had been adequately evaluated (U.S. Congress, Office of Technology Assessment 1978).

Frederick Mosteller is professor of mathematical statistics and Milton C. Weinstein is professor of policy and decision sciences, Harvard School of Public Health.

The authors wish to thank John Bailar, Leon Eisenberg, Rashi Fein, Howard Frazier, Alexander Leaf, and Marc Roberts for their comments and suggestions. They are especially indebted to David Freedman, Jay Kadane, and the other participants at the NBER Conference on Social Experimentation for their thoughtful criticism.

This research was supported in part by a grant from the Robert Wood Johnson Foundation to the Center for the Analysis of Health Practices and by National Science Foundation grant SES–75–15702.

An alternative response to the cost problem acknowledges that information on efficacy will not eliminate the need to face trade-offs between increasing incremental costs and diminishing incremental benefits. Given what we know about the benefits offered by available medical technologies, we expect a continuum from more cost-effective to less cost-effective; the more we are willing to spend, the more health we can purchase albeit at increasing incremental costs per unit of benefit. If we want to control costs without sacrificing health benefits, then we must learn how to assess the cost-effectiveness of medical practices and use this information to help us substitute more for less cost-effective practices. Examples of technologies for which proof of efficacy may not be the central issue, but for which cost-effectiveness is, include heart transplants, intensive care for the terminally ill, and possibly artificial implantable organs in the future. Moreover, information on efficacy will not resolve the highly individual and subjective judgments about the value of symptom relief or other aspects of improved quality of life.

These two responses to the health-cost problem are not mutually exclusive, although they lead to different emphases. While we concentrate on evaluation of efficacy as one approach to improving the public health and/or controlling costs, we acknowledge—and, indeed, seek to elucidate—some of the limitations of evaluation of efficacy in the health care system.

Evaluation has its own costs, and so we need to consider how much different kinds of evaluation are worth and what their benefits may be. The long-run goal of the research that we outline here would be to develop and demonstrate a methodology for assessing these benefits and costs.

To oversimplify for a moment, we can identify two possible scenarios that result from evaluating efficacy. In the first, a therapy or diagnostic method that proved ineffective (or, at least, cost-ineffective) would be dropped by the profession, and the money saved would reduce the national medical budget without substantially impairing health. In the second scenario, a procedure is proved effective, leading to more widespread use and the resultant health benefits. We have examples of both scenarios: gastric freezing, for the first, and antihypertensive medications, for the second. We return to these examples below.

Students of policy will recognize both of these scenarios as idealized and unrealistic. Technological changes and changes in practice are ordinarily slow, except in crisis situations. For the first scenario, funds not used for one purpose are quickly and smoothly diverted to other uses, possibly ones that compensate for an abandoned procedure. Advocates of a procedure let go slowly and use ostensibly (and sometimes legitimate) scientific arguments to cast doubt on the validity of the evaluation. For the second scenario, practitioners may be slow to adopt new procedures, even if proven efficacious, unless they perceive the benefits to be immediate and attributable to the intervention (a general obstacle to adopting preventive medical practices).

While we may doubt instant abandonment of procedures, immediate reduction in expenditures, or universal adoption of newly validated practices, we can hope that identifying better procedures will improve the use of medical resources. Improvement may be accomplished by increasing the use of underutilized or innovative practices or programs, by finding more cost-effective or less risky ways to administer care, by weeding out useless or harmful procedures, or merely by speeding up the process that grades procedures as better or worse.

Studies of the effectiveness of evaluations or of the diffusion of medical technology make clear that attempts to evaluate evaluations have a rocky road. For example, the innovation of gastric freezing for treating gastric ulcers was abandoned after substantial evaluations (Miao 1977), but perhaps the procedure was already out of style before the strongest trial had been completed (Fineberg 1976). If the latter was the case, then weaker studies may have had a substantial effect on the total process of introduction, use, and abandonment. At the same time, we know that some techniques such as bleeding, now believed to have no merit, lingered for centuries without evaluation. Consequently, we can afford to approach with modesty a study that aims to develop a basis for evaluating the benefits, risks, and costs of various methods of appraising effectiveness. It is not that we feel the effort unimportant, but that the path has new thickets that replace the old ones as fast as they are cleared.

Although we recognize the difficulty of the task, we are reminded of the need for some rational basis for allocating resources to clinical experiments. Budgets for clinical trials at the National Institutes of Health (NIH) are under constant surveillance, and vigilant congressmen will want to know that the resources have been well spent. Administrators of these agencies, facing contracting budgets, must constantly decide in what medical procedures to invest resources for a clinical trial, recognizing that a trial done in one area means a trial not done in another. Can these administrators not only improve their decision rules for internal-budget allocation, but also determine whether additional resources spent on clinical investigations have a greater expected return than resources spent at the margin elsewhere in the health sector? The economist's test of allocative efficiency (equal shadow prices across and within sectors of the budget) has more than a little conceptual appeal in this domain, but the analytical tasks are formidable.

We realize that the conceptual tools needed for such studies will require repeated refinement. Our first few efforts have no hope of being definitive. From our work thus far, we believe that we cannot get useful handles on this program until we have tried to evaluate a few situations.

We find the candidates extremely varied in their form and background information. Therefore it may be valuable to outline our beginning thoughts and what we foresee as difficulties, in anticipation that criticism will help us streamline and direct a long-term effort or that, informed by the evaluations of our peers, we may even be encouraged to abandon it.

6.1.2   Methods of Evaluation

Initially we defined the problem as that of evaluating the randomized clinical trial (RCT). What is it worth to evaluate a new procedure using RCT? Inevitably the question arises, "Compared with what?" One answer is, "Compared to what would have happened in the absence of an RCT." The possible procedures for comparison are varied: perhaps observational studies of procedures after they are widely practiced, perhaps clinic-based or community-based studies, perhaps systematic efforts using data banks, perhaps NIH consensus-development conferences, perhaps committee appraisals in the Institute of Medicine or the Assembly of the Life Sciences of the National Research Council, or perhaps the review papers in such professional journals as the *British Medical Journal, Journal of the American Medical Association, Lancet,* the *New England Journal of Medicine*, or those devoted to specialties. Whatever the alternatives may be, we do not seem to be able to deal with the RCT, or other methods, in isolation. Obviously this necessity for breadth multiplies our research effort enormously.

Moreover, we need to design the potential study (RCT or otherwise) before evaluating it. (The National Heart, Lung, and Blood Institute uses a planning phase when it prospectively evaluates its clinical trials in which the basic structure of the experimental design is formulated prior to a decision to proceed with full-scale design and implementation [Levy and Sondik 1978].) Since this planning step is also necessary in developing railroads and buildings and weapons systems, we seem to be stuck with it.

Usually we hope that the costs of processing information leading up to a decision, a sort of transaction cost, will be negligible relative to the value of the decision, but if heavy detail is required, such a simplication may be mistaken.

Some general qualitative or operating principles might be developed. For example, we could set up an operating principle that a study involving more than a million people to be followed for twenty years is hopeless. Or, given a choice, that acute-disease studies pay off better than chronic-disease studies, or vice versa. We are not endorsing these as principles, but as illustrations of policies that could emerge from a historical study of medical experiments.

We know that sometimes an RCT is impractical; other times it may not be helpful because other considerations, including value judgments, may overrule it. For example, an RCT helped establish the value of the Salk vaccine against paralytic polio. Today the Salk vaccine (killed virus) is widely used abroad, while Sabin vaccine (live virus) is largely used in the United States. Both vaccines seem to be highly effective, though it is said that the Sabin leads to a few cases of polio in those exposed to recently vaccinated people (Institute of Medicine 1977). The decision as to which to use seems to depend more on an analysis of the policy of enforcement of administration than on efficacy. A major reason for Sabin use in the United States seems to be our perceived inability to administer booster shots. At another level, some public health officials are considering trying to wipe out the virus totally by administering both Salk and Sabin vaccines to all children ("This Week in Review," *New York Times*, 25 January 1981). To consider and evaluate this idea would require evaluation methods different from the RCT. We will need to consider how to choose methods of evaluation for various purposes, taking into account the value of information produced on the acceptability, risk, cost, and effectiveness of the proposed procedures.

6.1.3   How Are Evaluations Used?

The value of an evaluation depends on how its results are translated into changes in practice. Our approach considers three classes of decision-making models in the presence of information from evaluations: the normative, the descriptive, and the regulatory.

In the normative model—the ideal—physicians act in the best interests of society. They process new information rationally. They allocate resources according to the principles of cost-effectiveness analysis, electing the procedures that yield the maximum health benefits obtainable from the health care budget. Although some future reconfiguration of incentives in our health care system (e.g., explicit resource ceilings, increased competition, increased central management) may move us closer to that state of affairs, the normative model of decision making is best thought of as an unattainable ideal; the value of information under this model is the best we can possibly expect.

In the descriptive model, or models, we would attempt to assess what the response of physicians and other decision makers *would be* to the information from a trial. Here we must rely on past experiences and on what economic, sociologic, and psychologic theories tell us. We need to learn how to predict when the response will be rapid, when slow, when nonexistent, and when paradoxical. Perhaps a model can be developed, based on data from past history, that would identify the characteristics of the procedure, the type of study (e.g., randomized versus observational, large versus small, multi-center versus single institution), the nature of the medical specialty, and other variables that can be combined into a prediction of response.

In the regulatory model, we would allow for the possibility of intervention (by government, by insurers, by professional societies) intended to make medical practice more responsive to information. For example, reimbursement might be preconditioned on evidence of efficacy or otherwise linked to the state of information. FDA-type procedures for practices other than drugs and devices would fall into this category. We recognize many problems inherent in such an approach: establishing criteria for efficacy where outcomes are multi-attributed (including survival and many features of the quality of life), establishing criteria for efficacy to apply to a heterogeneous population when the procedure cannot have been tested in all possible subpopulations. We realize that more decentralized approaches to altering incentives for practice in response to information on efficacy—or even to collecting the information itself—may be possible.

6.1.4   Our Objective

We propose, in section 6.2, a general conceptual model for evaluating the cost-effectiveness of clinical trials. This rather formal, oversimplified model will need more specificity when applied. It likely omits important policy or technological features, either because we have not thought of them or because modeling them presents frustrations.

In section 6.3 we discuss the range of medical problems that might be examined and the range of evaluative options that need to be compared. Our major aim in this section, however, is to describe the kinds of data that may be needed in evaluating the cost-effectiveness of a trial. These data requirements follow from the conceptual model in section 6.2 and from the realities that emerge when some of the simplifying assumptions are relaxed. For example, how do the results of the trial link to medical practice? Who are the decision makers, how will they use the data, and where does the burden of proof lie? We consider also the basis for the required probability assessments, the outcome measures that enter into the definition of "effectiveness," and the costs and risks of the clinical studies themselves. In section 6.4, we turn to some illustrative examples, sketched briefly to make more realistic some of the issues discussed. These sketches should not be confused with what a full study would require. Furthermore, we would presumably need collections of studies to help us base the models on empirical results.

Finally, in section 6.5 we discuss some of the kinds of studies that we believe are ultimately required to make this program a reality.

6.2   A Simplified Decision-Analytic Model for Assessing the Cost-Effectiveness of a Trial

6.2.1   Rationale

Let us clarify our thinking by beginning with a grossly oversimplified model based on admittedly unrealistic assumptions. By studying the simplified model and then relaxing the assumptions, we can identify the data requirements for actually carrying out a program of evaluating the cost-effectiveness of a clinical trial.

We should point out that ours is not the first attempt at applying decision-analytic concepts to the problem of evaluating evaluations. Thompson, for example, developed a model for evaluating social-program evaluations and applied it to an evaluation of a U.S.-supported health program in Yugoslavia (Thompson 1975). The author admittedly found it difficult to apply the model quantitatively, but did derive qualitative conclusions about the administrative and bureaucratic determinants of effective evaluation. Stafford developed a similar model in relation to evaluations of manpower training programs (Stafford 1979). In the domain of clinical trials, Levy and Sondik (1978) have presented a conceptual framework for allocating resources in the National Heart, Lung, and Blood Institute, but their approach stops short of a formal assessment of the expected value of information. We want to assess the value of information and the costs, risks, and benefits of obtaining it in a practical, but still quantitative manner.

6.2.2   The Cost-Effectiveness Model of
Health Care Resource Allocation

Economists turn to cost-effectiveness analysis when resources are limited and when the objective is to maximize some nonmonetary output. This technique is well suited to the assessment of medical procedures, where outcomes do not lend themselves to monetary valuation. The cost-effectiveness of a medical procedure may be evaluated as the ratio of its resource cost (in dollars) to some measure of its health effectiveness (Weinstein and Stason 1977; U.S. Congress, Office of Technology Assessment 1980). The units of effectiveness vary across studies, but years-of-life gained is the most commonly used. The rationale for using such a ratio as a basis for resource allocation is as follows. Let us suppose that the health care budget is B. (In the United States in 1980, B was about \$200 billion per year.) Let us further suppose that cost-effectiveness analyses have been performed on each of the N possible uses of health resources, perhaps defined by procedure and target population. (Of course, N is a very large number.) Suppose the expected net-resource burden of procedure i is C_i, and its expected net effectiveness is E_i. Consider only procedures for which C_i and E_i are both positive, (since the optimal decision rule for procedures with one positive and the other negative is obvious, and because doing a procedure with negative C_i and E_i is equivalent to not doing one with positive, but equal, absolute values). Finally, assume that society's objective is to allocate the budget to achieve the maximum total health effect (setting aside, for later reexamination, equity concerns). In other words, consider total effectiveness to be the sum of individual effectiveness values for each procedure, regardless of who benefits. Then the problem reduces to the programming problem

$$\max_{\{\delta_i\}} \sum_{i=1}^{N} \delta_i \, E_i \,,$$

subject to the usual constraints

$$\sum_{i=1}^{N} \delta_i \, C_i \le B, \; 0 \le \delta_i \le 1 \,,$$

the solution to which is to select procedures in increasing order of the ratios C_i/E_i until the budget B is exhausted. The C/E ratio for the "last" procedure chosen, λ, is the reciprocal of the shadow price on the budget constraint; that shadow price, in turn, may be interpreted as the incremental health value (in years of life, say, or quality-adjusted years of life) per additional dollar allocated to health care.

Although the cost-effectiveness model is far from being used as a blueprint for health resource allocation in practice, many studies along these lines have helped clarify the relative efficiency with which health care resources are being, or might be, consumed in various areas of medical technology (U.S. Congress, Office of Technology Assessment 1980; Bunker, Barnes, and Mosteller 1977; Weinstein and Stason 1976).

6.2.3 A Cost-Effectiveness Model for Clinical Trials

In the above formulation, the net costs (C_i) and net effectiveness (E_i) are uncertain. For purposes of today's decision making, it may be reasonable to act on their expected values, but we must not obscure the possibility that new information might alter our perceptions of these variables (in the Bayesian sense of prior-to-posterior revision), thus permitting reallocations of the budget in more health-producing ways. In terms of this same objective function, it is reasonable to ask what is the value of information about the effectiveness of a medical procedure. Moreover, since resources for providing such information (e.g., for clinical trials) are limited, it is reasonable to ask what is the cost-effectiveness of a clinical trial, where the "cost" would be the resource cost of the trial and the "effectiveness" would be the expected increase in the health benefits produced, owing to the information. We would also want to take into account the possibility that, if the utilization of a procedure drops as a consequence of the trial (e.g., if the procedure is found not to be effective), the result might be a freeing up of health care resources for other beneficial purposes.

6.2.4 A Simple Model of Two Treatments

We are wary of constructing an elaborate model that is too restrictive in some fundamental way, so we think it best to start with a simple formal model that can be made more realistic as we gain insights from studying specific examples. For illustrative purposes, this simplified model rests on a strong normative assumption of behavior in response to the information from a trial. If the model were correct, it would yield an upper bound on the value of a trial. More realistic estimates might derive from a model based on predictions of actual decision making in the presence of trial data. Such a model with descriptive assumptions could also be constructed.

Our simple model rests on the following assumptions:
1. An old treatment has been used for some time. It has two possible outcomes: success and failure.
2. A new treatment, about whose efficacy little is known (except from laboratory studies), also may result in either success or failure.
3. Both treatments (a) tend to be used on repeated occasions in individual patients, and (b) make their effects known rather quickly; moreover, (c) we can distinguish "success" from "failure."
4. Let P_O and P_N be the probabilities of success for the old and new treatments, respectively. We start with a joint prior with density $f(P_O, P_N)$. The marginal means are π_O and π_N.
5. The probabilities of success apply to all patients uniformly. This fact is known and unalterable. (This assumption implies that there would be no advantage to stratification.)
6. A controlled experiment with sufficiently large sample sizes can compare the two treatments in such a way that it can be assumed to provide virtually perfect information on P_O and P_N.
7. In the absence of the experiment, the old treatment will continue to be used for T years, in X_t patients in the t_{th} year ($t = 1, \ldots, T$); the experiment lasts T_E years ($T_E < T$). T is known.
8. The unit costs of the treatments are known to be C_O and C_N, for the old and new, respectively.
9. With the experiment, the new treatment will be adopted if and only if its adoption is "cost-effective" in the sense defined in assumption 10 below. Its adoption will be universal, and it will replace the old treatment up to the horizon at year T. (This is the normative assumption of decision making.)
10. The new treatment will be considered cost effective if and only if

$$0 < \frac{C_N - C_O}{P_N - P_O} < \lambda V, \qquad\qquad (C_N > C_O),$$

$$P_N > P_O \text{ or } \frac{C_O - C_N}{P_O - P_N} > \lambda V, \qquad\qquad (C_N \leq C_O),$$

where V is the health benefit per "success" achieved (in years, or quality-adjusted years). (An important special case arises if $\lambda = \infty$; in this case health care resources are effectively unlimited, and the shadow price on the budget constraint $[1/\lambda]$ is zero.)

11. The cost of the experiment is C_E; there are no risks.

12. All decision makers are risk neutral.

Consider first the case in which the new treatment is at least as costly as the old ($C_N \geq C_O$). In that case, the trial has value only if it results in a cost-effective improvement in health outcome. This would occur if

$$P_N > P_O$$

and

$$(C_N - C_O)/V(P_N - P_O) < \lambda.$$

Let

$$\Omega = \{(P_O, P_N): (P_N - P_O) > (C_N - C_O)/V\lambda\},$$

and let

$$X = \sum_{t=t_E}^{T} X_t(1 + r)^{-t},$$

where r is the discount rate. Then the expected health benefit from the experiment equals

$$VX[\iint_\Omega (P_N - P_O)f(P_O, P_N)dP_O dP_N].$$

Note that we are discounting health benefits at the same rate as costs (Weinstein and Stason 1977). The costs consist of two components: the expected induced treatment cost if the new treatment is adopted, which equals

$$X(C_N - C_O)\iint_\Omega f(P_O, P_N)dP_O dP_N,$$

and the cost of the trial, which equals C_E.

One measure of cost-effectiveness would be given by the ratio of total expected costs to expected benefits:

$$\text{Cost-effectiveness} =$$

$$\frac{C_E/X + (C_N - C_O)\iint_\Omega f(P_O, P_N)dP_O dP_N}{V\iint_\Omega (P_N - P_O)f(P_O, P_N)dP_O dP_N}.$$

Now consider the case where the new treatment is less costly than the old ($C_N < C_O$). In that case, the value of experiment might consist of the potential cost savings if the finding is that the new treatment is no less effective than the old.

Let $\Psi = \{(P_O, P_N): P_N \geq P_O\}.$

Then the expected savings consist of

$$S = (C_O - C_N)\iint_\Psi f(P_O, P_N)dP_O dP_N,$$

and the expected health benefits would consist of

$$B = V \iint_{\Psi} (P_N - P_O) f(P_O, P_N) dP_O dP_N.$$

If the expected savings exceed C_E, then the experiment is clearly cost-effective; if not, then a measure of its cost-effectiveness would be given by $(C_E - S)/B$.

If we apply the cost-effectiveness model rigorously in this latter case, the new treatment might be found to be less effective than the old, but not so much less that it would not be cost-effective to adopt it anyway, taking into account its lower cost. This might happen if $P_N < P_O$, but

$$\frac{C_O C_N}{V(P_O - P_N)} > \lambda.$$

Thus, the effect of the experiment might be to make health outcomes a little worse, but in a cost-effective way when compared to other uses of resources. This situation is analogous to one in which an experiment, while proving no benefit, at least gives us reasonable assurance that the procedure in question is cost-ineffective compared to other available health interventions.

We do not want to attach too much importance to the cost-effectiveness ratios themselves. Their meaning depends on a rather stylized and fanciful notion of how decisions get made and how resources are constrained. Rather, we do want to emphasize the approach to estimating, for a trial, the expected change in health outcomes and the expected induced health care costs or cost savings.

6.2.5 Relaxing the Assumptions

Now, let us return to reality and see how, by relaxing the assumptions, we can identify the data required for the kind of evaluation we are proposing.

We will consider the following:
1. How will decisions be made once the information from the trial is in hand? How does this depend on the design and conduct of the trial? How does it depend on the health care institutional structure (e.g., regulation, financing)?
2. How would decisions have been made without the trial? What would have been the course of diffusion and adoption of the procedure?
3. How can the system be improved, by regulation or by imposing more appropriate incentives, so that the results of trials will be used more effectively and efficiently?
4. What do we do if the measure of efficacy is more complicated than "cure"? How do we handle risks, side effects, symptoms? At the very least, we need to estimate these attributes of outcome, but we may

also want to allow for the possibility that the trial will provide information on them. How do we handle effects on morbidity and the quality of life?

5. How do we handle a nonhomogeneous population in which the comparative efficacy (and risks, and perhaps costs) may differ among subsets of the population? Do we need to evaluate alternative experimental designs?

6. How do we assess the information from a trial that does not give perfect information?

7. How do we assess the information we would get from nonexperimental designs?

8. How do we establish the time horizon for the procedures in question, and how do we estimate the numbers of patients who would receive them? How should we decide when in the course of a procedure's dissemination to do a trial?

9. How do we assess prior probabilities of efficacy (i.e., prior to the decision to do the trial)?

10. How do we assess the costs and risks of the experiments themselves?

11. What are some of the other, less direct, benefits of doing trials?

6.3   Problems in Assessing Cost-Effectiveness of Medical Evaluations

In the enterprise we are suggesting, we would hope to have the aid of physicians as well as economists in bring additional realism to the evaluations. The tendency in medical studies, as in judicial review, is to avoid generalizations and focus strongly on specifics. As the following discussion illustrates, the diversity and incomparability of situations forces these constraints. Diagnosis, prevention, therapies, palliation, and health care delivery all fall within the scope of the studies we might try to evaluate. RCT's can be used for any of them or may be a component of evaluation. For example, in considering the dissemination of a new expensive technology, we may require an RCT to help measure the effectiveness of treatment as one component of an evaluation. Another component might relate to utilization patterns, and yet another to costs. We will probably focus on the RCT as a method of providing information on efficacy and take information on other aspects of cost-effectiveness as given. However, we may also want to consider how to assess the value of information on costs or on patterns of use of medical procedures and facilities.

6.3.1   How Decisions Will Be Made with the Experiment

In section 6.2, we offered a stylized model in which resources are allocated "rationally," as if by a benevolent Bayesian dictator. This model may be helpful to get us started, but it needs to be brought back to reality.

An alternative to the "rational" model is a model that captures the way procedures actually are adopted or abandoned. We do not know very much about how decisions are actually made. When a therapy is evaluated and found useful (or useless or damaging), what can we say of the events that follow? Recent research on the diffusion of medical practices sheds some light on this question (Barnes 1977; Miao 1977; Fineberg 1976), but, as noted earlier, the conclusions regarding the effect of the trial itself are often ambiguous. When the experiment on mammary artery ligation for relief of angina showed the sham operation to be as good as the experimental one (Barsamian 1977), we understand that the experimental operation was dropped. When studies showed that successive diagnoses of the need for tonsillectomy in groups previously diagnosed as not diseased produced the same proportion of "diseased" diagnoses as in the full group, as far as we can see nothing happened (Bakwin 1945).

We need a systematic set of historical studies that tells us the situation before, during, and after the evaluations. (We say evaluations because often more than one is available.) From these, it might be possible to identify the factors that tend to predict the impact of evaluations on practice. For example, how does the effect of an RCT on practice depend on the existence of an inventory of prior observational studies? Does it matter whether the RCT contradicts or confirms the previous studies? Does the second or third RCT make more of a difference than the first? Perhaps, as Cochrane (1972) suggested, we should systematically plan more than one trial, not just for scientific reasons, but because people will pay attention to the results.

Related to the hypothesis about multiple trials is the question of the importance of packaging and public relations for trials. Perhaps trials that show a dramatic effect (or that refute a generally believed large effect) more successfully affect practice than those that deal in small effects. Taking this into account, assuming it is true, should we give priority to trials that are believed ex ante, to be more likely to make a big splash, even if this strategy means sacrificing cost-effectiveness as defined by our hypernormative model?

We may also want to consider the value of making certain that a trial *seems* relevant to a physician's practice, e.g., by conducting it in a community setting, by using a seemingly "typical" cross section of patients. The probability of a successful result may have to be reduced in order to increase the probability of disseminating the findings in practice.

Finally, we observe that with the descriptive, rather than normative, view of decision making, it is very possible that a trial might have negative value. Results get misinterpreted. Expensive procedures found to be efficacious might be widely adopted even if they are not cost-effective. Procedures often are used in clinical circumstances beyond those for which they were evaluated. Efficacy in the hands of experts may not translate into effectiveness in the hands of a nonexpert, especially complex surgical or diagnostic techniques. Promoting a procedure of questionable efficacy to the status of a trial might give it credibility that it would otherwise lack if left to the "quacks." These and other concerns should be weighed against the benefits of trials, because the medical care system does not always use information, even good information, just as we would want it to.

6.3.2   How Decisions Will Be Made Based on the Literature and Record

Suppose we look at the observational study model when an innovation comes into society, is practiced (or experimented on) for a while, and reports appear about it. How do clinical practitioners respond to these reports and fragments of information? We can draw upon the literature for theoretical insights, but the empirical data base is thin. We see no way to handle this lack of data except to obtain a collection of situations, try to trace them as cases, and then to generalize to some models. For example, by systematically reviewing a surgical journal through the years, Barnes (1977) has provided examples of surgical innovations that later were discarded.

6.3.3   How to Design Institutions to Improve Incentives to Use Information Appropriately

Our third model of the response of health care providers to information from trials (the first two being the normative model and the descriptive model) would allow for intervention, or at least changes in the incentives for decision making owing to changes in the structure of health care insitutions. Regulation is one form of intervention. Weinstein and Sherman (1980) developed a structured framework for considering alternative regulatory and nonregulatory "levers" upon the health care system, taking into account the target of intervention (provider, patient, etc.), the nature of the lever (strict regulation, incentive, persuasion, etc.), and a variety of other dimensions. Our purpose here is not to enumerate all possible forms of leverage, but rather to mention a few as examples.

Various agencies at various levels have some leverage on practice, ranging from regulators such as the FDA to reimbursers such as the Health Care Financing Administration (HCFA) or Blue Cross–Blue Shield. Both HCFA and the Blues have ceased payment for some procedures found to be inefficacious. The National Center for Health Care Technology recommended to HCFA that heart transplants not be reimbursed on grounds of cost-effectiveness, although the recommendation was modified to permit certain providers to obtain reimbursement.

Direct linkage of reimbursement to demonstrated efficacy, while appealing in principle, has several limitations. Among these are problems in making the leap from efficacy in a study population to efficacy in individual patients. There would always be the need for some sort of escape clause in exceptional cases. Another problem in such a centralized approach is how to determine to what degree subjectively held concerns for symptoms and the quality of life are legitimate components of efficacy and, if they are, how to weigh them into the standard for reimbursement. Furthermore, fiscal intermediaries seem not to have much of an incentive to engage in such regulatory practices.

Another intervention that seems to work, at least in some settings, involves systematic persuasion within professional societies and peer groups. In one experience, physicians in one hospital reduced their utilization of tonsillectomy when told of their excessive rates relative to other hospitals (Wennberg et al. 1977; Dyck et al. 1977; Lembcke 1959). The Professional Standards Review Organization program was to have had this model as its raison d'être, although it is not clear how successful it has been.

At present we do not have a stable, but a rapidly changing system of control. Thus information, reimbursement principles, and changing regulations may be heavily confounded so that our ability to model a rational or irrational process may be heavily compromised. On the other hand, we may be able to gain insights into the kinds of institutional structures that are well suited to use information provided by clinical trials.

6.3.4   How Shall We Characterize Measures of Efficacy
         Required for Clinical Decision Making?

Acute and chronic diseases tend to give us different measures of outcome. In acute disease we usually focus on proportion surviving or proportion cured or degree of cure rather than length of survival. Morbidity, measured perhaps by days in the hospital, gives another measure of efficacy. Ideally we would compare costs, risks, and benefits from the new treatment with those from the standard treatment.

In chronic disease, we may be especially concerned with length of survival and with quality of life. Although it is generally agreed that quality of life is important, indeed often the dominant issue, its measurement, evaluation, and integration into cost-benefit studies must still be regarded as experimental (Weinstein 1979). Studies are proceeding in various places. For example, at Beth Israel Hospital, John Hedley-Whyte, M.D., and Allen Lisbon, M.D., are pilot testing a questionnaire on quality of life following surgery. Although the patient reports on the various aspects of life (leisure, family, happiness, ambulatory ability, etc.), a summary that could be integrated with other attributes of outcome is not in sight. Instead, comparisons of results for different operations is readily available. For another example, in a body of research dealing with "health-status indexes," subjects assign weights to various health states, and a single measure of "weighted life expectancy" or "quality-adjusted life expectancy" is derived (Torrance 1976; Kaplan, Bush, and Berry 1976). Applications of these techniques to specific procedures, using real subjects, are rare.

Another problem arises especially in the evaluation of diagnostic procedures. If a new method of diagnosis successfully detects cases of a disease for which we have no effective treatment, how valuable is the technology? It may be useful for counselling or for research, but the effect on health outcome may be negligible.

6.3.5   Problems with Heterogeneous Populations

Information on homogeneity of response to treatment across patients and providers tells about the uncertainty of improvements a therapy offers. If community hospitals get different results from teaching hospitals, or if various ethnic, age, or sex groups produce differing responses, then efficacy becomes difficult to measure. In these circumstances, we have difficulty nailing down the amount of gain owing to new information.

The problems are especially severe when we must deal with groups that have no theoretical connections among them. Let us mention first a favorable situation. In dose-response-curve work, we often have rough theory and experience to guide the choice of a relation. Since differences in shape of the relation may have modest impact, we can use the information from several groups, and then, say, weight the groups to estimate the effect; we do not lose much information by spreading the information across the groups. But when groups may not be related in their response, the total size of the investigation must be increased. In the extreme case, when we cannot argue from one group to another, each group must be considered separately: pre- versus postmenopausal women, men at various ages and in various stages of diseases. The total sample size for the study would equal the sum of the sample sizes for each group. As groups proliferate, samples become small, too small to determine anything for each group separately. The typical situation lies between these extremes, and we need to learn more about how to model them.

The central point here is that a trial may be valuable in telling us who can benefit from a procedure and who cannot. Such information could save lots of money, even if most procedures are beneficial for some people. But learning how to describe the subpopulations that can benefit may not be easy, especially if we do not have a good predictive model when we allocate patients to treatments and decide how to stratify.

6.3.6   Assessing the Informational Content of Alternative Experimental Designs

The precision of outcome achievable by various designs depends on their size, on their stratification, and on the uniformity of individual and group response. In addition, the measurement technique sets some bounds on precision because simple yes-no responses may not be as sensitive as those achieved by relevant measured variables. When the outcome variables measured are not the relevant ones but proxies for them, we lose both precision and validity.

The RCT, however, is likely to give us values for a rather narrow setting and would need to be buttressed by further information from before and after the investigation.

6.3.7   Assessing the Informational Content of Nonexperimental Designs

Nonexperimental designs run the gamut from anecdotes or case studies of single individuals through observational studies.

Current behaviors toward such studies have great variety; prevailing attitudes include ignoring them, regarding them as stimuli for designing studies with better controls, and regarding them as true, even overriding contradictory results from better-controlled studies. Although it is easy to list reasons often given for these differing behaviors of people and institutions, (reasons such as: physicians like the medical theory; institutions like the implied reimbursement policy; no one has a better therapy, and patients need something; a new generation of physicians is required to understand the new biological theory; patients won't comply), we have difficulty developing a normative basis for judging the information content of the data from the studies.

A Bayesian approach used by Meier (1975) and extended by others in considering the precision of historical controls might be helpful here. In spite of a large sample size, historical control groups may give substantially varying performances depending on the physician or the institution where treatment is given. When we assign reliability to them as if they came from an experiment with sample size n and standard deviation of measurement σ, i.e., using $\sigma/\sqrt{n}$, we overlook the group-to-group variability. By introducing this variability Meier is able to show how much the total variability increases. A difficulty with the approach is agreeing on the size of the group-to-group variability to be introduced. That difficulty arises because (1) we have to define "groups like these," and (2) we have to provide data for the groups, thus establishing a prior distribution for the situation at hand. The first of these may not present much more difficulty than the usual fact that the scientists differ in how they think of their populations. The second requires us to find the data and implies extensive information gathering and evaluation either in the field or from the literature.

Currently some theoretical work has been going on in statistics oriented toward using Bayes or empirical Bayes methods to evaluate the effects of treatments in studies where the investigator has weak or no control over the allocation of treatments to subjects or patients and where the choice of allocation may itself be related to the probability of a favorable response from the treatment, over and above the value of the treatment itself (Rosenbaum 1980; Lax 1981). For example, more of the slightly ill patients may be allocated to treatment A and more of the seriously ill to treatment B. These investigators are trying to provide ways of untangling such effects. The investigators must, of course, model the various components of the problem.

Since the efforts in this direction are fairly recent, two steps seem appropriate. One is to discover if these approaches can be applied to our problem. The other step is to attempt to find any circumstances where such efforts can be verified. So far, although the methods have been applied, we have no verification.

6.3.8 Predicting the Utilization of Procedures

By assessing numbers of patients with a specific disease and the rates at which the disease occurs and progresses, we can estimate the importance of a procedure and its value. We are, of course, concerned with the value of the information leading to the establishment of the importance or unimportance of a therapy or procedure.

The value of one innovation depends on how soon another at least as good comes along and is adopted. If we have both a new treatment and an old treatment, and the new treatment is better $(P_N > P_O)$, then the value of an experiment to establish that fact depends on (1) the rate at which better treatments $(P_B > P_N)$ come along to supplant the new, and (2) the rate at which treatments of intermediate efficacy $(P_N > P_I > P_O)$ would have come along to supplant the old, prior to the introduction of the better. The situation might develop as shown in figure 6.1, where the shaded area represents the benefit of the trial.

Of course, if physicians are allowed to use the new treatment without a trial, then things get more complicated. We would hope that the more effective the new treatment, the more widely used it will be (as anecdotal evidence spreads and as a sort of "osmotic pressure" builds). Compared with the benefit of the experiment that would pertain under the assumption that the burden of proof falls on the innovation, the benefit will be less if $P_N > P_O$; but it will be positive (and therefore greater) if $P_N < P_O$.

Thinking about the course of diffusion over time raises another important question: At what point in time should a trial be conducted? If we wait too long, the procedure may be established, and practice will be hard

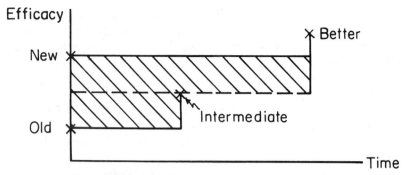

Fig. 6.1   Assessing the potential benefit from a newly validated treatment.

to change. But we also don't want to do the trial too soon, because (*a*) the technology may not be technically mature and may improve over time (in anticipation of which improvement, no one will pay attention to the trial if it shows no benefit), and (*b*) the innovation may turn out to be a poor performer with bad side effects and sink into obscurity. We need to develop strategies that adapt to early signals of a procedure's likely course and to respond promptly (but not prematurely) with a trial when appropriate. In other words, the decision whether to do a trial must be thought of as dynamic, not static.

6.3.9   Assessing Priors

Gilbert, McPeek, and Mosteller (1977) took a small step in the direction of assessing priors by reviewing randomized clinical trials in surgery over a ten-year period. They estimated the distribution of the size of the improvements (or losses), and they separated the experiments into two classes: those innovations intended to improve primary outcomes from surgery and anesthesia, and those intended to prevent or reduce complications following surgery and anesthesia. They found the average gain across studies to be about 0 percent improvement, the standard deviation for the gain in the primaries about 8 percent, and for the secondaries about 21 percent.

Such empirical studies help us assess the prior probabilities of improvements of various sizes brought by innovations. (This is a second-order value of the information from a trial.) Many other research possibilities are available, from observational studies to estimate group variation, from discussions with experts, and sometimes from reasonable considerations of naturally occurring bounds.

6.3.10   Costs and Risks of Studies

If we already have an experimental design, we can probably evaluate its direct costs. Although quarrels can arise about whether the cost of treatment, for example, should be allocated to the cost of the investigation, we should not have much difficulty evaluating the price of a given trial. On the other hand, in certain cancer trials, the incremental cost may be small because the fixed cost of a multicenter "study group" has already been paid. It is understood that incremental cost is the appropriate measure.

An exception would arise if we had a wholly new therapy or if the insurance system changed suddenly as it did during the swine-flu vaccination program, but we would have to be careful to sort out real costs from transfer payments.

The question of risk is a thorny one that arises when human subjects are given a treatment less effective than the alternative (Weinstein 1974). For treatments with reasonably long horizons, this risk should be considered minor compared to the long-term value of knowing which is the better treatment. However, if horizons are short, these problems may be more important. We may wish to consider alternative experimental designs that reduce the efficiency of the study in order to reduce risks to subjects, e.g., play-the-winner rules and variable allocation formulae, (Zelen 1969; Cornfield, Halperin, and Greenhouse 1969). On balance, we do not want to be diverted too deeply into this thicket, since it is probably not productive. It would be better to concentrate on the primary benefits and costs of studies.

6.3.11   Other Benefits of Trials

One of the great values of combining well-founded facts with good theory resides in the bounds that can be set. For example, with a little theory and a little empirical information, we can reassure ourselves that man need not look forward to running the two-minute mile unless a new method of locomotion (or, should we say, ambulation) is discovered.

Thus a study that gives us solid information about death rates, recovery times, and rates of complications for a variety of treatment groups is likely to provide extra values that go beyond its own problem. The National Halothane Study, for example, not only studied the safety of anesthetics generally, but also provided data used to design other studies, stimulated the further Study of Institutional Differences (in operative death rates), and acted as a proving ground for a variety of statistical methods and encouraged their further development. How shall such information be evaluated? Can we assess a prior distribution for unanticipated benefits, without necessarily being able to imagine what those benefits might be?

Another benefit of clinical trials is that they may reinforce a general professional awareness of the value of scientific evidence of efficacy. The publication of trials in key medical and specialty journals is thus seen as a kind of continuing education, fostering alertness and healthy skepticism with respect to innovations, and setting high standards for the data base upon which to support clinical decisions. Other benefits that may be attributed to trials include enhancement of the quality of patient care for participants (although perhaps at some added cost), and insights leading to improved efficiency in administration of health care services.

6.4 Examples

Earlier we mentioned the need for a few examples that might be examined with a view towards helping us learn to evaluate the contribution of studies.

6.4.1 Two Fables

We begin with two fables because we need to be more realistic about some problems of evaluation. The examples draw on ideas in the history of gastric freezing and blood pressure control.

Gastric Freezing

Gastric freezing was invented by a famous surgeon, Owen Wangensteen, to replace surgery as a treatment for gastric ulcers. The procedure was supported by biological theory: as a result of cooling, the stomach would have a better chance to heal itself. The patient swallowed a balloon, and coolant from a special machine entered and was withdrawn from the balloon.

A sequence of observational studies reported the performance of treated patients for the period 1962–69, with percentage of relief or definite improvement and sample size as shown in table 6.1. Although the outcomes in tables 6.1 vary a great deal, one notices decreasing performance as follow-up time increases.

Aside from these observational studies, several randomized double-blind trials were carried out comparing improvement following gastric-freezing treatment with that of controls. Table 6.2 shows the outcomes of these investigations. The study labeled "sham" at the bottom of the table was an especially well-controlled study that employed sham freezing as well as regular freezing. The sham and the freezing treatments produced nearly identical results. After this investigation, enthusiasm for the technique waned (Miao 1977). However, some studies of gastric freezing (Fineberg 1976) suggest that the treatment was falling into disfavor already and that the key experiment may have had only a slight effect.

We can probably collect information on the manufacture and sale of gastric-freezing machines; we may not be able to discover actual numbers of treatments. Assuming that we can obtain year-by-year information for treatments, how shall it be used?

The virtues of the findings of a good study are several. If the benefits of

Table 6.1   Gastric Freezing Observational Studies

Follow-up Period	Relieved (%)	Number Treated and Observed
Up to 6 weeks	100	19
	majority	86
	100	10
6 weeks–8 months	72	150
	13[a]	13
	78	53
	65	33
8 months–1.5 years	69	185
	14	29
	18	22
	21	60
	31	91
1.5 years–3 years	no studies	
Over 3 years	20	85

[a]A percentage of 13 is not compatible with $n = 13$, but we are not able to recheck this.

Table 6.2   Gastric Freezing Randomized Trials Together with Sample Sizes (n)

Time of Follow-up (months)	Gastric Freezing		Control	
	% Improved	n	% Improved	n
6	57	20	30	20
	75	19	29	17
	47	30	21	30
18	76	28	46	24
24	0	8	25	8
24 (sham)	34	82	38	78

treatment are positive, we have strong evidence of a gain. If, on the other hand, the benefits of treatment are zero or negative, we are released from further use of the treatment and can open our minds and resources more wholeheartedly to the use of and search for other treatments.

Hypertension

The association between high blood pressure and cardiovascular mortality and morbidity has been well known for some time. The life insurance industry, for example, published its so-called Build and Blood Pressure Study in 1959. The Framingham Heart Study published its early follow-up results some time thereafter, and they were impressive. Meanwhile, drugs that effectively lower blood pressure were generally available, and their risks seemed small compared to the hypothesized benefits. And yet no randomized trial had proven the benefits of high-blood-pressure control. The practice of antihypertensive medication was limited to cases of malignant hypertension, so-called because of its immediate, dire consequences.

Then in 1967, the first report of the Veterans Administration randomized trial on antihypertensive medication was published (Veterans Administration Cooperative Study Group 1967). The trial established the efficacy of treatment in "severe" hypertensives (those with diastolic blood pressure or DBP above 115 mm Hg). A later report, in 1970, established efficacy in "moderate" hypertensives (DBP between 105 and 114 mm Hg) (Veterans Administration Cooperative Study Group 1970). The findings regarding mild hypertensives (DBP between 90 and 104 mm Hg) were inconclusive. Most of the hypertensives in the United States are mild hypertensives (perhaps 20 million of the 25 to 30 million hypertensives, the remainder being moderate or severe).

Prescriptions for antihypertensive drugs increased following publication of the VA study, but not so rapidly as one might have hoped. By 1973, it was estimated that perhaps 25 percent of hypertensives were receiving medication (although only 15 percent were taking it); however, the diffusion rate in mild hypertension was not markedly less than in moderate hypertension. The Secretary of HEW, Elliot Richardson, launched the National High Blood Pressure Education Program to try to accelerate the practice of treating high blood pressure. This program apparently has been somewhat successful; at least, the proportion of hypertensives who are taking medication has been rising steadily.

About the same time, interest arose in developing a controlled trial that would resolve the uncertainty about the efficacy of treating mild hypertension. This led to the Hypertension Detection and Follow-up Program (HDFP), a community-based, randomized trial in which the controls, instead of receiving a placebo, were allowed to seek whatever treatment they wished.

Many were skeptical whether the results of the HDFP would be useful. Therefore, plans were set for a true double-blind placebo trial in mild hypertension. However, estimates of the study size required to establish a statistically significant ($\alpha = 0.05$) effect with high power ($1 - \beta = 0.90$) ranged from 36,000 to over 200,000, depending on assumptions about compliance, degree of blood pressure reduction, etc. (Laird, Weinstein, and Stason 1979). The prior expectations were based on the Framingham Heart Study.

A calculation of the potential benefits and costs of such a trial was made at that time by one of the authors and his colleagues (Laird, Weinstein, and Stason 1979). First, the cost of the trial was estimated at $135 million, assuming 28,000 subjects followed for five years. Next, the size of the population at risk was estimated to be 20 million, of which 10 percent were already being treated. Now, to simplify considerably, there were three possible results of the trial: not efficacious, efficacious, and inconclusive. If it was found that treatment was not efficacious, and if this finding was translated into practice, then 2 million persons per year would *not* spend an average of $200 on treatment, for a total of $400 million per year. Over ten years, with discounting at 5 percent per annum, the present value is $3 billion.

Now we need to assess some priors. Let us say we assigned a 0.1 probability to the event that treatment is not effective and a 0.2 probability that the study will show conclusively the effect is either zero or small enough to be considered outweighed by risks and costs. (The latter estimate can be made more rigorous by considering study size, a prior distribution of the efficacy parameters, e.g., mortality rates, and the probability that each particular finding would result in reduced utilization.) Under these assumptions, the study has a 0.02 chance of saving $3 billion over ten years, an expected value of $60 million; so this contingency would pay back half the cost of the study. Then we would have to repeat the analysis under the possibility that treatment is efficacious and that the study will so demonstrate. (Now we would have to estimate the health benefits—as Weinstein and Stason [1976] have done—and the additional treatment costs owing to increased utilization.) We would also have to consider the false-negative case (treatment is efficacious, but the study says it is not), and the false-positive case (treatment is not efficacious, but the study says it is). We would then plug all this into the cost-effectiveness model and assess the value of the study.

The epilogue to this fable (although it is by no means over) is that the HDFP reported its results in 1979 (Hypertension Detection and Follow-up Program 1979). There was a significant and important treatment effect, especially in the mildly hypertensive group. Now the controversy continues around whether this community-based study was really measuring the effects of antihypertensive medication or whether other differences between the treatments could have accounted for the difference in mortality. The value of the HDFP—and of the placebo trial that was never conducted—is still not known.

6.4.2 Examples with Other Complications

In the area of large-scale studies that have complications of various sorts we note:

1. *Studies of coronary bypass surgery.* Some coronary bypass surgery studies are experiments, and some are observational studies. Among other difficulties, they present the welcome problems of the improving ability of therapists, the reduction of costs as technology improves, and thus possibly changing findings over time. Although much can be made of these matters, they are a commonplace of the passage of time and improvements in science and technology. Evaluators should have ways of dealing with them. In this sense any therapy is always in an experimental or dynamic state.

2. *Prostate cancer.* A large-scale study of prostate cancer led to dosage and therapeutic recommendations (Byar 1973). As far as we know, the study is not now the subject of controversy, although it was attacked for some time.

3. *Portocaval shunt.* Many portocaval-shunt studies with varying degrees of control show that the weaker the control, the more favorable the outcome of the investigation to the treatment. These studies, and many like them for other diseases collected by Chalmers and his colleagues, go a long way towards undermining the informational content of poorly controlled studies (Grace, Muench, and Chalmers 1966).

4. *University Group Diabetes Project (UGDP).* This diabetes study illustrates many difficulties that arise in practice from optional stopping, from hypotheses generated during the experiments, from data deemed to be important though not collected, and from results that are unpopular with physicians and commercial institutions.

5. *Salk vaccine trial.* This trial went well.

6. *Gamma globulin study.* This gamma globulin study, weakly controlled, was intended to prove the medication effective against polio. At the close of the study little was known.

Although we could lengthen this list, we need to discuss what considerations should go into the choices for detailed study: Can we define a population of studies? Should we study both RCT's and observational studies? Can we measure the follow-up effects of the studies? How?

6.5   Conclusion

The purpose of this paper is to outline a general program of research and the reasons for it. We will benefit from criticism and discussion, recognizing that the total problem is a bit like dipping one's head into a bowl of fruit salad and opening one's eyes.

Are there parts of the research program that can profitably be broken off and studied separately? The approach described has a rather worm's eye view of the problem. We write as if we need to know, or at least make an estimate of, everything before we can reach conclusions. Are more global, decentralized attacks possible? Meanwhile, three observations seem likely to stand up to further scrutiny:

1. In planning a controlled trial, it would be valuable for those expert in effectiveness, costs, and other data pertinent to the health area of the trial, to perform at least a rough, back-of-the-envelope calculation of potential benefits and cost savings. This sort of meta-analysis cannot hurt, and even if we don't yet know how to implement a full-blown planning model of the type we have outlined, the rough calculations may help.

2. Evidence of efficacy from controlled trials will not solve the health-care-cost problem and will not even eliminate uncertainty from medical decisions. Value judgments related to multi-attributed outcomes (including quality of life) will remain, as will uncertainties at the level of the individual patient. Moreover, the problems of what to do about procedures that offer diminishing (but positive) benefits at increasing costs will always be with us.

3. Clinical trials can help, and we need to learn their value and how to increase it. As a nation, we may try various institutional changes to encourage the use by practitioners of trial information, perhaps by linking reimbursement to demonstrated efficacy, but more likely by providing incentives to be both efficacy-conscious and cost-conscious.

Comment   Joseph B. Kadane

Any governmental activity on which millions of dollars are spent is a worthy subject of analysis. Medical experimentation is a good candidate for such analysis, not only because of the amount of money involved, but also because we are all prospective beneficiaries of the improvements in medical techniques made possible by such experimentation.

In this very interesting paper, Mosteller and Weinstein give us an initial model to guide the choice of which medical experiments to support. The heart of that model is in section 6.2.4 of their paper. Some of their twelve assumptions are heroic, particularly the ninth assumption that all medical decision-makers will instantly adopt a new procedure if it is shown in the experiment to be cost-effective. The authors recognize in section 6.3.1 the desirability of substituting for this normative model a descriptive model of the spread of medical innovation. But they also point out how little we know about the history and sociology of medical innovation. Yet we need good descriptive models of this process to predict what would

Joseph B. Kadane is professor of statistics and social science, Carnegie-Mellon University.

happen in medical decision-making if the experiment were conducted and had various specified outcomes, and what would happen absent the experiment.

Certainly Mosteller and Weinstein are correct to call for rough, back-of-the-envelope calculation of the potential benefits and cost savings of each planned controlled medical trial. I do not understand quite so well, however, what research strategy they would use to make such calculations better informed. What would their research priorities be? Without this information, even a rough calculation of benefits and costs for their own research proposal seems impossible.

References

Bakwin, H. 1945. Pseudodoxia pediatrica. *New England Journal of Medicine* 233: 691–97.

Barnes, Benjamin A. 1977. Discarded operations: Surgical innovations by trial and error. In *Costs, risks, and benefits of surgery*. See Bunker, Barnes, and Mosteller 1977.

Barsamian, Ernest M. 1977. The rise and fall of internal mammary ligation in the treatment of angina pectoris and the lessons learned. In *Costs, risks, and benefits of surgery*. See Bunker, Barnes, and Mosteller 1977.

Bunker, John P., Benjamin A. Barnes, and Frederick Mosteller. 1977. *Costs, risks, and benefits of surgery*. New York: Oxford University Press.

Byar, D. P. 1973. The Veterans Administration Cooperative Urological Research Group's studies of cancer of the prostate. *Cancer* 32: 1126.

Cochrane, A. L. 1972. *Effectiveness and efficiency: Random reflections on health services*. London: Nuffield Provincial Hospitals Trust.

Cornfield, Jerome, Max Halperin, and Samuel W. Greenhouse. 1969. An adaptive procedure for sequential clinical trials. *Journal of the American Statistical Association* 64: 759–70.

Dyck, Frank J., Fergus A. Murphy, J. Kevin Murphy, David A. Road, Martin S. Boyd, Edna Osborne, Dan deVlieger, Barbara Koschinski, Carl Ripley, Alfred T. Bromley, and Peter Innes. 1977. Effect of surveillance on the number of hysterectomies in the province of Saskatchewan. *New England Journal of Medicine* 296: 1326–28.

Fineberg, Harvey V. 1976. Gastric freezing: A study of the diffusion of a medical innovation. Washington, D.C.: National Academy of Sciences.

Fuchs, Victor R. 1974. *Who shall live?* New York: Basic Books.

Gilbert, John P., Bucknam McPeek, and Frederick Mosteller. 1977. Progress in surgery and anesthesia: Benefits and risks of innovative therapy. In *Costs, risks, and benefits of surgery. See* Bunker, Barnes, and Mosteller 1977.

Grace, N. D., H. Muench, and T. C. Chalmers. 1966. The present status of shunts for portal hypertension in cirrhosis. *Gastroenterology* 50: 684.

Hiatt, Howard H. 1975. Protecting the medical commons: Who is responsible? *New England Journal of Medicine* 293: 235–41.

Hypertension Detection and Follow-up Program Cooperative Group. 1979. Five-year findings of the Hypertension Detection and Follow-up Program. *Journal of the American Medical Association* 242: 2562–77.

Institute of Medicine. 1977. *Evaluation of poliomyelitis vaccines.* Report of the Committee for the Study of Poliomyelitis Vaccines. Washington, D.C.: National Academy of Sciences.

Kaplan, Robert M., James W. Bush, and Charles C. Berry. 1976. Health status: Types of validity and the index of well-being. *Health Services Research* 11: 478–507.

Laird, Nan M., Milton C. Weinstein, and William B. Stason. 1979. Sample-size estimation: A sensitivity analysis in the context of a clinical trial for treatment of mild hypertension. *American Journal of Epidemiology* 109: 408–19.

Lax, David A. 1981. Inference with unobserved variables: Analysis of a non-randomized study. Ph.D. diss., Department of Statistics, Harvard University.

Lembcke, Paul. 1959. A scientific method for medical consulting. *Hospitals.* 33: 65.

Levy, Robert I., and Edward J. Sondik. 1978. Decision-making in planning large-scale cooperative studies. *Annals of the New York Academy of Sciences* 304: 441–57.

Meier, Paul. 1975. Statistics and medical experimentation. *Biometrics* 31: 511–29.

Miao, Lillian L. 1977. Gastric freezing: An example of the evaluation of medical therapy by randomized clinical trials. In *Costs, risks, and benefits of surgery. See* Bunker, Barnes, and Mosteller 1977.

Mosteller, Frederick, John P. Gilbert, and Bucknam McPeek, 1980. Reporting standards and research strategies for controlled trials. *Controlled Clinical Trials* 1: 37–58.

Rosenbaum, Paul R. 1980. The analysis of a non-randomized experiment: Balanced stratification and sensitivity analysis. Ph. D. diss., Department of Statistics, Harvard University.

Stafford, Frank P. 1979. A decision theoretic approach to the evaluation of training programs. *Research in Labor Economics*, Supplement 1: 9–35.

Thompson, Mark S. 1975. *Evaluation for decision in social programmes.* Westmead, England: Saxon House.

Torrance, George W. 1976. Social preferences for health states: An empirical evaluation of three measurement techniques. *Socio Economic Planning Sciences* 10:129–36.

U.S. Congress, Office of Technology Assessment. 1980. *The implications of cost-effectiveness analysis of medical technology*. Washington, D.C.: GPO.

——. 1978. *Assessing the safety and efficacy of medical technologies*. Washington, D.C.: GPO.

U.S. Department of Health and Human Services. 1980. *Health United States 1980*. DHHS publication no. (PHS) 81–1232. Hyattsville, Md.: GPO.

Veterans Administration Cooperative Study Group on Antihypertensive Agents. 1970. Effects of treatment on morbidity in hypertension, II: Results in patients with diastolic blood pressure averaging 90 through 114 mm Hg. *Journal of the American Medical Association* 213: 1143–52.

——. 1967. Effects of treatment on morbidity in hypertension, I: Results in patients with diastolic blood pressures averaging 115 through 129 mm Hg. *Journal of the American Medical Association* 202: 1028–34.

Weinstein, Milton C. 1979. Economic evaluation of medical procedures and technologies: Progress, problems, and prospects. In *Medical technology*, U.S. National Center for Health Services Research, DHEW publication no. (PHS) 79-3254. Washington, D.C.: GPO.

——. 1974. Allocation of subjects in medical experiments. *New England Journal of Medicine* 291: 1278–85.

Weinstein, Milton C., and Herbert Sherman. 1980. A structured framework for policy intervention to improve health resource allocation. In *Issues in health care regulation*, ed. Richard S. Gordon. New York: McGraw-Hill.

Weinstein, Milton C., and William B. Stason. 1977. Foundations of cost-effectiveness analysis for health and medical practices. *New England Journal of Medicine* 296: 716–21.

——. 1976. *Hypertension: A policy perspective*. Cambridge: Harvard University Press.

Wennberg, John, Lewis Blowers, Robert Parker and Alan Gittlesohn. 1977. Changes in tonsillectomy rates associated with feedback and review. *Pediatrics* 59: 821–26.

Willems, Jane Sisk, Claudia R. Sanders, Michael A. Riddiough, and John C. Bell. 1980. Cost-effectiveness of vaccination against pneumococcal pneumonia. *New England Journal of Medicine* 303: 553–59.

Zelen, Marvin. 1969. Play the winner rule and the controlled clinical trial. *Journal of the American Statistical Association* 64: 131–46.

7 The Use of Information in the Policy Process: Are Social-Policy Experiments Worthwhile?

David S. Mundel

Social-policy experiments are very expensive and therefore should only be undertaken in very particular—and perhaps, relatively infrequent—situations. The intent of this article is to stimulate a discussion of the factors that increase the potential utility of experiments, so that in the future this information-gathering technology can be used more appropriately and effectively.

The factors that contribute to the high cost of experimentation are very clear—money, time, people, and institutions. Experiments cost a lot of *money* because the data-gathering activities are extensive—much data needs to be collected on many subjects—and because the cost of treatments is usually paid for by the research effort itself. Because social experiments usually involve increased benefits, the costs of research efforts usually include, at a minimum, the net benefit costs. Experiments are costly in terms of *time*—the time between the conception of an experiment and the availability of useful data is longer than in other research techniques. Often experiments have taken more than a decade to produce reliable and available evidence. Experiments are also costly in terms of *people and institutions*—there are very few policy researchers and research institutions that can successfully implement a large-scale social experiment. The use of these resources for experiments raises the question of whether these individuals and institutions might be more effectively utilized in other projects.

The factors that contribute to the potential utility of social experiments are less clear. Among the factors that are important are:

David S. Mundel is president, Greater Boston Forum for Health Action, Boston, Massachusetts.

251

- Can experiments answer the questions that are important to policy makers?
- If experiments can answer important policy questions, can the answers be understood?
- If experiments can provide understandable answers to important questions, can the answers alter the beliefs of policy makers?

7.1 Can Experiments Answer the Questions That Are Important to Policy Makers?

In order to assess the desirability of a potential social experiment, one must ask which questions are important in a policy debate and whether an experiment is a cost-effective means of answering them.

There are many types of questions or issues that influence the policy process and only some of them can be resolved using social experiments. The questions include: Is "A" a problem? (For example, are middle-income families experiencing difficulties in financing their children's postsecondary education? And, if "A" is a problem, who has it? Why do they have it? Does it deserve social attention?

A great deal of social policy making depends on the answers to these questions, and these answers are not likely to be provided by social experiments. This does not mean that social science or policy research is unable to provide assistance in answering these questions, but only that nonexperimental methodologies, e.g., survey research and structural analysis, are more appropriate technologies.

Another set of questions that dominates the policy process relates to the implementation of programs or policies. The basic question one must ask is whether or not the institutions and individuals involved in a policy arena will act in such a way that a policy change will actually influence the intended policy target. For example, in the case of expanded federal assistance for college students from middle-income families one must ask whether state governments, banks and other lending institutions, colleges and universities and their financial-aid offices, philanthropic institutions/organizations, and others will "allow" a change in federal student-aid policy to result in a change in the level of student aid and pattern of prices facing students and their families. The fact that implementation problems and unforeseen or unintended consequences often limit or pervert the impact of well-intended policy choices is becoming increasingly apparent. Experiments can do very little to inform policy makers about this range of issues because the experimental treatments cannot be implemented on a broad enough scale or for a long enough time for these reactions and interactions to take place.[1] Policy demonstra-

1. The one effort to experimentally investigate this range of issues is the market-saturation segment of the housing-allowance experiments; the results of this attempt were neither satisfactory nor convincing.

tions are often implemented to investigate these phenomena but they, too, are often limited in duration and scope, and the character of the treatments is not sufficiently restricted to produce valid performance assessments.

A third set of questions relates to the behavioral consequences of policy treatments; for example, if middle-income students receive additional student assistance, will their college-enrollment rates or patterns change? This type of question is the natural focus of social experiments. However, structural and other analysis of survey data and theoretical analysis can also be used to answer these questions. Thus, one must ask, if these questions are the ones for which answers are sought, whether social experiments are the most cost-effective or appropriate means of answering them.

The potential realm of experimental techniques is thus quite limited. Of the three types of questions that are important to policy makers, only one appears amenable to experimental inquiry. Even that one type—behavioral consequences—is not solely approachable by experimental techniques.

7.2 If Experiments Can Answer Important Policy Questions, Can the Answers Be Understood?

If the purpose of a social experiment is to answer a "behavioral consequence" question that is important to policy makers, one must ask whether the answer will be understood by these individuals.

Policy makers are not skilled consumers of research. Policy makers are generally neither policy analysts, policy researchers, econometricians, nor statisticians. Consequently, their understanding of regression and other statistical-inference techniques is limited, and complex structural analyses that suggest that A "causes" B are rarely understood. If such an analysis suggests that the prior belief of the policy maker is true, policy makers may use the analysis to support their beliefs by repeating its conclusions, but their understanding of the analysis is itself limited. Policy makers with different beliefs than those supported by the statistical analysis will often discount the analysis because of its simplifying assumptions or because other studies show other results. These policy makers, too, do not generally understand the analysis itself.

One potential means of overcoming policy makers' lack of statistical understanding is to rely on policy analysts to translate the complex answers into understandable terms. This strategy is effective when policy analysts exist in an issue area, when they are strong enough methodologically to understand the statistical analysis themselves, and when the policy analysts are effective communicators so that their translations of the research are understood. Regretably, these three conditions are often not met.

Experiments themselves are another potential means for overcoming the problems caused by policy makers' limited understanding of statistical inference and the lack of an extensive policy-analysis community. If properly conceived and analyzed, social experiments can result in simply stated and easily understood conclusions. In theory, the results of an experiment can be adequately presented in a simple $Y \times N$ table, where Y is the number of treatments (one of which is the control) and N is the number of population groups affected.

But most social experiments have not been conducted in such a way that their results are easily understood. Often many experiments are not carefully enough conceived or planned so that a simple presentation of results is possible. Consequently complex structural analysis is undertaken, and thus the potential ease of communication is lost. For example, the income-maintenance experiments required complex structural analysis in order to reach conclusions. Also, most experiments involve many treatment options, either because a lack of agreement about treatment options exists or because once an experiment is proposed, its scale attracts the interest of advocates for a wide variety of treatments. These expanded sets of treatments result in a need for structural analysis of results because the number of observations is not increased sufficiently for simple comparisons between a treatment and the control group and among treatment groups to be possible. Thus these expansions result in greater difficulties in communicating the experimental results, which compromises the potential ease of understanding that could result from focused experimentation.

On balance, experiments can be designed and implemented so that they can produce easily understood results. To do so will require careful experimental designs and strong limits on the number of treatments considered. These limits will need to be enforced throughout the development and implementation of future social experiments.

7.3   If Experiments Can Provide Understandable Answers to Important Policy Questions, Can the Answers Alter the Beliefs of Policy Makers?

Most policy makers appear to be very certain about the effectiveness of policy options that they are considering. This appearance results from many factors; for example, policy deliberations are often only publicized late in the decision-making process—after policy makers have made up their minds. Policy makers often seek to limit the appearance of uncertainty because they perceive that uncertainty and indecisiveness are politically unattractive. A further source of apparent certainty is policy makers' efforts to improve bargaining positions should compromises be required.

This certainty is luckily more apparent than real. In general most policy makers are uncertain about the impact of the policies about which they are deciding. This uncertainty is particularly true early in the policy development process before lines are clearly drawn and coalitions are formed. Uncertainty is also present where leadership has declined and party discipline is diminished, conditions that characterize the U.S. Congress at the present time.

When policy makers are uncertain about the impact of potential policies, the results of experiments and other research efforts can play a role in influencing their beliefs. In this regard, policy makers are classically Bayesian—entering a problem with an estimate of the likely outcome and an estimate of the variance or uncertainty surrounding the likely outcome. When the variance is greater, additional evidence is more highly valued and has a greater influence on expectations.

All of this suggests that experiments are most appropriate early in the policy-development process when decision makers are uncertain and uncommitted. This notion seems to run counter to the view (expressed above) that experiments should focus on a very small number of treatments because a narrow range of options may only become apparent after significant policy deliberations. The apparent contradiction can be resolved by a realization that even early in most policy debates the range of options can be narrowed to one or two treatments versus the status quo. Furthermore, given the time lag between the design of an experiment and the availability of its findings, starting early in the policy process seems to be the only way to have the information available prior to the resolution of the policy problem.

Experiments may also be appropriate at later stages in the policy process if decision makers are again or remain uncertain. Doubt, skepticism, and uncertainty are not solely present early in the policy process. Often uncertainty is greater after clearly desirable options have been tried and found wanting.

7.4   Will Experiments That Meet These Criteria Be Undertaken?

This question regarding the likelihood of further social experimentation confronts the policy-making and policy-research communities with important choices. For the policy community the issue is whether resources will be allocated early enough—prior to a policy question reaching public awareness or crisis proportions—and in a concentrated fashion so that social experiments can be both worthwhile and possible. The current skepticism regarding the potential role of social science research within the policy-making community and the concomitant desire to reduce social science funding suggest that this issue will be resolved negatively. At the same time, the policy makers' uncertainty regarding the effectiveness of major policy options suggests that experiments could be influential.

For the policy-research community the issue is largely whether experiments can be focused on a narrow range of policy alternatives so that conclusive and understandable results can be obtained. The policy-research community may also oppose the concentration of resources needed to undertake experiments when the aggregate level of social science funding is declining. The capacity to concentrate resources during funding declines is limited.

In summary, although the criteria for designing influential social experiments are now more apparent and the potential utility of these experiments is now higher, the likelihood of further experimentation is probably declining.

8   Social Science Analysis and the
Formulation of Public Policy:
Illustrations of What the
President "Knows" and
How He Comes to "Know" It

Ernst W. Stromsdorfer

> All projects and programs are of course evaluated, with more or less accuracy and
> effectiveness, as decisions are made to continue, terminate, or redirect various
> activities. . . . How best to do the evaluation, what skills are needed by the
> evaluators, and what specific questions need to be answered for local, State and
> Federal purposes—these are problems that have not been fully resolved, and to
> which differing views and experience combine to give quite different answers.
> —*Education and Training: Opportunity
> Through Learning*. Ninth Annual Report
> of the Secretary of Health, Education,
> and Welfare to the U.S. Congress on the
> Manpower Development and Training Act.

8.1   Introduction

This study analyzes the manner in which social science analysis is
developed and utilized by legislators and policy makers to formulate
social policy. The initial charge for this study was to determine whether
information about social and economic behavior was more likely to be
used in policy development if it was developed from a classical experimental as distinct from a quasi-experimental method of analysis.
Based on the way policy makers behave, this charge proved to be too

Ernst W. Stromsdorfer is professor of economics and department chair, Washington
State University.
    The author would like to express his thanks for the helpful criticism of Henry Aaron,
Robert Boruch, Laurence Lynn, Fred Siskind, and David Whitman. Errors of fact and
misguided opinion are clearly the author's responsibility.
    An earlier version of this article entitled "The Impact of Social Research on Public Policy
Formulation" appeared in *Applied Research for Social Policy*, ed. Kenneth J. Arrow, Clark
C. Abt, and Stephen J. Fitzsimmons, Cambridge, Mass.: Abt Books, 1979. Kind permission
has been granted to use portions of that article.

narrow a focus. While it is certainly true that data on behavior derived from properly designed social experiments are more believable and do allow unambiguous assertions of cause and effect, it requires more than random assignment to a treatment and control group to make experimental data *usable* and *reliable*. This is borne out by the discussion of Dennis Aigner on residential electricity time-of-use pricing experiments and by experiments such as the National Supported Work Demonstration which, while yielding positive employment results for welfare women, still has a variety of methodological problems that reduce the reliability of the results and constrain its application (Masters 1980).

After reading commentary on the policy-development process and inspecting policy and budgetary documents and evaluations of actual social programs, it has become obvious that policy makers, while not totally subjective and nonrational, will use whatever data are at hand to support their case, regardless of the methodological purity by which it has been developed. Canons of scientific evidence are not ignored but are applied selectively. Taste or preferences for certain methods, such as the case-study approach, are as much determinants of what data are used as is any perceived methodological purity or rigor. Furthermore, the same person or agency, when evaluating two programs whose, say, economic effect on state and local governments is the same, is capable of using evidence quite selectively to support one program and reject another. As pointed out below, the cases of Public Service Employment (PSE) and educational block grants to state and local governments are an example of this interesting bit of policy rationalization. The phenomena of substitution and displacement are used to reject the former program while they are not mentioned for the latter where they also operate fully.

As a result, the initial question posed for this paper is probably not as interesting as is the general question of analyzing how information is generated and used. Thus, I shall instead discuss the following types of questions:

- To what extent does information lead to policy formulation or change?
- What is the context of the application of research to policy?
- Does analysis precede or follow development of policy?
- Does analysis ever account for the variance or change in policy formulation and application?
- How are research methods and the resulting information constrained by the political process?
- Under what conditions do research and analysis appear to have no impact?

The analysis of social policies and programs will always receive a weight of less than unity in policy development, given the complex nature of the political development of a program. Also, the results of analysis will sometimes be used in ways and for purposes that are not entirely consistent with the original objectives of the analysis. Furthermore, the political process will often dictate that some kinds of analysis simply cannot be performed, or if performed, the research must be carried out in a fashion inconsistent with the most appropriate scientific method. In fact, I would argue that the above phenomena are the rule rather than the exception in the conduct and application of social research. And finally, research based on a range of methods varying in their appropriateness to the specific problem at hand will be found to exist side by side in a given agency charged to provide information to policy makers. I do not really intend to paint a pessimistic and cynical picture of this process. Some information, if founded on an understanding of the policy in question, is better than none at all. And if one route of analysis, such as a benefit-cost analysis, is cut off, it is often possible to use alternative routes, such as an analytic treatment of program process and service delivery. Indeed, although we might prefer to think otherwise, a complex or expensive analysis of a program or policy is not always needed, especially if there is little or no conceptual development to guide the execution of such work. It has been the case that simple cross-tabulations of salient program data have been sufficient to effect major changes in programs. The Public Service Employment component of the Comprehensive Employment and Training Act (CETA) was significantly revised using such simple data. At the same time, it is depressing to recognize that occasionally the U.S. Congress will expressly prohibit the use of public funds to carry out certain types of analysis. For example, section III(b) of CETA prohibits use of CETA funds to conduct research on the subminimum wage. Classical experiments are also illegal with respect to analyzing the Employment Service and the Unemployment Insurance programs—at least as of 1977.

However, this same adversary relationship, given the existence of our open government and the canons of scientific evidence our system subscribes to, forces or induces the execution of research that is politically unpopular. The case discussed below of substitution and displacement within the PSE program is instructive of this. Highlighted by the work of George Johnson, this issue generated an incredibly heated and sometimes acrimonious debate within the Department of Labor throughout the late 1970s (Johnson and Tomola 1977). Nevertheless, the Department of Labor did fund a demand-side study in the Employment Opportunity Pilot Projects to study this phenomenon in the private, private nonprofit, and public sectors.

8.1.1 Plan of the Chapter

Before moving into the main body of the discussion, it is useful first to discuss the production of knowledge as it is generated by and for government and the general ways it is utilized by government.

Following this, the study will discuss examples of social research that have had an impact on public policy and other examples that have not. For both types I will describe cases where the research was on the cutting edge, initiating debate, and other cases where the research followed debate.

8.2   The Production and Use of Information

Analysis of this issue requires that the process of translation of analytical results into social policy be broken down into two broad components: 1) How is knowledge produced? 2) How is it utilized? Each of these two questions requires further breakdown.

8.2.1   Knowledge Production

The production of knowledge occurs through at least three processes:
1. *The production of management information-system (MIS) data.* Such MIS data can be classified into three general types:
   a. *MIS data developed within a behavioral context*; data on program inputs which can be related to program output. Such MIS data are generally rare, mainly because it appears to be beyond the capacity of bureaucracies to produce it.
   b. *MIS data not developed within a behavioral context*; situations where measures of input or output only are collected and cannot be related to their respective output or input. Most commonly, measures of input only are collected. When such data are used in policy development, output is assumed to be equivalent to input. Much educational-policy data are of this type, e.g., more teachers imply better education.
   c. *MIS data that measure neither input nor output directly*, for instance, simple counts of people receiving a broad, undifferentiated program treatment, such as the number of people covered by a new law. Program data on the federal minimum wage comes directly to mind. Depending on whether one is an opponent or proponent of minimum-wage legislation, legislation that implies wider coverage is worse or better.

The conditions under b and c above tend to arise out of two general contexts. First, the most common, most programs are not designed with the purpose of discovering their effectiveness. They are generally passed by Congress on the consensual assumption that they work. A major example is Title I of the Elementary and Secondary Education Act of 1965 (ESEA) or the (extinct) Neighborhood Youth Corps (NYC) (Rivlin 1971, 80). Second, it is intended that programs not be analyzed in terms of their behavioral impact. A good example is the Unemployment Insurance program, which wasn't analyzed behaviorally until the early 1970s; over the parallel time period, the Manpower Development and Training

Act (MDTA) and CETA both had an evaluation component built directly into them. In fact, the MDTA was the major catalyst for modern evaluation of social programs in the U.S. Department of Labor.

In general, the more political support there is for a program, the more limited will be the available systematic information on that program. The old National Alliance of Businessmen JOBS program is a case in point. In contrast, a relatively unpopular program, such as Job Corps during the Nixon administration, was required regularly to report very detailed *cost* data, though the first relatively valid study of Job Corps *benefits* did not occur until 1977 (Thornton, Long, and Mallar 1980).

2. *The production of knowledge through natural or quasi experiments.* Here, two general approaches are discernable:

    a. *Natural or quasi experiments that attempt to model an existing program's process and estimate its effect through econometric or other means.* All evaluations of the federal minimum-wage program and the Unemployment Insurance System are of this class.

    b. *Natural or quasi experiments in the form of (more or less) carefully designed demonstration projects.* Dozens of examples exist here, such as the Youth Incentive Entitlement Pilot Projects (YIEPP) or the Minnesota Work Equity project, both of which are subsidized employment and training/education programs, the former for disadvantaged youth and the latter for welfare clients. Following Rivlin, this form of analysis can be through either systematic development or through more or less unfocused innovation. The Youth Act of 1977, with a $1.1 billion combined research and program component, had both systematic development—the Youth Incentive Entitlement Pilot Projects—and unfocused innovation—the bulk of the act and its resources.

3. *The production of knowledge through classical experiments* wherein there is random assignment to treatment and nontreatment groups, thus allowing assertions of cause and effect to be made. Examples are the National Supported Work Demonstration, the Seattle and Denver Income Maintenance Experiments (SIME-DIME), and the Housing Allowance Demand Experiment.

Finally, a fourth form of knowledge production is possible: knowledge that arises in the form of untested but testable hypotheses through independent theoretical development. The human-capital revolution, and its extensive application in the War on Poverty, is in part an expression of this phenomenon.

8.2.2.   Knowledge Utilization

Not only are there diverse forms and qualities of information production, but decisions based on such knowledge are also diverse. Given the political drive to develop a given policy, it is the general case that any data at hand and supportive of the case will be used. Policy decisions are made on the basis of:

1. *No data or information at all but rather faith, bias, or political desire.* Someone wants something and has enough votes to get it. The decentralization of CETA is a straightforward example. This is discussed further below.

2. *Hypotheses suggested by impressions of regularities in data associated with a social problem.* Title I of the ESEA had this characteristic. Consider the following:
   a. Educated people are less likely to be poor—a datum.
   b. Children from poor families tend to perform badly in school—a datum.
   c. Therefore, provide poor children with compensatory education and you will break the cycle of poverty—a hypothesis to be tested; only, as Alice Rivlin points out, ESEA wasn't set up to test the hypothesis (Rivlin 1971).

   The Neighborhood Youth Corps was developed at about the same time and in a similar way. Consider the following:
   a. Rich kids are less likely to drop out of school than poor kids—a datum.
   b. The drop-out rate of poor kids is directly related to the business cycle—a datum.
   c. Therefore, give poor kids a job while they are in school and they will be less likely to drop out due to the opportunity costs of staying in school—a hypothesis to be tested. However, the program designers assumed the hypothesis was not rejected and proceeded to set up the NYC. Subsequent tests showed no effect on schooling retention (Somers and Stromsdorfer 1970).

3. *Hypotheses tested by data from natural experiments.* The Public Service Employment components, titles II-D and VI of CETA, have been under attack for several years in Congress and are currently scheduled for elimination, largely due to the econometric analysis performed to measure substitution and displacement. The argument that substitution reduces PSE effectiveness is directly employed both by the Congressional Budget Office (U.S. Congress, Congressional Budget Office 1981) and the Office of Management and Budget (U.S. Office of Management and Budget 1981) in suggesting budget cuts for the FY82 federal budget. For instance, the OMB argues that: "Charges that PSE is primarily a subsidy supporting State and local services are based on experience in the rapid 1977–78 build-up of Title VI and may not be as true today as then. . . . Independent estimates of the proportion of PSE jobs that

are substituted for regular State and local jobs range from a high of 90% (after three years) to a low of 20%."

Two observations are in order here. First although substitution undoubtedly exists and is probably high—consensus seems to fall in a range from 40 percent to 60 percent at this time—neither of the studies referred to from which the above numbers are taken are reliable. (Johnson and Tomola 1977, for 90 percent and Nathan et al. 1979, for 20 percent; see Borus and Hamermesh 1978 for a critique of these results.) Next, the Reagan administration, while objectively rejecting PSE due to the substitution phenomenon, does not mention the fact that the noncategorical block grants proposed for education are almost pure revenue sharing and, therefore, should result in 100 percent substitution (U.S. Office of Management and Budget 1981). Thus, one begins to wonder about the basis upon which research and analysis results are applied. The persons in question apparently also engage in this selective use of analysis in good faith and apparently are unaware of (or uninterested in) the inconsistency in their thinking and practice.

4. *Hypotheses tested by data from classical experiments.* Classical experiments are relatively new to the scene as well as rare in the area of social and economic behavior. With one or two exceptions, there are no classical experiments of existing Department of Labor (DOL) programs. In fact, as noted above, for the "old" DOL programs, such experiments are illegal. Thus, all of the policy development in the DOL has been based on quasi experiments as well as intuitive or impressionistic methods.

Where experiments have been conducted, we have had to undergo a considerable learning process. Experiments are not simple to design. Aigner rejects five of the fifteen residential electricity time-of-use pricing experiments as not useful. (Aigner, this volume). With respect to the negative-income-tax (NIT) experiments, only SIME-DIME appears to be highly reliable and usable. The Rural NIT Experiment appears to be useless. The National Supported Work Experiment's (Masters 1980) positive results for subsidized employment for welfare women are encouraging but are qualified because, in particular, substitution and displacement are not netted out of final program impact. The National Supported Work Demonstration employs a random assignment to an experimental/control group. Through closely supervised work experience in a supportive peer-group environment, the program seeks to improve job skills per se and change personal behavior such as work habits and motivation. AFDC women, drug addicts, ex-offenders, and disadvantaged youth represent the four treatment groups. The treatment period is constrained variously to twelve to eighteen months. The AFDC women had to volunteer for the program. Thus, this study group represented less than 18 percent of the AFDC population. Masters reports positive results on employment, though unsubsidized private-sector effects were not as large as hoped. The study is strongly indicative but not conclusive that such a program can reduce welfare dependency. The positive results are concentrated in just a few sites; there is apparent interaction between treatment and site effects; and, as noted above, there is an undertermined amount of displacement and substitution (Masters 1980). National Supported Work Demonstration represents our only experiment of subsidized public-sector employment. It is not clear that the Reagan administration even knew of the results before it moved against PSE. And, had the administration known, such knowledge may not have made any difference in its desire to eliminate PSE, since the evidence, while positive, is limited in scope.

Finally, the Housing Allowance Demand Experiments show a minor impact of housing allowance on increased consumption of housing, yet there is no attack on this program in the OMB budget document (U.S. Office of Management and Budget 1981) nor does the CBO budget document discuss this program (U.S. Congress, Congressional Budget Office 1981).

In short, a variety of experimental data exist, but they are of uneven quality and, in addition, they are not used consistently.

We turn now to a more detailed discussion of the use of research with respect to specific social programs.

8.3   Research with an Impact: Initiating Debate

Within the past few years policy research has initiated debate and forced the consideration of issues that would otherwise have received less attention by Congress and the several administrations. Examples of such issues are welfare reform, unemployment insurance, and Social Security.

8.3.1   Welfare Reform

The reform of welfare is a perennial policy issue. The basic concern with welfare services has been the presence of too many and too complex categorical aid programs whose eligibility requirements and cumulative tax rates have led to considerable horizontal inequity (unequal treatment of equals) and reduction in the work incentive. Milton Friedman, James Tobin, and others proposed substituting a negative income tax for the existing set of categorical aid programs. This idea was timely and struck a responsive chord among academics, government administrators, and policy formulators. As a result of this interest, a set of classical experiments was developed to test the impact on labor-market and other social and psychological behavior of differently structured income-maintenance programs. Experiments were conducted in New Jersey and

Pennsylvania; Gary, Indiana; Seattle, Washington; Denver, Colorado; and rural counties in Iowa and North Carolina.

Since the concern over the work-disincentive effects of welfare was high, initial analysis of the data from these experiments centered on estimating individual and family labor-supply behavior. Results based on three years of experimental treatment indicate that the labor supply of married white males with wives present in the household may be reduced by as much as 5 percent in response to a modest income-maintenance program. For white wives with husbands present in the household, labor supply may be reduced by over 20 percent (Robins and West 1980). The income and substitution elasticities of this study have been used in developing recent welfare-reform proposals to estimate the demand for low-wage PSE jobs and structured job search.

The five-year treatment shows larger labor-supply reductions and will most certainly solidify resistance to the NIT among the new administration (as well as others), though at present the administration's rejection of an NIT seems to be less due to the work-disincentive effects as due to the dilemma posed by the interdependence of the welfare tax rate, the minimum-income guarantee, and the income cutoff and the resulting budgetary cost implications (Anderson 1978, 1980; Stockman: Proposals for welfare reform 1981).

However, a propos the way in which experimental (and other) data are interpreted, we should note that, based on the results from the New Jersey experiment, the following policy implications were initially proffered:

> First, public opposition to coverage of all intact families by an income-related case transfer program—to the extent that such opposition is based on fear of large reductions in work effort—should decrease. Second, the concern of policy makers about the disincentive effects of particular tax rates and guarantee levels should diminish. . . . Third, the case for a work test in an income-related case transfer program covering intact families is weakened. (Barth, Orr, and Palmer 1975)

For a time, these attitudes probably did prevail. However, with the hearings held by Senator Moynihan in 1978, the previously "low" rates of labor-supply reduction were now seen to be "high" (Lynn and Whitman 1981). And the focus on a work test is paramount in the Reagan administration, whether one is discussing food stamps, AFDC, or unemployment insurance.

Workfare, in several forms and emphases, has been the polar alternative to the NIT. Versions of a strong work test and provision of PSE jobs were incorporated in the Family Assistance Program under President Nixon as well as proposals in discussion during the Ford and Carter administrations. Rejecting the subsidized-employment component of past workfare proposals, the Reagan administration is strongly fostering work tests for AFDC, food stamps, and the unemployment insurance program, (U.S. Office of Management and Budget 1981; "Donovan; Jobless Need New Careers," *Boston Globe*, 26 February 1981), without being fully aware that this work-test requirement is observed in the breech and significant enforcement of it has nontrivial budgetary costs. (The OMB document does note that projected cost savings do not net out enforcement costs.)

Currently, the Department of Labor is testing workfare or work-conditioned welfare reform in Minnesota, the first direct test of the guaranteed-jobs component of the Carter welfare-reform package, though the Supported Work results are strongly suggestive of the probable direction of effect (Rodgers et al. 1979). New Community Work Experience Program demonstrations are now being proposed by the Reagan administration to test out a decentralized local state-oriented workfare and training program for AFDC recipients.

The Employment Opportunity Pilot Projects (EOPP) currently underway is also a variety of workfare. It has an even stronger test treatment of structured job search. At this time some sites are placing almost 50 percent of their eligible clients in jobs, though there appears to be wide variation in these placement rates among pilot sites (ASPER/DOL officials, discussion with the author, December 1980).

8.3.2 Unemployment Insurance

Historically, the analytic focus of the administrators of the unemployment insurance (UI) system has been on the establishment of the optimum benefit level, mainly from the standpoint of the adequacy of wage replacement. A work test, often casually or indifferently administered, is the principal technique whereby the government reflects its concern over the potential work disincentive effects of this income-transfer program. In the wake of the 1975 recession, with benefit payments approaching $19 billion in fiscal year 1976, concern was expressed in some areas of the administration and in Congress over the effect on the aggregate unemployment rate of the weekly benefit level and the extension of benefits to a maximum of sixty-five weeks for eligible individuals. Economists in several branches of the Department of Labor funded a variety of studies to measure this impact; independent researchers conducted their own studies (Katz 1977). While the data in these analyses were faulty and the econometric techniques used to overcome these data problems were often inadequate, the analyses did indicate that the behavior of insured workers had several effects on the measured unemployment rate. For example, the duration of unemployment among UI recipients appeared to increase as benefits and their duration increased. Daniel Hamermesh argues that the best estimate is that a 10 percent increase in weekly benefit amount will increase an individual's unemployment by about one week. The overall effect of the current program on the civilian unemployment rate is to increase it by about half a percentage point (Hamermesh 1977). Overall, however, it was probably not the particular point estimate that was as significant in influencing policy on the UI system as was the breakthrough in this new way of looking at the UI program and the determination of the direction of effect.

Concern over the employment-disincentive effects of the program, particularly problems of financing the state trust funds and determining the adequacy of UI tax rates, led to a revision of the UI legislation in the fall of 1976. However, the only efforts made to reduce disincentives to work in this legislative revision were denial of summer benefits for school employees with contracts for the forthcoming term and for school employees with a reasonable assurance of postvacation employment, and reduction of unemployment-compensation benefits for retired individuals by the amount of any public or private pension based on a claimant's previous employment.

Interesting enough, the current OMB recommendations, while attacking the Unemployment Insurance Extended Benefits Program, do not focus on the possible disincentive effects of the program except to argue for a more stringent work test for extended benefit claimants (U.S. Office of Management and Budget 1981). Recent announcements by the Secretary of Labor suggest a major refocus of UI, however ("Donovan: Jobless Need New Careers," Boston Globe, 26 February 1981), and current legislative proposals for UI can be viewed as implicit recognitions of the disincentive effect.

8.3.3 Social Security

Evaluation research has had an interesting impact on the interpretation of the effects on labor supply of increased Social Security payments, marginal payroll tax rates, and changes in eligibility for retirement. From 1947 to 1974 the labor-force participation rate of men aged sixty-five and over dropped from 48 to 22 percent. Beneficiaries within the old-age and survivors' component of the Social Security Administration (SSA) rose from 15 to 67 percent of the total number of people aged sixty-five and over during the same time period. Studies conducted by the SSA staff as benefits were increased or extended concluded that almost all persons retired involuntarily as a result of bad health, difficulties in finding a job, or compulsory retirement age. The basic method used in these studies was a direct questionnaire—people were asked why they retired. Since American society places considerable emphasis on the value of work as well as the social and personal obligation to work—the secularized Protestant ethic—it is not surprising that people, when asked why they retired, cited illness or business downturn (i.e., socially acceptable reasons) rather than the financial and leisure opportunity associated with retirement (Munnell 1975).

In contrast to this method of analysis, the approach of the economist is to look for evidence of revealed behavior; that is, the focus is on measurement of actual behavior and the interaction among variables affecting this behavior, rather than on direct query concerning motives and actions. Studies using economic models that include variables representing the benefit and eligibility characteristics of the SSA system find that these variables have a large economic effect on retirement decisions. Indeed, as might be expected, there is an interaction between health and financial factors (Munnell 1975). This recognition of the voluntary nature of the retirement decision in response to increasing benefits has brought into sharper focus the financial problems of the Social Security system. The current administration is discussing changes in the retirement age, and the disability insurance (DI) component of SSA is under OMB revision and challenge (U.S. Office of Management and Budget 1981), perhaps due to OMB awareness of the above. Finally, Congress has mandated that an experiment be conducted of the disability insurance component to determine ways to reduce the drain on the DI funds. (*U.S. Code Congressional and Administrative News* 1980).

8.4   Research with an Impact: Following Debate

The best example of evaluation research that followed the lead of policy development is in the area of training and retraining programs for both prime-age workers and youth. These programs reflect the strong belief in American society that education is the key to economic growth and the assumption, though basically unproved and unmeasured, that there are large external benefits from any type of education. Also, training programs appealed (although for different reasons) to both conservative and liberal elements in Congress and the administration. Such programs were passed with minimal political and intellectual controversy, and as a result the major evaluations of such programs came after the fact of policy development and revision. Almost every one of the evaluations of training and retraining programs have been case studies impaired by selectivity bias, lack of proper control groups, nonresponse bias, and insufficient follow-up period. Over time, however, these studies suggested that there were positive and statistically significant effects on earnings large enough, under reasonable assumptions for a social discount rate and earnings projections, to cover program costs. Nevertheless, one cannot generalize from these case studies. The inconsistency in earnings benefits across studies, linked with the growing realization that training cannot create jobs in a period of cyclical unemployment, led to a disenchantment with training as a panacea for unemployment; thus, beginning in the early 1970s the view that retraining "did not work" became prevalent in government circles and among some academics, even though the basic evaluation results did not change (Aaron 1978a, 65). Indeed, it was in the mid-1970s that fairly accurate data on national samples of prime-age trainees and nontrainees were generated from SSA earnings records. Sophisticated econometric analysis of these records indicated that for males benefits averaged from $150 to $500 per year in the period immediately following retraining. The "decay rate" in those earning benefits was estimated to be about 15 percent per year. For women the benefits were between $300 and $600, with no apparent decline over the five-year period following retraining (Ashenfelter 1978). Given costs, the impact appeared to be marginally efficient.

However, the presumption that training did not work led to a major shift from a categorical-program approach to the provision of a unified set of services, under a decentralized program, that prime sponsors would employ in various combinations that would be more efficient and equitable. But this program change was made in the absence of reliable analysis.

To verify that the categorical training program did not work would have required a complex set of cost-benefit analyses for different types of program treatments, as well as training courses administered to different sociodemographic target groups. Such evidence simply did not then and does not now exist. Nevertheless, the decision to decentralize the programs prevailed. The conditions whereby this decentralization would have improved the effectiveness of training were not met, however. Namely, the detailed labor-market information necessary to specify the appropriate training programs was no more available under CETA than it was under MDTA. Decentralization reduced federal control, a positive gain given the mood of the period, but it surely did not increase program efficiency. At this time an elaborate longitudinal study of a national sample of trainees and other program participants is underway in the DOL. However, it is not designed such that one can test if decentralization has made any difference in program effectiveness. There is only one possibility for a crude test—to replicate the Ashenfelter analysis with SSA earnings data for the CETA period and compare the MDTA and CETA period results.

8.5   Research without an Impact: Initiating Debate

Retraining programs, job counseling, and other services for the cyclically and structurally unemployed gradually fell into relative disfavor during the early 1970s, though, as noted above, in the absence of reliable supporting evidence. The new hope for alleviating unemployment became public-service employment, first authorized under the Public Employment Program of the Emergency Employment Act of 1971 and made permanent in 1974 as the Public Sector Employment Program under CETA.

Two conditions have to be satisfied in order for PSE to be a socially effective method for alleviating unemployment. The more important of the two is that unemployed workers who are put to work on subsidized public-sector jobs must not displace other (similar) employed workers in the public or private sector or be used to perform work that would have been performed in the absence of the PSE program. Second, the output produced by PSE workers should have some positive social value.

George Johnson, who was then Director of Evaluation in the Office of the Assistant Secretary for Policy, Evaluation, and Research, U.S. Department of Labor, pointed out that the first condition was not likely to be fulfilled. In short, displacement would not only occur, it would occur very quickly; even when state and local governments were not in fiscal straits, they had every incentive to substitute federal funds and PSE workers for their own fiscal effort. If they were in fiscal straits, their regular employees, after a period of lay-off, would be rehired as PSE workers. Such behavior was endemic in New York City, for instance. Congress was not ignorant of the fact that such displacement might occur. Indeed, "maintenance-of-effort" clauses are consistently written into laws like CETA that have a revenue-sharing component. The error of Congress lay in believing that such legalisms could be enforced. To detect the extent of fiscal substitution requires a complex data set beyond the capability of local governments to provide or the federal government to finance and monitor. Both the General Accounting Office and the program auditors of the Department of Labor became cognizant of the great difficulty in measuring the degree of displacement or substitution so that maintenance of effort could be legally enforced. Ultimately, the Department of Labor auditors simply ceased to concern themselves with the problem.

Paradoxically, during the Ford Administration displacement was used as an argument *against* the expansion of PSE and *for* the expansion of conventional training within CETA. The advocates at that time did not recognize or discuss the fact that under a revenue-sharing program such as CETA, displacement or failure to maintain effort applied to any program so funded—training as well as public-service employment. And, of course, the fascinating behavior of the Reagan administration with regard to this substitution issue has been mentioned above.

With the rebirth of interest in welfare reform under Carter, PSE gained a new lease on life as an integral part of a workfare program. However, the displacement issue was still a nagging concern. Widespread displacement could eliminate the effectiveness of any long-term effort to combat the structural unemployment implicit in the welfare problem. With displacement, no net reduction in overall economic dependency need occur;

churning in the unskilled sector of the labor market may be the only result. This phenomenon strikes at the heart of section II-D of CETA which is aimed at alleviating long-term structural unemployment.

8.6 Research without an Impact: Following Debate

The most unfortunate recent example of social-program research and data collection that has had no meaningful impact on policy debate is the analysis of the Occupational Safety and Health Act of 1970 (OSHA). At present, the Bureau of Labor Statistics expends 4.7 million dollars annually to collect industrial accident statistics for OSHA. These data are used to help target safety inspections more efficiently. However, they are deficient in helping evaluate the net effect of OSHA safety inspections, and little of this expensive effort has helped clarify the policy cacophony that embattles this potentially useful program. Indeed, while there is a variety of data sets on industrial accidents and injuries in existence, such as state workers' compensation data, these data could not provide systematic information to guide congressional debate during the formulation of the act, and such systematic information still does not exist. The proposed Schweiker Amendment to OSHA (*Congressional Record* 1979), for instance, referred only to aggregate time-series data on nationwide accident rates as suggestive of the "failure" of the OSHA program. With a few notable exceptions (Smith 1979), only limited analysis of OSHA impacts exists. The Occupational Safety and Health Administration did not have a coherent research and evaluation plan between 1974 and 1977, even though this was a requirement in the annual budgeting process. During that time the OSHA administration was making no concerted effort to discover the net social impact of its policies. It was only ineffectively pressing forward selected health standards supported by ill-designed and ill-executed economic impact statements. Even so, by 1979 a total of approximately one billion dollars had been spent on the administration of OSHA (Bolle 1980). Even allowing for the extreme politicization of the agency, given the above costs plus the social costs imposed by the program on industry, it is difficult to understand that a more coherent and determined effort was not achieved to measure the effects of this program and collect more meaningful management-information data.

8.7 Concluding Remarks

It is clear that social research has a considerable impact on policy formulation and execution, but not exactly in the way a fastidious scientist would prefer. It is also true that political factors define or inhibit what will be analyzed with public resources and what will be applied in any practical political context. In some cases constraints are such that it is not possible to collect appropriate descriptive data, much less to perform a critical analysis of the program in question.

Lest I overemphasize the negative side, however, let me assert that program analysis and evaluation can be an extremely valuable policy tool. In particular, I have come to believe that analysis designed to reveal the administrative and operational process of a social program can be extremely valuable. As most social scientists who become members of government discover, program processes are not clearly thought out or understood by the people who define and operate them. The Trade Adjustment Assistance Act, for instance, which is predicated on the reasonable assumption that those workers ought to be compensated who lose their jobs due to structural economic change, e.g., auto workers, has been found to be very difficult to administer since the true losers and how much they lose cannot be properly identified. Providing understanding ahead of time of how a program might work through process analysis can render an invaluable practical, as well as social service when done correctly. A basically sound or deficient program can often be discovered by an effective process analysis. The installation of an effective work test is a prime example where such a process analysis can be helpful, and, the avoidance of the economic and political costs of TAA, discussed above, is another example.

And, finally, as the level of expertise increases within the bureaucracy and Congress, more attention and resources can be paid to formulating efficient MIS systems and systematic experiments and less on shot-gun approaches to program analysis as characterized by the ESEA of 1965 and the Youth Act of 1977. Gradually, experimental analysis just may gain an ascendancy which it most certainly does not now have.

Comment   Henry Aaron

Holding a conference on social experiments in today's budgetary climate is rather like holding a conference on dirigible flight a month after the Hindenburg disaster. One cannot escape a feeling of unreality.

I shall divide my comments on David Mundel's and Ernst Stromsdorfer's papers into three parts. The first is a summary of each of the papers. The second consists of specific comments on the two papers. The third part is a collection of comments inspired as much by the subject the papers address as by the papers themselves and in fair degree by the desire to provoke. I fear you may find them provoking rather than provocative.

Henry Aaron is senior fellow, Brookings Institution.

Mundel poses a series of questions about social experiments: Can experiments answer questions important to policy makers? Can the answers be understood? Can the answers alter the beliefs of policy makers?

The first question is divided into four subquestions. Can social experiments identify problems? Can social experiments pinpoint who has a problem and whether it is important? Can social experiments assist in the implementation of policy? Can social experiments identify the behavioral consequences of policy? Mundel answers no to the first three of these subquestions and yes to the fourth, qualified by the observation that other possibly more effective and certainly cheaper instruments are available.

The second major question concerns whether the results of social experiments can be understood. Mundel concludes that experiments can be designed to yield comprehensible results, but often they are not because the experiment is too complex or the experimenter too unclear.

The final question—can results alter the beliefs of policy makers?— also receives a qualified yes, if the experiment is simply designed and undertaken early enough in the process of policy development.

Mundel does not state whether any experiments undertaken to date have met his standards and fulfilled the rather limited potential he adumbrates, but he implies that the prospects are poor for social experiments in the future.

Ernst Stromsdorfer has attempted to draw specific lessons from a variety of social experiments, research projects, and evaluations. His theme is not so much social experimentation as it is the manner in which information, in general, has influenced policy and the generalizations that this experience supports. He stresses the fact that, willy-nilly, most policy research, experimentation, and evaluation comes sooner or later to smack of what Alice Rivlin in her review of Christopher Jenck's *Inequality* called "forensic social science." In the policy forum, social science research is "evidence" to be introduced as part of a frequently multifaceted adversary process in which each side builds its case to make it as persuasive as possible.

Stromsdorfer begins by placing knowledge production relevant to policy into a variety of categories: data produced in the course of program administration, the results of natural or quasi experiments such as a new program that changes the environment palpably, and findings of social experiments. Research based on census data or surveys does not fit comfortably in any of these categories, but one of them can be broadened to include it without affecting anything of substance.

Stromsdorfer then comes around from the other side and suggests that decisions may be based on faith without data, hypotheses suggested by regularities in data but not formally tested, hypotheses tested by data from natural experiments, or hypotheses tested against data from classical social experiments. Once again, other research can be appended to this list. He also mentions hypotheses untested or only weakly tested by data, such as the belief in human capital underlying Johnson's Great Society initiatives. In common parlance, we call such hypotheses faiths.

The succeeding four sections review a variety of research, categorized according to whether or not it had an impact in initiating debate on policy issues, influenced a debate already under way, or followed a decision already made. Because the issues treated—welfare reform, social security, employment and training programs—are continuing issues, one can quibble with the categorization, but the essential point is that most of Stromsdorfer's comments seem balanced and well informed. I shall return to a few with which I do not fully agree below.

Stromsdorfer concludes with a brief section in which he singles out analysis of administrative and operational process as likely to be particularly useful, a point flatly at odds with one of Mundel's observations, but demonstrably correct in my opinion. He also expresses the rather wistful hope that the accretion of expertise within the bureaucracy and Congress may promote experimental analysis to a position of influence from which it is now clearly absent.

Specific Comments

Mundel's paper is hard to discuss because it is a collection of generalizations not buttressed by specific examples. I found myself feeling uncomfortable with the generalizations and thinking "Yes, but . . ." He warns that experiments are costly in terms of people and institutions. Yes, but they produce analysts expert in a program whose know-how did not exist before the experiment and probably would not have existed without it. He states that experiments can do little to inform policy makers about problems of implementation, but how should one treat the findings of the NIT experiments on monthly reporting or of the housing-allowance experiments on the appropriate fees for agents under section 8? He points out that policy makers frequently do not understand what analysts tell them. Well, yes, but they can be made to understand and sometimes do. The answer may lie as much in the attitude of the policy maker as in the attributes of the analyst.

In general, Mundel asks whether experiments directly and clearly influence decisions. He finds that they seldom do. For reasons to which I shall return, I think that he has correctly answered the question posed, but that he has posed the question incorrectly.

The most striking aspect of Stromsdorfer's paper is that it does not confine itself to social experimentation. Rather he recognizes that social experiments can only be evaluated in comparison with other methods by which information finds its way into the process of political decision. In this connection, he emphasizes the selective application and disregard of scientific canons. He does not clearly say who is guilty of this dereliction, but I trust that he would level this charge not only at politicians and bureaucrats but also at analysts.

General Comments

I believe the lurking in the back of many of our heads is a view of how the evidence of social experiments ought to be used. This view is consistent with a number of statements in some of the papers. Inspired by genuine uncertainty about how to deal with a problem or by the belief that research evidence will persuade opponents, supporters of a policy initiate a social experiment. (In passing, I would suggest that social experiments have never preceded debate but have always followed its beginning. Results of other research may initiate debate.) Economists and other social scientists step in and design a test to estimate the key parameter. On the basis of the experiments, the parameter is found. It resolves doubts about which line of policy to pursue, and policy makers act on it.

Such is the Platonic image of the social experiment, and indeed of research in general, that many of us hold. Consciously, we recognize that it is hard to design experiments and that the results are often needlessly obscure. And we understand that many forces other than the rational application of science are involved in setting policy. But when things do not work out quite as we hoped, we go back to the drawing board to do things better. (It is hard to accept the metaphor of Hilton Head as drawing board, but there it is.) And that is precisely what we should do.

But as we sharpen our instruments, we should recognize that the process is quite unlike the naïve model I have sketched. As Stromsdorfer correctly puts it, the social experiment or the research paper with policy implications is part of an adversary process. What Stromsdorfer did not say, but what I know he recognizes and what needs saying, particularly in a group such as this, is the fact that the adversaries are contending for power, not truth. And deep down, that is what many of us are contending for too—how else can one explain the appalling lapses from analytical evenhandedness that Stromsdorfer mentions and documents. Through such lapses analysts have undermined their own credibility and persuasiveness and debased their own currency.

If the model of the social experiment on a straight line that passes through the truth on the way to action and power is so wide of the mark, what analogy fits better? Oddly enough, the model I would choose is that of efficient markets, although I make no claim of efficiency in any sense for the political process. A large number of actors, with divergent and conflicting interests and information, try to buy cheap and sell dear. The market efficiently digests all information and the result is a more or less determinant price. A rumor of some change in market conditions will alter expectations of some people in some degree, but the trend in prices is based on more basic market conditions.

Most research in the political market place is a rumor believed by one person, the analyst. Other analysts may accept his findings; more often they will try to better them or to alter them. The half life of rumors is short. The difference between results of work by the solitary investigator and the social experiment is a matter of scale. Experiments involve politicians who must vote large sums to support them after approving the idea of experimentation itself. They involve state and local governments and voluntary organizations, lots of administrators to run them, and analysts to plan them and to study their results. They must be expertly designed and implemented because if opponents can show errors in their execution, either the experiments will not be completed or the persuasive value of the effort will be destroyed. But the chief difference between a study by a solitary research worker and a social experiment is political and social, not intellectual. It is a mistake to seek important intellectual differences, as some of the papers presented here have pointed out.

The question then is whether social experiments serve the rumor-generating function more effectively than does solitary research. The fact that social experiments are political events would appear to give them a great advantage. Furthermore, their scale enables them to look at issues such as new administrative processes that small-scale research finds it harder to investigate. As I have pointed out elsewhere, serendipitous findings of the income-maintenance and housing-allowance experiments will more than repay the U.S. Treasury the cost of the experiments in very short order.

In the end, however, social experiments, like most research on social programs, have been a force for slowing the adoption of new policies. The evidence cited by Stromsdorfer points clearly in that direction. My point is not that such a result is good or bad, merely that it has occurred. Social experiments, like other analysis, show problems to be more complicated and subtle than we had thought, and results are harder to achieve than we had hoped.

I sometimes wonder what would have happened if Franklin Roosevelt had had the good fortune to be president when economics was further advanced than it was in the 1930s. Instead of appointing the Committee for Economic Security in 1935, he might have fielded a social experiment to find out how people would respond to retirement benefits, welfare for the aged, and cash payments to the unemployed. By 1937 we might have had the research design completed instead of the legislation Congress actually enacted. By 1940 we might have seen the completion of payments to the first wave of experimental subjects instead of the initiation of benefits under a new program. The Second World War, alas, would have interrupted the analysis of results and perhaps payments to the cohorts who were still receiving treatments to test duration effects. But we could have resumed treatments in, say, 1946 and completed analysis by the mid-1950s. We could have spent some time debating whether the decline in saving that we observed was attributable to the experiment or magnified by the expectation of the end of the Great Depression or by the postwar consumption boom, whether the increase in duration of unemployment was a steady-state reaction or was magnified by the change of postway labor-market conditions and hence transistory. Oh, what a missed opportunity!

Speculations such as these prompt the observation that Mr. Stockman is making a grave mistake in trying to put us all out of work. He has not realized that we are the instrumentality for inaction. By diverting us to teaching rather than research or even to still more reputable ways of earning a living, he will make easier the growth of ideas for activist social change undisturbed by critical analyses when the mood of the country shifts.

Comment   Laurence E. Lynn, Jr.

I must begin by confession that I find this subject—the use of social science in policy making—boring. One reason is that I have written on the subject and discovered that the number of interesting things one can say is limited. Another is that there is an extensive literature on the subject: the interesting things have already been said quite well by others. Additional papers constructed on no more than casual observations encased in the authors' unique taxonomies seem superfluous. To attract bored readers, an author must bring new data or insights to the subject, or else restate the received wisdom in an original and provocative way. Regretably, our two authors come up short.

David Mundel argues that social science experiments can answer only some of the questions of interest to policy makers: those of the form, If I implement policy X, what will be the behavioral consequences? The answers will be understood, and thus influential, only if (*a*) the experiments are limited in scope and rigorous in design, thus increasing the likelihood of unambiguous results, and (*b*) the results are available early in the policy-making game, before everyone's positions have hardened.

In keeping with a much-honored tradition, Stromsdorfer abandons the question he was assigned—Are findings from classical experiments more or less useful than findings from quasi experiments?—and addresses one

Laurence E. Lynn, Jr., is dean and professor, School of Social Service Administration, University of Chicago.

he finds more interesting: How is "information" generated and "used"? In his view, "knowledge" is produced through three processes: generation of data for management information systems (MIS), natural or quasi experiments, and classical experiments. Policy decisions are based on no data or information, hypotheses suggested by regularities in MIS data, or hypotheses tested by data from natural or classical experiments. He discusses the actual impact of several sets of data according to whether experimental findings initiated debate or followed debate.

Neither author has added to our store of insight and wisdom. Both appear to use criteria appropriate to the standard "rational actor" model of choice, though Stromsdorfer notes (ruefully) that "politics" has something to do with the initiation and use of research. That is, both appear to define "use" as an identifiable official reacting rationally and directly to the findings of a study, presumably embracing them. Neither has bothered to refer to the much richer formulations of the issues available in the literature. (For the best single essay, see Weiss 1978). Both suggest that it is better to introduce social science "early" rather than "late" in policy formulation, "before" debate rather than "after" it. Unlike many of their brethren in the academic community, both would manipulate the research product to enhance its usefulness or impact. Neither offers any recommendations concerning changes in research administration which would improve matters.

They reach opposite conclusions, however, concerning the future use of social experiments in policy making. Stromsdorfer believes that "gradually experimental analyses just may gain an ascendancy which it most assuredly does not now have." Says Mundel, "the likelihood of further experimentation is probably declining." Perhaps this difference reflects the authors' differing faiths in the social-research enterprise. Mundel is clearly circumspect, a bit skeptical. Stromsdorfer is an enthusiast: research should be used, and it would be if there weren't so many political "constraints." The authors of these views are capable researchers with substantial experience in government. Take your pick.

References

Aaron, Henry J. 1978a. *Politics and the professors*. Washington, D.C.: Brookings Institution.

———. 1978b. *On Social Welfare*. Cambridge, Mass.: Abt Books.

———. 1975. Cautionary notes on the experiment. In *Work incentives and income guarantees: The New Jersey negative income tax experiment*, ed. J. A. Pechman and R. M. Timpane. Washington, D.C.: Brookings Institution.

Aaron, Henry J., and John Todd. N.d. The use of income maintenance findings in public policy, 1977–78. Office of the Assistant Secretary for Policy and Evaluation, Department of Health, Education, and Welfare. Washington, D.C.: GPO.

Ashenfelter, Orley. 1978. Estimating the effects of training programs on earnings. *Review of Economics and Statistics* 60 (no. 1): 47–57.

Anderson, Martin. 1980. Welfare reform. In *The United States in the Eighties*, ed. Peter Duignan and Alvin Rabuska. Stanford, Calif.: Hoover Institution Press.

————. 1978. *Welfare: The political economy of welfare reform in the United States*. Stanford, Calif.: Hoover Institution press.

Barth, Michael C., Larry L. Orr, and John L. Palmer. 1975. Policy implications: A positive view. In *Work incentives and income guarantees: The New Jersey negative income tax experiment. See* Aaron 1975.

Bolle, Mary Jane. 1980. Overview of S.2153: "The Safety and Health Improvements Act of 1980" (Schweiker, Williams, Church, Cranston, and Hatch), including background and pro-con analysis. Congressional Research Service, Library of Congress, Washington, D.C.

Boruch, Robert F., and David S. Cordray. 1980. *An appraisal of educational program evaluations: Federal, state, and local agencies.* Evanston, Ill.: Department of Psychology, Northwestern Unviersity.

Borus, Michael E., and Daniel S. Hamermesh. 1978. Estimating fiscal substitution by public service employment programs. *Journal of Human Resources* 13 (no. 4): 56–65.

Caplan, Nathan, and Eugenia Barton. 1976. *Social indicators 1973: A study of the relationship between the power of information and utilization by federal executives.* Ann Arbor, Mich.: Institute for Social Research, University of Michigan.

Caplan, Nathan, Andrea Morrison, and Russell J. Stambaugh. 1975. *The use of social science knowledge in policy decisions at the national level: A report to respondents.* Ann Arbor, Mich.: Center for Research on Utilization of Scientific Knowledge, Institute for Social Research, Univerity of Michigan.

Congressional record. 1979. Occupational Safety and Health Improvements Act of 1979. Washington, D.C.

Gramlich, Edward M. 1980. Future research on poverty and income maintenance. In *Poverty and public policy: An evaluation of social science research*, ed. Vincent T. Covello. Boston, Mass.: G. K. Hall and Co.

Hall, Arden T. 1980. The counseling and training subsidy treatments. *Journal of Human Resources* 15 (no. 4): 591–610.

Hamermesh, Daniel S. 1977. *Jobless pay and the economy*. Policy Studies in Employment and Welfare (no. 29). Baltimore, Md.: Johns Hopkins University Press.

Haveman, Robert H. 1977. Introduction: Poverty and social policy in the 1960s and 1970s—An overview and some speculations. In *A decade of Federal antipoverty programs*, ed. Robert H. Haveman. New York, N.Y.: Academic Press.

Johnson, George E., and James D. Tomola. 1977. The fiscal substitution effects on alternative approaches to public service employment policy. *Journal of Human Resources* 12 (no. 1): 3–26.

Katz, Arnold, ed. 1977. The economics of unemployment insurance: A symposium. *Industrial and Labor Relations Review* 30 (No. 4): 431–37.

Levin, Henry M. 1977. A decade of policy developments in improving education and training for low-income populations. In *A decade of federal antipoverty programs*. See Haveman 1977.

Levy, Frank. 1978. The harried staffer's guide to current welfare reform proposals. In *Welfare reform policy analysis series: Number 4.* Washington, D.C.: Urban Institute.

Lynn, Laurence E., Jr., ed. 1978. *Knowledge and policy: The uncertain connection.* Washington, D.C.: National Academy of Sciences.

———. 1977. A decade of policy developments in the income-maintenance system. In *A decade of federal antipoverty programs*. See Haveman 1977.

Lynn, Laurence E., Jr., and David Whitman. 1981. *The president as policy maker: Jimmy Carter and welfare reform.* Philadelphia: Temple University Press.

Masters, Stanley. 1980. The effect of supported work for the AFDC target group. Mathematica Policy Research, Inc., Princeton, N.J.

Munnell, Alicia H. 1975. *The future of social security.* Washington, D.C.: Brookings Institution.

Nathan, Richard P., Robert F. Cook, V. Lane Rawlins, and Associates. 1981. *Public Service Employment: A Field Evaluation.* Brookings Institution.

O'Neill, David M., and June A. O'Neill. 1981. Employment, Training, and Social Services. In *Agenda for progress: Examining federal spending*, ed. Eugene J. McAllister. Washington, D.C.: Heritage Foundation.

Rivlin, Alice M. 1971. *Systematic thinking for social action.* Washington, D.C.: Brookings Institution.

Robins, Philip K., and Richard W. West. 1980. Labor-supply response over time. *Journal of Human Resources* 15 (no. 4): 524–44.

Rodgers, Charles, Ernst Stromsdorfer, Shari Ajemian, Erica Groshen, Audrey Prager, Kristina Varenais, and Stephanie Wilson. 1979. *Minnesota work equity project: First interim report.* Cambridge, Mass.: Abt Associates Inc.

Schultze, Charles L. 1968. *The politics and economics of public spending.* Washington, D.C.: Brookings Institution.

Schiller, Bradley R. 1973. Empirical studies of welfare dependency. *Journal of Human Resources* 8 (supplement): 19–32.

"The Seattle and Denver Income Maintenance Experiments." 1980. *Journal of Human Resources* 15 (no. 4).

Smith, Robert S. 1980. Data needs for evaluating the OSHA safety program. School of Industrial and Labor Relations, Cornell University. Mimeo.

————. 1979. The impact of OSHA inspections on manufacturing injury rates. *Journal of Human Resources* 14 (no. 2): 145–70.

Somers, Gerald G., and Ernst W. Stromsdorfer. 1970. *A cost-effectiveness analysis of the in-school and summer neighborhood youth corps program*. Madison, Wis.: Industrial Relations Research Institute.

Stockman: Proposals for welfare reform. 1981. *Socioeconomic Newsletter* 6 (no. 2).

Thornton, Craig, David Long, and Charles Mallar. 1980. A comparative evaluation of the benefits and costs of Job Corps after eighteen months of post program observation. Technical report K. Princeton, N.J.: Mathematica Policy Research, Inc.

U.S. Code Congressional and Administrative News. 1980. St. Paul, Minn.: West Publishing Co.

U.S. Congress. Joint Economic Committee. 1979. *Hearings on the effects of structural unemployment and training programs on inflation and unemployment.* 96th Cong., 1st sess. Washington, D.C.: GPO.

————. Congressional Budget Office. 1981. *Reducing the federal budget: Strategies and examples, fiscal years 1982–1986.* Washington, D.C.: GPO.

————. 1977. *Welfare reform: Issues, objectives, and approaches.* Washington, D.C.: GPO.

————. 1976. *Employment and training programs.* Staff working paper. Washington, D.C.: GPO.

U.S. Office of Management and Budget. 1981. *Schedule for Reagan budget revision.* Washington, D.C.: GPO.

Weiss, Carol H. 1980a. *Social science research and decision-making.* New York, N.Y.: Columbia University Press.

————. 1980b. Three terms in search of reconceptualization: Knowledge, utilization, and decision-making. Paper presented at the Conference on the Political Realization of Social Science Knowledge: Toward New Scenarios, 18–20 June 1980, Vienna, Austria.

————. 1978. Improving the linkage between social research and public policy. In *Knowledge and policy: The uncertain connection*, 23–81. *See* Lynn 1978.

————. 1977. *Using social research in public policy making.* Lexington, Mass.: Lexington Books, D.C. Heath and Co.

Contributors

Henry Aaron
Brookings Institution
1775 Massachusetts Avenue N.W.
Washington, D.C. 20036

Dennis J. Aigner
Department of Economics
University of Southern California
Los Angeles, California 90007

John Conlisk
Department of Economics
University of California, San Diego
La Jolla, California 92093

Paul B. Ginsberg
Congressional Budget Office
2nd and D Streets, S.W.
Washington, D.C. 20515

Zvi Griliches
Department of Economics
Harvard University
Littauer Center, Room 125
Cambridge, Massachusetts 02138

Jeffrey E. Harris
Department of Economics
Massachusetts Institute of
  Technology
E52-563
Cambridge, Massachusetts 02139

Jerry A. Hausman
Department of Economics
Massachusetts Institute of
  Technology
E52-271A
Cambridge, Massachusetts 02139

Gregory K. Ingram
World Bank
1818 H Street, N.W.
Room I8115
Washington, D.C. 20433

Paul L. Joskow
Department of Economics
Massachusetts Institute of
  Technology
E52-280B
Cambridge, Massachusetts 02139

Joseph B. Kadane
Department of Statistics
Carnegie-Mellon University
Pittsburgh, Pennsylvania 15213

Laurence E. Lynn, Jr.
School of Social Service
  Administration
University of Chicago
969 E. 60th Street
Chicago, Illinois 60637

Daniel L. McFadden
Department of Economics
Massachusetts Institute of
 Technology
E52-271D
Cambridge, Massachusetts 02139

Frederick Mosteller
Department of Biostatistics
Harvard School of Public Health
677 Huntington Avenue
Boston, Massachusetts 02115

David S. Mundel
Frank B. Hall and Company of
 Massachusetts
89 Broad Street, 8th Floor
Boston, Massachusetts 02110

Lawrence L. Orr
Office of Technical Analysis
A.S.P.E.R.
U.S. Department of Labor
200 Constitution Avenue, N.W.
Washington, D.C. 20210

John M. Quigley
Graduate School of Public Policy
University of California, Berkeley
2607 Hearst Avenue
Berkeley, California 94720

Harvey S. Rosen
Department of Economics
Princeton University
Princeton, New Jersey 08544

Sherwin Rosen
Department of Economics
University of Chicago
1126 East 59th Street
Chicago, Illinois 60637

Frank P. Stafford
Department of Economics and
 Institute for Social Research
University of Michigan
Ann Arbor, Michigan 48109

Ernst W. Stromsdorfer
Department of Economics
Washington State University
Pullman, Washington 99164-4860

Lester D. Taylor
Department of Economics
University of Arizona
Tucson, Arizona 85721

Milton C. Weinstein
Department of Biostatistics
Harvard School of Public Health
677 Huntington Avenue
Boston, Massachusetts 02115

David A. Wise
John F. Kennedy School of
 Government
Harvard University
79 Boylston Street
Cambridge, Massachusetts 02138

Author Index

Subject Index